What people are saying about ..

AND THE LAMB WINS

"Most of us approach the Bible's teaching on end times like we would a 2000-piece jigsaw puzzle with no picture on the box to help us assemble it. We are similarly clueless about God's future and our hope from God's Word. This is tragic. Simon Ponsonby's book is a sane, balanced, thorough, and consistently stirring guide to the complexities of Bible eschatology. He deals with everything important as he takes us 'Back to the Future' as God sees it, handles all the tough questions, and never fails to excite the reader. More than that, I agreed with 99 percent of what he says!"

Greg Haslam, minister, Westminster Chapel, London

"Simon Ponsonby's *And the Lamb Wins* tackles a most controversial and seemingly quite timely topic. You will find it an extremely well-researched and clearly presented 'answer book' of the myriad points of view regarding the end times. You may also find yourself thinking a bit deeper about this topic, and possibly disturbed on occasion, as many long-taught socially religious conclusions are challenged; but in the end, I think you will find yourself hopeful. The Lamb wins, and so do those who follow him."

Michael L. Simpson, international business strategist, life coach, and author of Gold Medallion–winner *Permission Evangelism* and *I Believe, Now What?*

"An incredibly thorough and insightful look into God's eschatological program. It is, by far, the very best book I've ever read on the end times. The author has taken a subject that is very confusing for many people but made it understandable and exciting. All I want to do these days is talk about what I learned from this book!"

Chris Bennett, pastor, Bakersfield, California

"And the Lamb Wins had me praising and repenting! Balancing scholarship, long-time reflection, and the courage to review the Christians' response to the 'faith that was handed down to us,' Simon digs deep into the truths angels long to look into. My initial reaction recalled the apostle Paul's words, 'I am debtor to the Jew and the Greek.' Bravo, Simon!"

Michael Modica, Assembly of God pastor, police chaplain

AND THE LAMB WINS

AND THE
LAMB WINS

WHY THE END OF THE WORLD IS

REALLY GOOD NEWS

SIMON PONSONBY

transforming lives together

AND THE LAMB WINS
Published by David C. Cook
4050 Lee Vance View
Colorado Springs, CO 80918 U.S.A.

David C. Cook Distribution Canada
55 Woodslee Avenue, Paris, Ontario, Canada N3L 3E5

David C. Cook U.K., Kingsway Communications
Eastbourne, East Sussex BN23 6NT, England

David C. Cook and the graphic circle C logo
are registered trademarks of Cook Communications Ministries.

The Web site addresses recommended throughout this book are offered as a
resource to you. These Web sites are not intended in any way to be or imply an
endorsement on the part of David C. Cook, nor do we vouch for their content.

All Scripture quotations, unless otherwise noted, are taken from the *Holy Bible, New
International Version®. NIV®*. Copyright © 1973, 1978, 1984 by International Bible Society.
Used by permission of Zondervan. All rights reserved. Scripture quotations marked KJV are
from the King James Version of the Bible. (Public domain.) Scripture quotations marked
ESV are taken from *The Holy Bible, English Standard Version*. Copyright © 2000; 2001 by
Crossway Bibles, a division of Good News Publishers. Used by permission. All rights reserved.
Scripture quotations marked RSV are taken from the Revised Standard Version Bible, copyright
1952 [2nd edition, 1971], Division of Christian Education of the National Council of the
Churches of Christ in the United States of America. Used by permission. All rights reserved.

LCCN 2008928479
ISBN 978-1-4347-6755-4

© 2008 Simon Ponsonby

The Team: Don Pape, Melanie Larson, Amy Kiechlin, and Jaci Schneider
Cover Design: Gearbox, David Carlson
Cover Image: © Getty Images, Chip Simons
Interior Design: Gearbox

Printed in the United States of America
First Edition 2008

1 2 3 4 5 6 7 8 9 10

051608

To my sons, Joel and Nathanael—may they play their part in bringing the gospel to the nations and live to welcome the victorious and glorious return of the Lamb

CONTENTS

PREFACE

They will make war against the Lamb, but the Lamb will
overcome them because he is Lord of lords and King of
kings—and with him will be his called, chosen and faithful
followers. (Rev. 17:14)

This book began life as a series of lectures at St. Aldate's School of
Theology. I embarked on the course reluctantly. My colleagues and
editor had suggested that I teach and write on the area of eschatology
(the study of the last things, from the Greek *eschaton*, meaning "last"),
and the words "fools rush in where angels fear to tread" immediately
sprang to mind. Even if I could pull together the various scriptural
threads and make sense of them, I knew that this was one area in which
people held passionate but disparate views. My Anglican disposition
for a sort of middle-class, middle-English middle way might not hold.
I knew enough to know that eschatology was a minefield. But it has
proved to be a gold mine.

Once into it I was hooked. Whole new areas of theology opened
up to me. Like a botanist with a new plant or a scientist with a new
insight, I was excited to find things in Scripture that I had never noticed
before. In particular my discoveries about the place of Israel in God's
plans were unexpected, undeniable, and even a little uncomfortable.
The hint that we the church have a part to play in hastening the return
of the Lord through worldwide evangelism and holy pursuit (see 2 Peter
3:10) challenged the Calvinist in me, but it also caused me to worship

more passionately the Lord who would include me in his plans. Reflecting on the physicality of the resurrection and the new life on the new heaven and earth had a great impact on me. I had been rather gnostic and overspiritualized before. I was surprised by the fact that the Bible meant what it said and that, generally, what it said could be taken literally rather than figuratively. This held true particularly in terms of the Antichrist, heaven, hell, and Israel: Such things were not mere symbols or ciphers to be interpreted or deconstructed, but could often be taken at greater face value than I had previously believed.

Probably the greatest impression I have received has been of the hope to which we are called and the great victory of the King of heaven. My former students will know that, as a chaplain in Oxford, I have often used the term "the Lamb wins" as a catch-all phrase to show the victory of the Lord over their fears, failings, and future. But that phrase also resounded through my study of eschatology. The Lamb wins: He defeats sin; he defeats death; he defeats Satan. Scripture is the story of the victory of the Lord who loves. Accompanying this victory has been the profound hope that frames the Christian life—hope in the return, restoration, recompense, and reign of the victorious Lamb.

While I have resolved certain issues in my own thinking, I have rather resisted finding a systematic overall plan. I have looked at various charts drawn up by certain traditions, giving precise dates and details of what will happen when. But at present we only know in part, and what constitutes Scripture's end-time prophecies is debatable, and their interpretation elusive. Only after the fact, when Christ has returned, will we know fully as we are known and, looking backward, see the whole story. So I have purposely not constructed a graph or time line to show how I think all the eschatological features fit together chronologically.

I have consulted widely in writing this book—no doubt too widely for some and not widely enough for others. No particular book stands out, but I have drawn on Augustine's *City of God* repeatedly and profitably; and, though often differing on conclusions, I have found David Pawson's *When Jesus Returns* to be a thorough, rewarding, and provocative companion on my journey. The World Wide Web has proved invaluable, and the bibliography reflects my constant trawling of its highways and byways. As a side note, I have not read any of the books in the fictional Left Behind series.

During the course of writing this material, I have unsettled old friends and gained new ones. I genuinely came to this study without any preconceived theology, other than the belief that the Lamb will return and win the day. Eschatology is a notoriously contentious area of theology. While I have taken my own stance over issues like the nature of hell, the millennium, Israel, the state of the dead, and so on, these are secondary matters to the ultimate victory of Christ and the eternal salvation of the saints. These last two alone I would defend to the point of breaking fellowship.

I would like to thank Charlie Cleverly and my colleagues for encouraging me to undertake this course and for giving me the time to read for, write, and teach it; Richard Herkes of Kingsway (David C. Cook) for his incisive insights and support of the project; and attendees at the St. Aldate's School of Theology for their stimulating engagement with the material. The Rev. Tom Finnemore helped to run the School of Theology. Sam Longair, an Oxford history graduate and my research assistant, located numerous materials as well as helping to run the events and compile the bibliography. Mark Porter once again came to the rescue, formatting the lectures into book form and checking references. My father, Pastor J. B. Ponsonby, prayerfully supported the project, working with me through the materials and finally succeeding in changing my mind on Israel! The Rev. David Cooke throughout made me laugh and kept me sane. Anita Cleverly allowed the book to intrude on her summer holiday and made numerous suggestions to improve the prose and content. I am also extremely grateful for the gracious and professional editing by Bryony Bénier, and the outstanding editorial and publishing team at David C. Cook, who I have been so privileged to work with. Lastly, Canon David White, Neville Jones, and Bishop David Pytches, seasoned students of eschatology, offered critical and constructive comments on the material and, though not always agreeing with my conclusions, encouraged and supported me. Their input, insights, and attention to detail have improved the book considerably.

I dedicate this study to my sons, Joel and Nathanael. May they play their part in seeing the world evangelized, and may they live to welcome the Lord returning in glory.

THE WHOLE WORLD
LOOKING FORWARD

He has ... set eternity in the hearts of men.
(Eccl. 3:11)

FASTEN YOUR SEAT BELTS

Interest in the end times has reached boiling temperature. The megablockbuster Left Behind series[1] has gripped the minds of the Christian world, fueling anticipation and speculation of an imminent millennium, Antichrist, rapture, tribulations, witnesses, judgment day, and the like. The series may not be regarded as literature to compete with a Tolstoy or even a Tolkien, but the sixty-five million copies sold in a decade indicate just how interested many are in its themes.

Alongside religious narratives we are daily bombarded by a litany of angst, accompanied by statistics concerning depletion of the ozone layer, irreversible climate change, depletion of fossil fuels (estimated by scientists to run out by 2050), erosion of natural rain forests, melting polar ice caps, imbalanced ecosystems, tidal rises, and increasing natural disasters like famine, tsunamis, and earthquakes, plus the fear of pandemics such as bird flu and AIDS. These have brewed a concoction powerful enough to fuel a sense that just possibly the old man on the street corner with his billboard announcing that "the end is nigh" might indeed be a real prophet. While we have always had the apocalyptic birth pangs such as wars, rumors of wars, famines, and earthquakes, impending ecological disaster is quite new in human history and, if unchecked, threatens to drive us headlong into an abyss. The apocalyptic imagery in John's Revelation depicting a scorched earth (see 8:7), a sterilization of the sea (see 8:8; 16:3) and the polluting of the rivers (see 8:10; 16:4) no longer looks so bizarre in the light of current ecological crises and the effects of global warming.

The academics are taking matters seriously. Social scientists are developing a whole discipline of "futurist studies," in which they seek to assess statistically various social, economic, political, and technological factors and guess intelligently where we are heading and how long we have.[2] In world-class universities like the Massachusetts Institute of Technology and Oxford, one can find whole departments endowed to research the future. Whatever the future holds, it is not going to go away.

The so-called Rapture Index,[3] defined as a "Dow Jones Industrial average of end-time activity, or a prophetic speedometer," factors in forty-five criteria including floods, occult prevalence, liberal theology, and Russian politics to guestimate how close the rapture is. An index of 85 or below counts as "low prophetic activity," 85–110 as "moderate prophetic activity," and 110–145 as "heavy prophetic activity," while above 145 means "fasten your seat belts." When I last looked, we had a Rapture Index of a staggering 158! But some years ago it was even higher—what goes up may come down—so I am still planning on my retirement and pension, while keeping an eye on the clouds.

WHAT IS ALL THE FUSS ABOUT?

I must confess that, until deciding to write this book, I had given little emotional or intellectual attention to the whole cultural and theological debate surrounding the end times. This may betray a personality trait of someone who rarely feels led to follow the crowd; perhaps also a theological persuasion as a moderate[4] Calvinist, relaxing in the sovereignty of a God who holds the end in his hands, who has decreed and kept secret the times and dates of his return (see Acts 1:7). I have struggled to be the best Christian man and minister, husband and father that I can and, like the psalmist, have tried not to concern myself with great matters or things too difficult for me (see Ps. 131).

My earliest awareness of end-time theology came at a meal table when I was a boy, listening in as my parents discussed whether Christ would return for a remnant church, for the faithful few (maybe those of my background, the Exclusive Brethren and a handful of Strict Baptists?), or for a worldwide glorious church. I was intrigued by this, and in my gut sensed what I have subsequently come to believe—that despite the increase of wickedness, there shall be a great increase of God's kingdom. Christ must have the supremacy in all things; Jesus' yes is greater than Satan's no; Christ's glory will cover the earth as the waters cover the sea, and he will return for a conquering church, not one hiding and dwindling in a dark bunker.

As a Christian in my late teens, I listened to the Larry Norman song "I Wish We'd All Been Ready," watched films like *Thief in the Night*, and read Hal Lindsey's *The Late Great Planet Earth*. But all this failed to fire a sense that the end was nigh. I knew enough Scripture to believe that Christ would return for a *prepared* bride, and I doubted whether the church was in fact quite ready and right for the wedding feast. I also believed that Jesus would return for a glorious *global* bride, with representatives from every *ethne* in the world going to worship at the throne. (*Ethne* is a word closer in meaning to "tribe" than "nation," and there are many more tribes than there are nations.) Having been challenged by a Wycliffe Bible translator about how many peoples and places still remained unevangelized, I became convinced that the Father will delay Christ's return until the gospel has reached and been received by "the uttermost ends" of the earth (see Acts 1:8; 2 Peter 3:9).

Studying theology as both an undergraduate and a postgraduate, I can recall no set of lectures devoted exclusively to eschatology; perhaps it was taught and I paid little attention, though I rather think it was not core to the curriculum. The themes associated with the end times and eternity have not been a significant feature in my fifteen years of teaching and preaching ministry. Of course, I have spoken on judgment, heaven, and hell, especially in the context of preaching the gospel; but ancillary matters like the millennium, rapture, identifying antichrists, and the like have seldom been mentioned. This apparent lack of focus on the end times and eternity seemed reasonable to me. The apostolic and historic creeds made little of them. Pastoral experience showed that often those most concerned with the end times were rather off-center. I followed John Wimber's dictum that our focus should be on the "main and the plain"—whereas end-times theology, often relying on abstract interpretations of singular biblical texts in Daniel or Revelation, seemed neither main nor plain. After this study, however, I realize that it is more central a theme than I previously thought.

STILL WAITING?

Having always loved church history, even teaching courses on it, I am only too aware that in every age of the church her theologians and prophets have assumed the end is nigh, have identified the Antichrist, and have anticipated and dated an imminent millennium and the return of Christ. To date, all have obviously been proved wrong. The Corinthian church members believed they were already living a resurrection life (see 1 Cor.

15:12); the Thessalonian church was disturbed by prophecies that Christ had already returned (see 2 Thess. 2:1–2); the second-century Montanists literally set up shop and waited at Pepuza for the New Jerusalem to descend on them; the nineteenth-century giddy Irvingites filled London with excitement. Someone somewhere has always been declaring that the end is nigh. In the late fourth century, even the heavyweight theologian Ambrose of Milan, perhaps influenced by the traditional Roman sentiment of "the world grown old," declared that the wars and disasters of his own age signaled that the end was near.[5] When the Teutonic barbarians overturned Rome in the fifth century, many again thought the end was nigh. During the Middle Ages, Pope Gregory IX wrote in his Papal Bull I that "the evening of the world is now declining,"[6] and several tracts such as *The Last Age of the Church* were published, stirring up end-time expectation.[7]

If on the one hand we have a theology giddy with expectancy, on the other we have a theology whose logic appears to leave little room for the end times and as a result could lead to a passive attitude to mission and discipleship. In recent years the rise of a particular theological movement that claims biblical evangelical roots but that asserts the future is unknown to God and open-ended, has caused me concern. This "open theism" proposes that God may know what *might* happen but not what *will*. He has no foreknowledge and cannot predict or prophesy or plan the future. Some might say that the "open theists" have created God in their image. As William Craig has observed, "Their God is ignorant of virtually all humanity's future since even a single free choice could turn history in a different direction ... At best God can make intelligent guesses."[8] In debating with a minister who held to this view, I was aware of my passionate pointing to Christ's gospel predictions of the climate, chronology, and criteria of the end. I guess I held a stronger theology of end times and eternity, underpinned by my committed Reformed theology.

So why am I now embarking on this study? Apart from the reasons given in the preface, I genuinely think it is important to understand and teach the whole counsel of God and not avoid contentious and difficult themes. And however far we may be from the end, we are nearer than when Paul first wrote and prayed *"Maranatha*—come, Lord Jesus" (see 1 Cor. 16:22).

ESCHATOLOGY—THE END AND THE BEGINNING

Eschatology is a catch-all phrase that derives from the New Testament Greek term *eschaton,* meaning "last." In classical and biblical Greek, *eschaton* was a wide term that could speak of being last in rank or at the last place on Earth, or of the last days. It conveyed a sense of extremity. In Jewish usage it often referred to death. In the New Testament it occurs over fifty times in reference to such finalities as resurrection (see John 6:39, 40, 44, 54), judgment day (see John 12:48), the end of history (see John 11:24), and the last days as the times we live in (see 2 Tim. 3:1; James 5:3).

The term *eschatology* itself was possibly coined by Abraham Calovius in the seventeenth century, but came into common usage in the nineteenth. According to the *Oxford English Dictionary,* it first entered English usage in 1844 with one G. Bush. In its current usage it conveys all aspects relating to the first and second coming of Christ, the tribulation, the day of the Lord, the millennium, the rapture, the Antichrist, death, resurrection, judgment, heaven, and hell.[9] It represents the concepts that in the medieval period were each called *novissimus*—a Latin superlative of *novus,* meaning "new." Thus, for the medieval church, the end things were the new things. This held together the end things of death and judgment and opened up the new things of heaven and hell. Eschatology is *novissimus*: The end times begin the new times. Jesus is the First and the Last, the Alpha and the Omega, the Beginning and the End. Reformed theologian Robert Culver rightly states, "Christianity ends with Christ in his glorious return ... there is a last one to meet us, not just an *eschaton*, a last thing."[10]

CHRISTIANITY IS ESCHATOLOGY

The seventh-century Apostles' Creed, which owes its origins to the earliest church fathers, sums up Christian eschatology succinctly:

> *[Jesus] will come again in glory to judge the living and the dead and his kingdom will have no end ... we look for the resurrection of the dead and the life of the world to come.*

Implicit in this judgment and eternal kingdom are the conquering of evil and the establishment of Christ's righteous rule.

Although accepted across the traditions and repeated by believers throughout the generations, the creed's influence as a major narrative has waxed and waned across church history, generally coming to the fore only at the close or start of centuries, on the turn of the first or second millennium, or whenever there were major cultural shifts or social crises. The significant discovery of Scripture for the laity in the Puritan era brought a revival of interest in prophecy and eschatology and a search for a remarkable end-time manifestation of God's purposes. Conversely, the Enlightenment's emphasis on reason, the individual, progress, and the drive of history influenced liberal theology, which replaced the eschatological concept of God's inbreaking rule with ethics, projecting the kingdom of heaven onto the historical, cultural, and moral frame.

The nineteenth-century liberal theologian Ernst Troeltsch observed, "The eschatology office is usually closed."[11] That was generally true for the nineteenth century, but rather the opposite was true for the twentieth, when a renaissance in New Testament studies showed how crucial eschatology was to the mission and message of Christ. Two powerful voices were Albert Schweitzer and C. H. Dodd. Schweitzer advocated what was termed "consistent eschatology," focusing on a disappointed Christ who, having failed to see the kingdom come as he expected (see Matt. 10:23), threw himself to death on the wheel of history, hoping to force the *Parousia*,[12] only to fail—yet ironically shaping history far more by his failure than if he had achieved his misconceived ambition.[13] C. H. Dodd was noted for his realized eschatology, which he drew from his study of Jesus' parables. For him the kingdom was not to be understood in apocalyptic and futurist ways, but as an already present and experienced reality: "The *eschaton* has moved from the future to the present, from the sphere of expectation into that of realized experience."[14] While Dodd gave due credit to the imminence of the kingdom in Jesus' ministry, both he and Schweitzer failed to do justice to the futurist aspects of Christ's and the apostles' eschatological teaching.

The distinguished twentieth-century theologian Karl Barth, writing in the rubble of World War I, thundered, "Christianity that is not wholly and utterly eschatology has nothing whatever to do with Christ"— although he understood this perhaps more in the existential sense of the God behind Time breaking in now, rather than the ultimate, definitive wrapping up of history by God.[15] Barth's pupil Jürgen Moltmann wrote the explosive *Theology of Hope*,[16] at times more indebted to philosophical Marxist theory than biblical theology, but recognizing that a historical eschatological framework was the foundation to the Christian faith. This text revolutionized modern theology, causing us to reconsider eschatology not as the last subject in the textbook of theology, but as the first.

> *From first to last, and not merely in the epilogue, Christianity is eschatology, is hope, is forward-looking and forward-moving, and therefore also revolutionising and transforming the present. The eschatological is not one element of Christianity, but it is the medium of the Christian faith as such, the key in which everything is set, the glow that suffuses everything here in the dawn of an expected new day.[17]*

This present study will demonstrate that Moltmann was right: Christianity is eschatology. Jesus began his ministry proclaiming, "Repent, for the kingdom of heaven is at hand," and he left promising that he would return to take his disciples to be with him. This book will seek to explore what it means for Christians to live life framed by Jesus' first coming and the hope of his second coming. We will show that the deep-seated angst felt by many as history hurtles toward a climactic chasm of decay and disaster is not without biblical commentary. The innate fear of death, judgment, and punishment is one to which Christianity directly responds, and the profound longings for eternal life, utopia, even union with God can be satisfied by what is on offer through Jesus Christ.

ONE

CHRISTIANITY IS HOPE

A faith and knowledge resting on the hope of eternal
life, which God, who does not lie, promised before the
beginning of time. (Titus 1:2)

LONGING FOR A BETTER SONG

In the film *Educating Rita,* Rita (played by Julie Walters) is a
hairdresser by day and an Open University pupil by night, seeking
to create a better future for herself. Talking to the English tutor Dr.
Frank Bryant (played by Michael Caine), she explains why she wants
to study, describing a family night out at the pub: "I did join in the
singing but when I turned around, me mother had stopped singing
and she was crying. I said, 'Why are you crying mother?' and she said,
'There must be better songs to sing than these.' And I thought, 'Yeah,
that's what I'm trying to do—sing a better song.'"[1]

In the Bible, John records his vision of heaven:

> *And they sang a new song.…*
> *In a loud voice they sang:*
> *"Worthy is the Lamb…!"*
> *Then I heard every creature in heaven and on earth and under*
> *the earth and on the sea, and all that is in them, singing:*

"To him who sits on the throne
and to the Lamb
be praise and honor and glory and power,
for ever and ever!"
(Rev. 5:9; 12–13)

The optimistic bubble that followed World War II, expressed in the slogan "We've never had it so good," was soon deflated by the Cold War that lasted more than four decades. Although this threat has now evaporated, it has been replaced by the ominous shadow of Islamic fundamentalist terrorism. The postmodern era has been dominated by what Anthony Giddens terms "anomie"—an empty apathy, the careless "whatever" popularized by the Vicky Pollard character in the *Little Britain* comedy sketches. But while some may say "whatever," others say "no more," as they glimpse no sign of hope on the horizon, no new song to sing. Worldwide, over one million people commit suicide each year; every forty seconds someone sees nothing to live for and ends his or her own life. This figure has increased by 60 percent since 1940. Failed attempts at suicide multiply it by twenty—and those are just the statistics the authorities know about and report. Perhaps most shocking for us is the rise in suicide among young Western males.[2]

In its technical sense pessimism is a term that indicates that the world always tends to the worst possible state. Everything naturally tends toward evil. Optimism suggests that the world is the best possible world that could have been created. Everything naturally tends toward good. The suicidal individual has a pessimistic belief that the future is bleak and futile. Rita the hairdresser has an optimistic belief that education will improve her future. She has hope. As we saw in the introduction, Christianity is eschatology, and eschatology is hope:

Christianity looks to the future and ultimately that future is a glorious one for the Christian.

"THERE IS NO HOPE FOR THE FUTURE, SO HELP YOURSELF NOW"

While some people live lives of quiet despair and others take drastic steps to remove themselves from such despair, poets often find an outlet in describing it. Take Theodore Roethke's haunting lines, for example:

> *I know the purity of pure despair—*
> *my shadow pinned against the sweating wall.*[3]

Others, however, seek to change either the despair-causing situation, or at least their response to that situation. Karl Marx refused to give in to life's melancholy, or to live on the basis of wishful thinking (pie in the sky when he died), but instead sought to bring hope into the situation by changing it here and now, not waiting for heaven but creating it, after the inevitable apocalyptic birth pangs of bloody revolution.

Those involved in the twentieth-century existential movement offered a different response to hope and hopelessness. Like Marx they refused to entertain a theological eternal perspective. But unlike Marx, rather than change the situation, they emphasized the idea of changing their *perception.* Living now, in time, in the face of the inevitability of death, one must confront this despair and choose life, autonomy, freedom, today. Each moment confronts the individual with the possibility of sinking into despair, being preoccupied by futile hope, or merely following the crowd. But individuals can live authentically in their situation, in that crisis moment, by choosing for themselves how they will respond.

The philosopher Albert Camus sought to exorcise all hope from his thought: "Hope as a rule makes a fool." In its place he put, "Thinking clearly and hoping no more."[4] Whereas Marx took inspiration from Prometheus's presumption against the gods, Camus turns to Sisyphus, who was condemned to heavy daily toil pushing a giant boulder up a hill, only for it to roll down the next day and having the toil begin again. For Camus this picture of reality (utterly hopeless in itself) can be transformed, not by hoping that one day the boulder will stay at the top, or by hoping that the gods will take pity on Sisyphus and end the punishment, but rather by Sisyphus choosing to think differently about his situation. I fear that all Camus has to offer here is the manipulation of emotions. The situation, punishment decreed by the gods, still remains.

Jean-Paul Sartre emphasized the idea that we are beings bound by time. We must renounce eternal future hope and create our own reality here and now by choosing to act authentically and freely. In an absurd passage in *The Age of Reason*,[5] the character Mathieu sees his uncle's three-thousand-year-old Chinese vase. This priceless object that has been lovingly preserved and protected for three millennia provokes Mathieu. He will not follow the crowd and tiptoe around it. Rather he picks it up and smashes it to the floor. "I did it and felt quite proud, freed from the world, without ties or kin or origins, a stubborn little excrescence that has burst the terrestrial crust." The pot remains smashed, wealth has been lost, beauty destroyed, a family annoyed—but yes, Mathieu did act "existentially"!

Existentialists loathe the Christian hope of eternal life. They fear that it brings passivity, lack of change, failure to choose authentically—it masks the reality of the human condition as despair. However, all its detractors can offer as an alternative is either to aggressively change the current situation, or to change one's attitude to the situation. In response to Marx's attempt to format fate on the canvas of human history, we point to a God who has stepped into history to change its course. In response to Sartre's emphasis on human will and decision to change our state of mind, if not our state, Christianity says that, through a free choice to accept Christ, our state of mind, state of being, and eternal state are all reformatted—or, in biblical terms, we are "born again."

Marx's Promethean presumption could not alter Prometheus's punishment. Similarly, Camus's Sisyphus still faced the punishment of the gods, even with his smile and his scorn. But the Christian hope is one of total deliverance. The decision of the individual in time affects both the state in which the individual lives now *and* in the future. Anthony Kelly speaks of Christian conversion as a move from worshipping idols to entrusting oneself to the living God. Through God-given, God-directed hope, the Holy Spirit draws us out of ourselves into a self-surrender that goes beyond the limited horizons of optimism or pessimism.[6]

CHRISTIANITY IS HOPE

Living hope in God as a key religious attribute is largely absent from the Greek and Roman religions, although it is found in the Egyptian. In the Old Testament the main word for hope was *qawah*, from the root *qaw*, meaning "to stretch toward, to expect." Related words are *batah*, "to trust"; *yahal*, "to wait/long for God"; *hakah*, "to wait"; and *sabar*, "to wait, hope, trust, fly to."[7] In the Old Testament, half of the 176 passages relating to hope refer to hope in Yahweh by a faithful Israel. The Old Testament hope looked to Yahweh's coming in glory, his reign over the earth, the conversion of the nations, and a new covenant for the forgiveness of sins. In the book of Job, we see this hope lifting

Job's despair above the immediacy of his appalling situation (see Job 7:6) to the expectation that one day he will arise with his Redeemer, be reclothed in flesh, and see the One for whom his heart yearns (see Job 19:26f.).

The New Testament Greek concept of hope is attached to the verb *elpizo* and the noun *elpis*. In the Septuagint (the Greek version of the Old Testament), the verb *elpizo* often translated the Hebrew verb meaning "to trust." It conveys a similar sense to that described above for the Old Testament—of hopeful expectancy concerning God's promises—but now the promises of God are the basis of hope because the God who made the promises has proven himself in Christ (Acts 26:6f.). Although not a frequent theme in the Gospels, it is prevalent throughout the Epistles, most notably in Paul's.

Paul is always eager for believers to understand the "one hope" (Eph. 4:4); the hope to which we are called (Eph. 1:18); the hope that only the believer knows (1 Thess. 4:13); the hope "stored up ... in heaven" through the gospel event (Col. 1:5); the hope set on Christ (2 Cor. 1:10), who will make a "glorious appearing" (Titus 2:13), raising the dead to new life (Acts 24:15; 26:6; 28:20) and bringing our hoped-for salvation (1 Tim. 4:10; 1 Thess. 5:8). This gospel hope in Christ's return with our salvation (Rom. 8:24) is a hope of justification to eternal life (Titus 1:2; 3:7); a hope of righteousness (Gal. 5:5); hope of re-creation into glory as God's children (Rom. 5:2; 8:20; Col. 1:27). It is a hope that is stirred by the Holy Spirit (Rom. 5:5), encouraged by Scripture (Rom. 15:4), for Jew and Gentile alike (Rom. 15:12), and that elicits joy and peace by the Spirit (Rom. 15:13). This hope as a permanent virtue stems from faith and leads to charity (1 Cor. 13:13).

These are all big brush strokes rather than fine detail. There is sparse treatment of the specifics of the hope stored up for us in heaven, perhaps because it is alien to human experience (John 3:12). Paul can say that "no eye has seen, no ear has heard, no mind has conceived what God has prepared" for those who hope in him, though we glimpse this by the Spirit (1 Cor. 2:9). So glorious is it, so far beyond our comprehension, that any analogy would tend to absurdity.

Hope is at the heart of Christian tradition

Patristic scholar Brian Daley has noted that "one thing is clear from the beginning of Christian literature, hope for the future is an inseparable, integral dimension of Christian faith."[8] The early church fathers were often more occupied with Christology than with eschatology. They were, however, in general agreement on the content of Christian eschatological hope.[9] They all held to a linear view of history with an origin and an end, rooted in the creative power and sovereignty of God, against the Gnostics' more cyclical view. They also held to the fulfilment of history ending in the resurrection of the dead, who would bodily share in the promised salvation. Finally, they maintained that a universal judgment would take place at the end: Justice would be enacted, and retribution and reward would be meted out, resulting in perfect happiness for the righteous and permanent misery for the wicked. There was some disagreement over how near the end was, ranging from very near to very far.

The medievalists spoke of "wanhope" (the absence of hope) as a blasphemy against the Spirit.[10] The mystic Julian of Norwich typified this in her *Showings*: "All will be well and all shall be well ... all manner of thing shall be well."[11] In Bunyan's *Pilgrim's Progress*, Mr. Hopeful accompanies Pilgrim from Vanity Fair, through beatings and imprisonment to the Celestial City. Calvin encouraged us to "hope boldly then, more than we can understand; he will still surpass our opinion and our hope."[12]

CHRISTIAN HOPE HAS A FOUNDATION

As we shall see, Christian hope is not wishful thinking—that is what Custer had at the battle of the Little Bighorn. Nor is it blind faith in the future—that is what Sartre showed on his deathbed, betraying his existentialism, saying, "I know I shall die in hope—but hope needs a foundation."[13] His failure to believe and trust in Christ showed that his hope was forlorn. Poet Samuel Taylor Coleridge understood that "hope without an object cannot live."[14] But Christian hope is not without object and foundation. St. Augustine spoke of "the great buttress of hope."[15] Christian hope is built on a firm foundation and directed to a focused object. It is not an optimistic mind-set, but a reasoned belief that affects my life. The philosopher Søren Kierkegaard said, "Hope is a passion for the possible." Christian hope is a possibility proven by God's previous action.

Christian hope is founded on the God who has promised and acted in Christ

Christian hope is based not on an idealized future prospect, but on a person who has proved himself trustworthy. Biblical hope is focused on a good God of the future, a God who has acted in love for us through Christ, reversing the downward spiral of our lives, removing the curse of judgment and death. As Hoffman has said, "Yahweh was the object, embodiment and guarantor of his people's hope."[16] Heathens can be described as being without hope (1 Thess. 4:13) because they are without God. Hope stems from relationship with God (Col. 1:27); hope is placed first and foremost in the God who makes the future, and only secondly in the future made by God. Romans 15:13 tells us that God is the "God of hope." Hebrews 6:18 makes it clear that hope is confidence in God who promises and delivers. We hope in God's "unfailing love" (Ps. 33:18).

Hope is related to faith, of course (1 Cor. 13:13), and faith is not blind, but rather confidence in and commitment to a God who has shown he is trustworthy by dying and rising from the dead. Peter says that ours is "a living hope" (1 Peter 1:3), because it is hope in the living One, who has come back from the dead. This demonstration of love and power confirms God's Word. He can be trusted, his Word can be relied upon, and hope may find a home here.

The resurrection reveals his eternal purposes. Jesus is the firstfruits of those raised from the dead, and we who trust in him shall also be raised glorious. Hope is faith in Christ (Rom. 4:18; 2 Cor. 1:10; Eph. 1:12; 1 Tim. 1:1). The writer to the Hebrews tells us that this hope is "an anchor for the soul, firm and secure" (Heb. 6:19)—a hope anchored in Christ, who lived, died, rose again, entered heaven, and is coming back on our behalf. This anchor of hope became an early Christian symbol, carved by the persecuted Christians on the walls of the Roman catacombs.

God promises and delivers. He did so preeminently through Christ and we rest assured and hopeful that through Christ he will do so again. John's apocalyptic vision is shadowed by future dread and woe. Evil will be abroad in the land, and there will be trials, tribulations, and persecutions for those who love Christ. Powers will set themselves up against Christ and his own. But over it all, and after it all, Christ reigns. Hope takes God at his word. The God who in the past promised and delivered does the same for the future. He will win through; he will ful-fill his purpose and promise to overthrow utterly every evil foe, and to establish an eternal home for those who hope in him, where there will be no sickness, sorrow, suffering, sin, or Satan. God will reign eternally, freely, fully, in glory with all who trust in him. This is our future hope, our story, our song.

HOPE HOLDS AND HEALS

Hope is an antidote to anxiety

Christian hope refuses to faint with fear at what the future holds, knowing him who holds the future. Indeed, looking into the future is forbidden (Lev. 19:31; Isa. 44:25). Berkouwer warns, "The only legitimate expectation is the one orientated to Israel's God."[17] Hope rests in God's sovereignty, rejoices in God's victory. We are not given a detailed plan of times and dates, just the big picture. Those who stray into straining out the end-time details to the last drop have actually lost the vision of future hope, leaving themselves at risk of being trapped in the shadows cast by the light. Hoffmann says that biblical hope leads to a "renunciation of all calculations of the future, the humble recognition of the limits set to our knowledge."[18]

Hope refuses to be alarmist

"Hand in hand with confident anticipation of God's gracious dealing goes submission to the sovereign rule of the Almighty—the time and manner and fulfilment are left to Him."[19] Hope permits no bunker mentality, no dread speculation; hope sees the dark clouds gathering and knows that dawn is running up fast behind them. Hope looks to and through the prophesied end-time trials and tribulations. Through the birth pangs the hopeful rejoice in a life soon to come. As Jesus said, look up, lift up your head: Your salvation draws near (Luke 21:28).

Hope steadies the Christian in life's storms

Despite the gathering darkness, the psalmist says:

Put your hope in God,
for I will yet praise him,
my Savior and my God.
(Ps. 42:11)

Such hope sustains (Isa. 40:31), even through death, when the dead in Christ rise on eagles' wings. Hope sees beyond the temporal trials and tribulations to the glory beyond. This is a key theme in the letter to the Hebrews, where the community is facing persecution and is tempted to pull away back to the synagogue. In the face of such trials, our future hope gives us present strength and enables us to endure. That is what keeps martyrs faithful to the end and through to the new beginning. Dietrich Bonhoeffer demonstrated this hope when he sent a message to Bishop Bell as he awaited his death: "This is the end, for me the beginning of life."

Hope is attractive to the hopeless

Joy is the mark of the hopeful who, by the Spirit, are touched by the power of eternity (Rom. 5:1–5; 12:12). This hopeful joy, in a world of hopeless sorrow, draws people to Jesus. It is a protest against the depression and despair that are pockmarking our culture. Anthony Kelly rightly encourages us:

> *The ecclesial community, breathing an atmosphere of Trinitarian communion, must cultivate a culture of hope to counter and cure the social culture of despair and violence. Hope takes on its historical form in the flesh and blood reality of the church as it reaches forward to the full arrival of the Reign of God over all creation.*[20]

Hope is communal

We do not hope alone, nor is hope for the few. It is the hope of Israel, the hope of the Gentiles, the hope of the church (Rom. 15:12). Hope in Christ invites the hopeless to join the people of hope. "The bearer of the promises is not primarily the individual but the people, the covenant, the remnant ... the horizon of hope becomes more universal ... the whole cosmos and all peoples are embraced."[21]

CHRISTIAN HOPE LEADS TO ACTION

The creedal statement "and he will come again to judge the living and the dead and his kingdom will have no end" is God's great "Yes!" against every evil, self-willing, demonic "No." It is the cry of triumph. Those who hope in faith hear this "Yes!" and the result is a revolution in their soul, heart, and life.

There is nothing passive about hope

Hope follows faith and produces charity (1 Cor. 13). Those who trust, hope; those who hope, love. Philosopher Ernst Bloch has said, "Hope is the driving force of all human initiative, from it he looks for the coming of the new."[22] The future is what is decisive for the present, not the past. Eschatological hope does not allow us simply to sit back and wait for God's future, but compels us to work for it and to welcome it. Hope does not lead to resignation, but to action.

Hope is disciplined waiting

We wait actively (1 Peter 1:13). Hope transforms the present in the light of God's future.[23] Hope of a better future causes me to act differently now—to see with the eyes of faith what may be and to meet the future coming toward me in action. Moltmann says that hope sets action in motion. We live between the present and the promise, but glimpsing the promise, we seek to draw it into the present. We want to meet the future by working toward it.[24] The vision of eternity must shape our present reality. If that is what God wants the future to look like, we must work for it now. Brian Haynes notes that "anyone who really believes in the last judgment will act in certain ways."[25] A T-shirt is available that says, "Jesus is coming back, look busy." Intended as a subversive dig at the Christian faith, it nevertheless conveys some truth, although we need to do more than just look busy. Hope in Christ's return means that when he comes, I want to be found working out his will.

Hope inspires a moral conversion[26]

Such a conversion occurs at both the personal level and the political level. Those who have this hope, as John says, will purify themselves (1 John 3:3). The bride will wish to be awake on her wedding day beautifully prepared to receive the King of Holiness. Caught by a heavenly vision of how reality will be, we echo eternity in time, seeking righteousness in our economics, international politics, and ethics. Hope is an antidote to modernity's materialism, which seeks immediate, material satisfaction. Hope-filled Christians reject a quick fix of comfort; we take the long-term view. We will not be dragged down to the immediate values of this world, but look beyond to heaven's horizon.

Hope leads to mission

Hope cannot be contained, it must be communicated. We who hope are always prepared to give an account for the hope within us (1 Peter 3:15). Indeed, such hope makes us bold in witnessing (2 Cor. 3:12). Moltmann puts it like this: "The *promissio* of the universal future leads of necessity to the universal *missio* of the church to all nations."

Knowing that Christ will return for his bride in love and for his Enemy in judgment, we seek with our last breath to call people to accept Christ, so that when he returns he will not be a dread stranger. C. S. Lewis rightly observed:

> *Hope is one of the theological virtues. This means that a continual looking forward to the eternal world is not a form of escapism or wishful thinking, but one of the things a Christian is meant to do. It does not mean that we are to leave this present world as it is. If you read history, you will find that the Christians who did most for the present world were just those who thought most of the next. The Apostles themselves, who set on foot the conversion of the Roman Empire, the great men who built up the Middle Ages, the English Evangelicals who abolished the Slave Trade, all left their mark on Earth, precisely because their minds were occupied with Heaven. It is since Christians have largely ceased to think of the other world that they have become so ineffective in this.*[27]

CONCLUSION

So the church is the community of hope—those who have put their hope in the God who has acted on our behalf in the death, resurrection, ascension, and expected return of Christ. This God promises those who trust in him that we, too, will rise again, will be justified from all sins, glorified as sons and daughters, and will enter eternity with him. Such hope carries us through.

I began this chapter with *Educating Rita* and Rita's hope to sing a better song. As I was writing in an Oxford coffee shop, a friend came to tell me of her grandfather's death the previous day in Australia. This man had loved God and had served him faithfully as a missionary. He died unexpectedly, a few weeks after he and his wife had celebrated their sixtieth wedding anniversary with a thanksgiving service. My friend informed me that, at the exact hour of his death, thousands of miles away at Trinity College in Cambridge, England, her sister was having a tutorial and suddenly over the PA system, a choir had burst out singing the hymn:

> *No more we doubt thee, glorious Prince of life;*
> *Life is naught without thee: aid us in our strife;*
> *Make us more than conquerors, through thy Deathless love:*
> *Bring us safe through Jordan, to thy home above.*
> *Thine be the glory, risen conquering Son,*
> *Endless is the vict'ry, thou o'er death hast won.*[28]

The tutorial group was amused, not knowing how or why this hymn had suddenly burst out around the college. My friend's sister noted the time. Later that day she was told of her grandfather's death, which had occurred at exactly the time when the hymn rang out. Coincidence, perhaps, but a meaningful one. At death all who hope in Christ will join with the angels around the throne, singing new songs of hope fulfilled.

Two

THE KINGDOM RULE OF GOD

The kingdom of the world has become the kingdom of our
Lord and of his Christ, and he will reign for ever and ever.
(Rev. 11:15b)

In the last chapter we considered how hope is a primary feature of
Christian eschatology: Christians look and long for the return of Christ
and the restoration of all things in heaven and on earth under God.
That future hope is also, in part, a present reality, brought about by the
inbreaking of God's kingdom through Christ.

We are all familiar with the concept of "kingdom." We speak of the
United Kingdom, the historical, social, political, and financial union
between the four nations that form the British Isles. Scientists speak of
biological kingdoms, distinct categories of life forms such as bacteria,
fungi, plants, and animals. Historians speak of the areas and peoples
conquered and controlled by military powers, such as Alexander the
Great's kingdom in Europe, Africa, and Egypt, or the expansive kingdom of the Roman Empire. But these definitions only do not sufficiently
reflect the biblical usage of the word "kingdom."

The definitive biblical Greek dictionary[1] defines the word *basileia*
as "kingship, royal power, royal rule, kingdom," and theologically as "a
chiefly eschatological concept." In terms of its origins, *basileia* carries the

sense of base or foundation. Generally speaking, however, a kingdom is the area and people over which a king reigns. One cannot accurately speak of a kingdom without also speaking of a king, nor of a king without a kingdom.

The New Testament usually speaks of the term *kingdom* in connection with God or heaven. These are not two separate kingdoms, but are essentially synonymous. Generally, Luke and Mark speak of the "kingdom of God," *basileia tou Theou*, whereas Matthew prefers to speak of the "kingdom of heaven," *basileia ton ouranon*, no doubt reflecting his target audience of devout Jews who always tried to avoid using the name of God and instead searched for a synonym.[2] Occasionally, the New Testament speaks simply of the "kingdom" and once or twice of the kingdom of Christ or the Son. They are all one and the same—the domain or the reign of the royal King God through his right-hand executive Son, Jesus Christ. The kingdom of God or heaven is central to the teaching and ministry of Christ and the church. The term occurs more than a hundred times in the New Testament, and the majority of the instances are found in the Synoptic Gospels. While it also embraces existential, ethical, and governmental categories, the theme of this book will direct our study to the term's eschatological significance.

THE KINGDOM OF GOD AND THE OLD TESTAMENT

The particular phrase "kingdom of heaven" or "kingdom of God" is not found in the Old Testament, although the *concept* it conveys is an important one even there. D. L. Moody was right when he said, "If Yahweh reigns he has a realm—if he is *melek* (king) he has a *malkuth* (kingdom)."[3] Rodman Williams says that Yahweh's kingship was the "great concern" of the Old Testament.[4] Yahweh is the present and everlasting king over Israel (Num. 23:21). Approaching death, Moses sang of the kingship of God over Israel (Deut. 33:5). Israel was called to live under the royal rule of King Yahweh, to serve him as a kingdom of priests (Ex. 19:5–6). They were a theocratic nation who, even when they appointed kings after human fashion, recognized God's ultimate kingship. The Israelites' request to have a king like other nations grieved God, but he acquiesced and appointed a monarchy—first Saul, then David and his line, but it was always understood that these monarchs ruled only by appointment of the great King (1 Sam. 12:12). Solomon sat on the throne of the Jewish kingdom, but he functioned as executive officer of Yahweh's kingship (1 Chron. 28:5, 7). The psalmist sang of God's kingship over an everlasting kingdom (Ps. 145:11, 13; 103:19), and said that Israel was to herald the reign of God among the nations (Ps. 96:10). The early national prophet Micaiah saw God seated on a throne (1 Kings 22:19), as did the later prophet Isaiah (Isa. 6:5), who prophesied that this God would reign on David's throne as king eternally (Isa. 9:6; Obad. 21; Dan. 7:13f.) and universally (Ps. 22:28; 99:1; 103:19).

THE KINGDOM OF GOD IN THE GOSPELS

Almost the first declaration of the angel Gabriel to Mary concerning Jesus was that he would reign as king over the house of Jacob and that his kingdom would be everlasting (Luke 1:32f.). The visit of the Magi took place because they had come to worship "the one who has been born king of the Jews" (Matt. 2:2). Herod's attempted assassination of the Christ child was motivated by jealousy and an attempt to secure his own throne (Matt. 2:13f.) because the Messiah was expected to be a political leader.

The forerunner, John the Baptist, came preaching repentance because "the kingdom of heaven" was near (*engiken*) (Matt. 3:2), and it demanded an immediate response. The present perfect tense used here suggests the unmistakable imminence of the kingdom, which has become a present reality through the visitation of Jesus. This is further conveyed by the Greek term *ephthasen*, meaning "arrived, come, actually present."[5] Jesus said that the "kingdom of God has come upon you" when deliverance from the demonic has been experienced (Matt. 12:28). "In the person and work of Jesus the kingdom of God has intruded into the world."[6]

The disciples' prayer that Jesus instructed them to pray daily invokes the rule of God on earth as in heaven (Matt. 6:9–10). This kingdom rule, evidenced by God's *will* being enacted, was not restricted to Israel but was destined for the whole earth. Although initially this gospel of the kingdom came only to Israel, the wider world was always in view. In fact Jesus tells us that the kingdom would be rejected by Israel who had received the prophecies and anticipated it, and it would be given to others—the Gentiles (Matt. 21:43).

This kingdom is "good news" (Mark 1:14–15), manifested in signs and wonders that do not simply confirm the Word, but illustrate the nature of the kingdom—where lepers are healed, lives are restored, the demonized are set free, the hungry are fed, hope is restored, and sins are forgiven (Matt. 10:7–8). David White speaks of this inbreaking of the kingdom through Jesus as "God's right to rule over sin, sickness, demons, death and disaster."[7] The kingdom is not for the self-righteous and religious, but for those who are humble and only too aware of their sinfulness (Matt. 5:3). Nonetheless, it is a righteous kingdom, seen and entered not on the basis of ancestry or DNA, but through spiritual rebirth (John 3:3, 5). Being spiritual, it is an internal kingdom, a reign "within you" (Luke 17:21). The kingdom comes to those who exercise childlike faith (Matt. 18:3), and to those who are willing to renounce all wealth, work, and family ties that stand in the way (Matt. 19:23; Luke 18:18–30). But God's kingdom economy also promises repayment of "many times as much" as we gave up to gain him (Luke 18:29–30).

This kingdom is worth giving everything for (Matt. 13:44f.)—but it does involve sacrifice. The kingdom is not entered by the passive or nonchalant: It advances forcefully, it is contested forcefully, and only forceful, tenacious people lay hold of it (Matt. 11:12). The eighteenth-century philosopher and politician James Burgh said that "no kingdom can be secured otherwise than by arming the people—the possession of arms is the distinction between a freeman and a slave."[8] Christ armed his disciples, not with clubs and swords (Luke 22:52), but with spiritual weapons of warfare, the power and authority of the Spirit, and the Word, which enacts the will of God. Christ's kingdom is a kind kingdom, where violence is a spiritual assault on the demonic realm. Rather than a kingdom of military arms, this kingdom is frequently described as a wedding party, or a banquet (Matt. 8:11; Mark 14:25). Invitations to the feast are sent out, but regrettably not always accepted. There are also degrees of honor within the kingdom (Matt. 5:19), but those who participate are all sons and daughters of God (Matt. 8:12). Like a mustard seed that becomes a giant bush, this kingdom is growing from its inception (Matt. 13:31). Its true members are not initially always distinct from the false (Matt. 13:24–30), but the King knows those who are his. Distinctions will be made, and God's children will shine like the sun in his eternal kingdom.

Although it breaks into this world, the kingdom is not of this world (John 18:36), where Satan temporarily holds sway and uses his dominion over earthly kingdoms to manipulate matters for his own ends. Clearly, there is a polarity to the presence of the kingdom: Jesus says that his kingdom is not of this world (John 18:36), yet also that it is near (Matt.

10:7). Jesus can say that it is a personal and spiritual kingdom located inside you (Luke 17:20–21), yet he can also say that it will take a universal political form following a period of apocalyptic preparation (Luke 21:31).

At the Last Supper, Christ links his death with his kingdom when he makes the sacramental signs of his imminent crucifixion, which will consecrate the new covenant. After breaking the bread and offering the wine to his disciples, he says he will not partake of such a meal again until he shares it with them "in my Father's kingdom" (Matt. 26:29). Thus the Passover meal, which becomes the church's family memorial meal, is a kingdom event that holds together in our minds the death of Christ at Calvary and the hope that is won there, of his return in glory, and the establishment of his reign.

THE KINGDOM OF GOD IN THE EPISTLES

The theme of the kingdom is not so prominent in the postgospel material, although Kim suggests that the kingdom of God is the central theme of Acts.[9] Following the resurrection, the disciples, who still do not understand the nature of the kingdom, ask whether it will now be established in a nationalistic, political manner (Acts 1:6). Jesus immediately responds, "It is not for you to know the times or dates the Father has set." This surely suggests that dates are indeed set and a restoration of the kingdom is a future prospect, but this is not to be their mission, not even their concern. Their mission is to witness to Christ to the ends of the earth in the power of the Spirit. This witness to the king and the kingdom is enabled by the same Spirit who anointed Christ to usher in the kingdom in word and deed: The disciples' mission will further extend the reign of God on earth. The date set by the Father for restoring the kingdom is intricately bound to their faithfulness in taking the gospel to the uttermost ends of the earth. The kingdom is not a nationalistic Jewish state, but a spiritual community of Jew and Gentile. The signs that accompanied and illustrated Jesus' preaching of the kingdom will also accompany the apostolic church, and the coming of the Spirit at Pentecost signifies the enthronement of Christ as King on David's eternal throne (Acts 2:30). The apostles' proclamation was of the inbreaking kingdom of God (Acts 8:12; 19:8; 20:25), and the early church story ends with Paul in Rome, the power center of the Roman Empire and the known world, where he proclaims God's kingdom with a challenge (Acts 28:23, 31). Indeed, this claim to the coming reign of God challenges Emperor Nero's rule to such an extent that it provokes him to kill Peter and Paul, the leaders of the church. But murder is powerless to stop the relentless advance of the kingdom of Christ, and as we know, the Roman Empire would bow its knee to Jesus in the early fourth century under Emperor Constantine.

Paul understood his ministry as an ambassador of the kingdom (Col. 4:11), a powerful kingdom that was evidenced in signs, wonders, and changed lives (1 Cor. 4:20). As in the Gospels, Paul's epistles convey the now-but-not-yet tension of the kingdom. It is a present reality, effected through the redemptive and reconciling work of Christ: Those who trust in him have *already* been transferred from the domain of darkness into the kingdom of the Son whom God loves (Col. 1:12–13). But Paul also speaks of the kingdom in terms of a *future* hope, one that the sinful will not inherit (1 Cor. 6:9; Gal. 5:21). God calls us into this kingdom (1 Thess. 2:12), manifested by the righteousness, peace, and joy brought about by the Holy Spirit (Rom. 14:17), but it is yet to appear (2 Tim. 4:1; 4:18) and will be inherited not in our flesh and blood, but in a resurrected spiritual body (1 Cor. 15:50). This now-but-not-yet tension is conveyed clearly in the later epistles. The writer to the Hebrews speaks of the kingdom as the place where Jesus is worshipped and enthroned as king (Heb. 1:8; 2:9), and also as something that the believers are currently receiving and that cannot be shaken by their trials (Heb. 12:28). James speaks of the kingdom in terms of future inheritance (James 2:5), and Peter similarly speaks of it as an eternal prospect (2 Peter 1:11).

John's apocalyptic vision in Revelation, notoriously difficult to interpret, has produced strongly competing theologies and eschatologies. Some see it largely as a *futurist* vision yet to be fulfilled. Others see it as a commentary on the *historical* political Roman context in which John wrote. Still others understand it as a *concurrent* history of the church through the ages. Some interpret it as literal history, others as figurative. What is clear is that it presents to us two realms in conflict, with the ultimate victory going to Christ the Lamb who sits on his throne victorious over every enemy, be that death or the Devil. Jesus' kingdom is already shared by John and the persecuted saints (Rev. 1:9) who have been delivered from Satan's authority and now serve as priests in the kingdom (Rev. 1:6; 5:10). Satan makes war against the church, the outpost of the kingdom of heaven (Rev. 12:13—13:18), but Christ's army is victorious (Rev. 14:1, 4; 17:14) through resistance to idolatry and fidelity to the testimony of Jesus (Rev. 12:11; 19:10). The conflict with Satan's dominion is ultimately ended when he is utterly vanquished by Christ (Rev. 16:16—18:24; 19:17—21; 20:10), whose victory at Calvary is consummated at the second coming (the *Parousia*), after which Jesus will reign as King of Kings and Lord of Lords (Rev. 17:14; 19:16; 22:5). Whatever the time frame of interpretation—historic, present continuous, or future—Revelation makes the unmistakable announcement that the kingdom of God, initiated by

Christ at his first coming, will be consummated at his second coming, when the Lamb wins and is worshipped as king by all.

THE KINGDOM OF GOD IN THE CHURCH'S REFLECTION

The early church

The early postapostolic literature generally speaks of the kingdom in terms reminiscent of the New Testament treatment. The notable feature in the widely respected *Clement* is the futurist perspective, in which the kingdom is seen as something we wait for, prepare for, and will inherit, and which is associated with God's appearing and bringing eternal life. The Gospel of Barnabas suggests that the kingdom was already present, through the death of Jesus at the cross (Gos. Barn. 8:5–6), while the *Didache* distinguishes the kingdom from the church, offering prayers for the Lord to gather the church from the four corners of the earth into his kingdom (*Didache* 9:4; 10:5–6).

The postapostolic fathers rarely wrote about the kingdom as such, but when they did, they tended to focus on the future millennial reign. Augustine recognized the anticipatory and fragmentary relationship between the church present and militant and the kingdom:

> *On the one hand, the church even now is the kingdom of Christ and the kingdom of heaven. This age is the millennial reign. On the other hand, it is a church composed of wheat and tares. Therefore, the church is a "kingdom militant," that is, a kingdom at war with the enemies of Christ and with the lusts that rage within its members.*[10]

The Middle Ages and the Reformation

In the medieval period Thomas Aquinas generally ignored the concept of the kingdom, while Joachim of Fiore's studies in Revelation led him to articulate a vision of establishing a visible kingdom of God in this world, which influenced several radical religious groups of the time.

The Reformation era did not produce much deep reflection on the kingdom, as the Reformers were more concerned with issues relating to justification, faith, the priesthood, and the church. Martin Bucer wrote a treatise on the kingdom that he sent to the young king of England, presenting a vision of the kingdom as the rule of God over the elect now—a community expressing the two great commandments to "love God" and "love one's neighbor." With Martin Luther, he argued that both church and civil government may be vehicles for this kingdom rule.[11]

John Calvin tended to equate the kingdom with the true church of the elect, but he also spoke of the kingdom in individual and spiritual terms: "By the kingdom of God which he declared to be at hand, he meant forgiveness of sins, salvation of life and every other blessing which we obtain in Christ."[12] Calvin's Geneva ministry was in some respects an attempt to order society in a political manner along the lines of kingdom principles. Similarly, the Puritans under Cromwell and in America were inspired by a notion of setting up the living kingdom on earth in a social and political form. The major Reformed formularies do not refer to the kingdom, although the Mennonite Confession of 1580 and the Particular Baptist Second London Confession of 1677 identified the elect with the kingdom.

Orthodox and Catholic thought

The kingdom has not been a major theme in Orthodox theology, although some understood the Byzantine state as an image of the kingdom of heaven on earth.[13] Orthodox theology generally equates the presence of the kingdom with the presence of the Spirit. Thus all prayers that invoke God's kingdom are immediately followed by an invocation of the Spirit.[14] The Holy Spirit is the heavenly king who makes the kingdom imminent in the life of individuals, drawing them into ever deeper communion with God.

Modern Catholic theology, post-Vatican II, tends to understand the kingdom as a future hope, but one that is "budding forth" in the church now through her sacramental life and her efforts to live and work for the future kingdom now.[15]

The Quakers and pacifism

The American artist Edward Hicks painted several canvases reflecting the Quaker understanding of the kingdom as an ethical, peaceful society. In a famous picture titled *The Peaceable Kingdom,* he expresses Isaiah 11:6, where the lion lies down with the kid and the calf. He painted these creatures cuddled together while in the background he depicts the signing of the treaty between the Lenape Native Indians and William Penn at the founding of Pennsylvania.[16] Similarly influenced by the pacifist Quakers, Leo Tolstoy wrote a thesis called "The Kingdom of God Is Within You,"[17] in which he portrayed the kingdom in terms of nonviolent resistance to evil, a notion that impressed itself on the young Gandhi and would prove particularly effective in his political life and work.

The liberal tradition

The outspoken church antagonist Friedrich Nietzsche understood Christ's kingdom in nonpolitical and noneternal terms, saying, "The kingdom of heaven is a condition of the heart—not something that comes upon the earth or after death."[18] In many respects he was repeating what was maintained by many nineteenth-century liberal theologians who, following Albrecht Ritschl, understood the kingdom as the ethical gathering of the redeemed inspired by love, living as the brotherhood of man under the fatherhood of God—a kingdom marked as ethical, moral, and relational, but generally devoid of all eschatological concepts.

This liberal conception held sway well into the twentieth century, tending to treat the kingdom primarily in terms of godly influence in society for social good—a notion more at home in socialist political categories than apocalyptic ones.[19]

The dispensationalists

There were, however, some who rejected this line, notably Ritschl's son-in-law Johannes Weiss and the so-called dispensationalist movement. Weiss emphasized the eschatological, future orientation of Christ's teaching—that Christ's was a kingdom in conflict with Satan's kingdom; that it was a work solely of God, apocalyptic in nature, that would sweep away the present order.

The dispensationalist theology of J. N. Darby, Cyrus Scofield, Lewis Sperry Chafer, and others asserted that when the Jews rejected Christ's alleged offer of the Davidic kingdom, the kingdom was withdrawn and the church was set up as a substitute. The current age is therefore an interlude, a parenthesis in God's dealings with Israel, during which time God deals with us through the church. This will continue until the return of Christ, when the church is to be taken away and the kingdom established.[20] It is interesting to note that for the dispensationalists the kingdom and the church are two completely separate entities, while the opposite conception is presented by the

Reformed theologian A. H. Strong, who entirely equates the two: "The Church is identical with the spiritual kingdom of God."[21]

Twentieth-century contrasts

The twentieth century saw an increase of interest in the kingdom—and further polarity of thought, most notably between those two giants Albert Schweitzer and C. H. Dodd, the former believing that "the kingdom never came" and the latter believing that it is "fully here." Schweitzer claimed that Christ understood himself as an eschatological and apocalyptic figure who, frustrated by the failure of the kingdom to come as expected through the Twelve's mission (Mark 6:7–13), threw himself heroically to death on the wheel of history, hoping to force God's hand to bring about the last days. Jesus was mistaken and failed, Schweitzer argued, though ironically his influence continues to expand, despite the fact that the kingdom cannot be regarded as a significant aspect of present-day eschatology.

C. H. Dodd, through his study of the parables, emphasized a "realised eschatology"—the kingdom did indeed come with Christ and is a present reality (as we saw earlier with the Greek words *engiken*, for example in Mark 1:15, and *ephthasen* in Matt. 12:28). The exorcisms and miracles prove its presence. Dodd played down the future eschatological perspective in Christ, emphasizing that the end had come in and with the kingdom of Christ, displayed in his miracles and through his death and resurrection. Rudolf Bultmann, meanwhile, sought to remove any sense of the *eschaton* as a historical future event. He also sought to eradicate any trace of apocalyptic motifs, which he saw merely as ancient literary baggage. He focused his eschatology existentially—that is, on neither a retrospective nor a future historical event, but on the personal experience of Christ by the individual now.[22]

Among the most balanced and biblical presentations of the twentieth century is that of G. E. Ladd, for whom the coming of the kingdom was preeminent proof that history and humanity cannot save themselves.[23]

> *The kingdom of God has created the Church and continues to work in and through the Church … however, the Church is not the only instrument of the kingdom—it ever stands under the judgment of the kingdom.*[24]

For Ladd the kingdom is seen in the initial defeat of Satan evidenced by the miracles, the gospel, the gift of forgiveness, the exorcisms of demons, and the conquering of death by Jesus' resurrection. All these constitute evidence that the kingdom has come through Jesus.

Inadequate reflection of Scripture

Many of the views of the kingdom presented above fail to do justice to Scripture and diminish the extensive power, glory, and majesty associated with God's kingdom. J. N. Darby's attempt to divorce the kingdom from the church simply will not stand up to biblical scrutiny: The gospel of the kingdom and the King of the kingdom provide the church with the ethics of the kingdom that frame her discipleship. The liberals who equate the kingdom with the existential spiritual experience of Jesus, or with mere ethics, fail to take into account the clear apostolic hope (Phil. 2:10f.) of a rule of Christ not just over the willing believer, but over history, humanity, and ultimately all powers in heaven and on earth. Any attempt simply to equate the church with the kingdom is to diminish the scope of God's rule and to exclude the kingly reign of God in the heavenlies where he rules over all angels and demons—a kingdom rule for which we are to pray here on earth as in heaven (Matt. 6:10). Indeed, the kingdom constitutes whatever and wherever is ruled, commanded, and exercised by the will of God, and must surely include the whole cosmos, which he sustains by his powerful word (Heb. 1:3).

NOW AND NOT YET

It is no mean feat to try to make sense of two thousand years of church reflection on the vast New Testament material and the often-opposing interpretations that have been put forward. But it is essential that we attempt to systematize and summarize what we have learned. Understanding something of the kingdom of God, the kingdom of heaven, the kingdom of the Son whom God loves is the key to unlocking Christian eschatology.

In discussing terms like *ephthasen* (Matt. 12:28), Caragounis has suggested that the imminence of the kingdom demonstrated by the miracles implies the advance of the kingdom, though not quite its presence, which remains in the future. The miracles are preliminaries of the kingdom that look forward to the cross and resurrection and the ultimate consummation at Christ's second coming.[25] We live between the inbreaking of the kingdom at Christ's first advent and the fulfillment of the kingdom at his second coming. Larry Kreitzer says that "the kingdom of God is something that straddles the dimensions of time being both present and future."[26] But in what sense?

Oscar Cullmann helpfully used the military analogy of D-Day, when the decisive battle was fought, and V-Day, when the ultimate defeat of Hitler was achieved. Paul says that until "perfection" (i.e., Christ) comes, "we know in part," but then we will "know fully" (1 Cor. 13:9, 12). Similarly, now we experience the kingdom in part, but when the perfect One comes again, we will experience the kingdom fully. Only by holding the tension between such polarities can we rightly understand the kingdom. It is both now and not yet. Perhaps the initial self-declaration of Jesus in John's Revelation as the one "who is, and who was, and who is to come" (1:8) may also be said of the kingdom. It was, it is, and it is to come: It was anticipated in the Old Testament by Israel; it broke out with the ministry of Christ in Judea; it continues with Christ present by the Spirit among the church; and it will be consummated by Christ returning and reigning supreme over all heaven and earth.

H. G. Wells, in his chapter on Jesus in *A Short History of the World*, summarized: "The doctrine of the kingdom of heaven which was the main teaching of Jesus, is certainly one of the most revolutionary doctrines that ever stirred and changed human thought."[27] Indeed it is. In fact it is that and far more. Jesus did not simply teach it, but at his first coming he inaugurated it, and at his last coming he will consummate it. It is a revolution that changes everything, turning this world upside down and right side up.

KINGDOM, CROSS, CHURCH

The kingdom arriving with Christ creates the church. The church is the community of those who have entered the kingdom by repenting and receiving the gospel (Mark 1:15) and been reborn by the Spirit (John 3:3, 5). The Holy Spirit applies the redemption and forgiveness purchased by Christ's blood, transferring them from the rule of Satan to the rule of God (Col. 1:12–14). This church, living in obedience and holiness (Matt. 5—7) under the kingship of Christ as the outpost of heaven, is a kingdom of kindness, happiness, and righteousness (Rom. 14:17) where, through the presence of the Spirit and the power of the gospel, lives are restored into the image of God in Christ.

Armed by the power of the Holy Spirit and the gospel of Christ, the church of God's kingdom continually clashes with the kingdom of Satan, rescuing lives from his grip (Matt. 9:2; Luke 11:19) and advancing heaven's rule on earth, even to the center of the Enemy's kingdom (Acts 28:31). Wherever and whenever individuals or communities live under the royal rule, doing the will of that King, the kingdom is come. The true church, the elect body of Christ, preaches, practices, prophesies, and prepares for the kingdom, which will come in all its fullness when Christ returns and joins his bride the church (Acts 1:7). When he comes, the Lamb's scepter will stretch over every person who has ever drawn breath, over every animal or angelic being ever created, over every place in every space, every star, galaxy, and universe—that is kingdom rule.

I'VE READ THE END OF THE BOOK, AND THE LAMB WINS

The title of N. T. Wright's massive treatment on the kingdom is *Jesus and the Victory of God*—a perfect title for all that the term "kingdom of heaven/kingdom of God" conveys. Despite appearances to the contrary, when human history seems to display the very opposite to God's kingdom rule, ultimately the King in his kingdom will reign. Then every spurious and pretentious kingdom will be overthrown, whether in individual souls, in the structures of society, or in the spiritual realms. All anti-kingdoms of the Antichrist Satan will be obliterated and God will reign in all, over all, forevermore (Rev. 20).

History shows that earthly kingdoms rise and fall. The Babylonian Empire was destroyed by the Medes, and the Persian Empire was superseded in its turn by the Greek Empire, which was replaced by the Roman Empire, itself subsequently eroded by the Barbarians. We have seen the rise and fall of the Ottoman Empire, Napoleon's Empire, the British Empire, the empires of Stalin and Hitler. Others may yet rise and fall. But ultimately, finally, decisively, all human and demonic empires and kingdoms will come and bow before the King of heaven and earth, Jesus Christ (Phil. 2:9–11).

> *Then the sovereignty, power and greatness of the kingdoms under the whole heaven will be handed over to the saints, the people of the Most High. His kingdom will be an everlasting kingdom, and all rulers will worship and obey him. (Dan. 7:27)*

THREE

DEATH AND LIFE

For as in Adam all die, so in Christ all will be made alive.
(1 Cor. 15:22)

THE REALITY OF MORTALITY

According to Benjamin Franklin, death and taxes are the only certainties in life. Death is the universal experience of all humankind: No matter what gender or race, no matter what social, financial, or intellectual status, no one escapes it. Lifestyle, genetics, health regimens, medications, and operations may hold it back a little longer for some, but eventually, and inevitably, all pass this way. Statistics can be made to say all manner of things, but the statistic that 100 percent of humans die has yet to be seriously challenged, even by those who speak of death as a mere illusion. Death is no respecter of persons. Sooner or later it comes to us all: "Every community has its cemetery."[1] Consequently, this generation would do well to heed the wise words of Solomon, who says,

> *It is better to go to a house of mourning*
> *than to go to a house of feasting,*
> *for death is the destiny of every man;*
> *the living should take this to heart.*
> *(Eccl. 7:2)*

This chapter will examine the Christian claim that death is neither final nor irreversible. Vernon White has correctly noted that "the death of the afterlife is often confidently announced along with the death of God, but it refuses to lie down and die. Instead it is the death of death which continues to fascinate the world and haunts our hopes."[2] White has said that rumors of heaven remain in postmodernity as much as in premodernity, in the young and the old. Wordsworth spoke of "intimations of immortality," Shakespeare of "immortal longings," Nietzsche of "all true delight desiring eternity." Surprisingly, though, in the mid-1990s a sociological survey by Douglas Davies concluded that up to a third of Anglicans and a similar percentage of Methodists believed that life ended at death. Only a third of those surveyed were clear that there was a spiritual life after death.

Perhaps the uncertainty about life after death is related to our detachment from death. Despite the certainty of death, despite the endless portrayal of violence in the media and the movies, here in the West in the twenty-first century, with the exception perhaps of the military, police, or medical services, most people have rarely seen a dead body, let alone sat with someone as they take their last breath. The old and sick generally die in relative comfort, in a hospital, sanitized and anaesthetized. We turn up and all we see is a box that contains the remains of someone we once knew, lowered into the ground or disappearing behind a curtain to be cremated. The ancients lived much closer to the mechanics of death and reflected more deeply upon it.

THE RESPONSE TO MORTALITY

People face death alone, and they face death differently. The following are some of the attitudes people display in response to mortality.

Some mock death

Immediately, one might think of the gravediggers in Shakespeare's *Hamlet*, singing and making puns as they dig graves and disturb skeletons. The classic modern illustration of this attitude is Monty Python's provocative *Life of Brian*, which ends with the macabre scene of Brian and his followers on the cross singing "Always Look on the Bright Side of Life." A fellow member of the clergy recalls being at a funeral of a professed atheist who wrote in his will that his funeral should end with everyone singing this Python song! Oscar Wilde famously mocked his own imminent death with his last words: "This wallpaper is dreadful— one of us will have to go." This tone is reflected in the words on an unknown tombstone that declared, "I expected death, but not yet," and in Spike Milligan's acidic epitaph, "I told you I was ill."

Some protest death

I was once the chaplain to a community for the elderly, and I will never forget a very elderly Irish lady shouting indignantly at me when I tried to broach the subject of death and the life to come. She would enter it soon, but so great was her fear that the very mention of it reduced her to panic. Others were uncomfortable with me wearing my clerical collar—as if I represented the grim reaper. Vicars turn up for three things—births, baptisms, and funerals—and for a few of these elderly people, my presence reminded them of only one thing— and it wasn't giving birth or being baptized! As a young priest I took seriously my vows and charge at ordination to "minister to the sick and prepare the dying for their death." For the first time I sat with dying people and held their hand as they left this world. I witnessed one lady fight indignantly to the very end, unprepared and unwilling to go—almost as if she were defying some unseen foe. The matron

commented knowledgeably, "She isn't dying well." The angry words of
Dylan Thomas seem apposite for many:

> *Do not go gentle into that good night ...*
> *Rage, rage against the dying of the light.*[3]

Some resign themselves to death

"There's not a lot you can do about it, so it's best just to live well
now." This was the line taken by the Greek Stoics, who presented the
view that death loses its terror when it is accepted as inevitable. Being in
the process of death, we need to cultivate an ability to die calmly.[4]

Life has the first word, death the last, but until death speaks, we
must live life. Death brings focus and coherence to the present. In the
face of the fact of death, we should reject despair, choosing to live life
to the full, not necessarily in the pursuit of present enjoyment as advocated by the ancients—"Eat, drink, and be merry, for tomorrow we die"
(see Isa. 22:13; 1 Cor. 15:32)—but rather in the personal exercise of
freedom. Because death deprives the individual of freedom, until that
moment we must act freely, of our own volition, not hoping for some
future fulfillment but fulfilling the present moment for ourselves.

Some embrace death

Tragically, as a parish priest I had to bury some young people who—
while still in their teens—felt that life was not worth living and took
matters into their own hands, refusing to let their life run its course. I
have also buried the world-weary old and infirm, who simply wanted
to expire. In my church we had a dear old saint who reached the age of
one hundred before retiring to heaven, but there was not a single time in

my nine years of meeting with her when she did not voice her weariness and declare her readiness to go to Christ. This echoes Paul's heart when he declares that he longs "to depart and be with Christ, which is better by far" (Phil. 1:23). For the believer death is not grim, but a glorious homecoming. Thus the poet George Herbert can say that death "wast once an uncouth thing," but is now "grown fair and full of grace."[5]

Christians, however, are not the only ones to have welcomed death. The Egyptians anticipated and hoped for a better life after death for the righteous and undertook great ceremony and expense to prepare their "tomb of life." Aristotle and Plato believed that the body imprisoned the soul, thus death was the soul's freedom. The Gnostics' dualistic conception of the universe held that the body trapped them, but death brought liberation from this flesh whereby the soul could migrate ever nearer to the divine spirit. Greek warriors like the Spartans, as with certain Norse tribes, could turn death into a triumph by dying courageously in battle and in so doing both leave honor behind them and take it with them.

THE REASON FOR DEATH

Death may come for various reasons: through sickness, violence, a random accident, or old age. In some cases death is a direct act of God—for example, Korah's destruction following his rebellion (Num. 16). Jesus said that Satan was a "murderer from the beginning" (John 8:44). Indeed, in *Paradise Lost*, John Milton presents Death as the son of Satan, an illegitimate child born from the incestuous liaison with his daughter Sin. But Scripture says that ultimately death comes through sin: Sin created the context in which violence and sickness take lives. The very wearing out of the body, the ceasing of its functions that sustain life, is ultimately a consequence of the disobedience of our first parents. God warned Adam and Eve that if they ate of the tree of the knowledge of good and evil they would surely die (Gen. 2:17). Not heeding the warning, they ate, and their rebellion was rewarded with the judgment that they would "return to the ground, since from it you were taken; for dust you are and to dust you will return" (Gen. 3:19). Paul picks this up and offers a commentary on it, stating that this death, this state-in-sin of our first parents, has been transmitted to all their subsequent offspring, and we all face death because of their disobedience (Rom. 5:12f.; 1 Cor. 15:20f.).

Augustine dealt with the experience and theology of death at length in his magisterial *City of God* (Book XIII, Ch. 19), where he asserted that humans would have been immortal but for sin, and Adam and Eve would have passed to heaven without death. Boettner says, "Death is not just a natural end of life … we are doomed to die because we are sinners. Death is a penal evil—an evil inflicted in accordance with law and as a penalty."[6] Millard Erickson says that humankind was born immortal; death is the result of sin; we were meant to live forever; though universal, death is unnatural, a curse, a penalty, an enemy.[7]

Death comes by decree and by degree. It is the consequence of rebellion against God's law—it unravels God's creational intent, bringing the death of the body, separation of the soul from God when enfleshed, and ultimate eternal separation from God. Death is more than the end of the functions of the human body. That is *physical* death. But the Bible also speaks of *existential* death, a dissipation of the life intended (John 10:10), and *spiritual* death, an alienation between our spirit and God (Rom. 8:10).

DEATH IN THE OLD TESTAMENT
The presentation of death in the Old Testament is not obviously coherent, leading to opposing views among scholars even within the

same traditions.[8] What we may say is that the New Testament, with its developing revelation by the Spirit, sheds further light and expands on the Old Testament understanding of death and the afterlife.

The curse of Adam presents death as the end, finite, a returning to dust. There is no hint of any existence after death. Later, however, although the psalmists bemoan death as separation from God (Ps. 6:5; 30:9; 88:5, 11), they also speak of Sheol as the place where the dead go—presumably somewhere distinct from where the body turns to dust. There is some hope that this Sheol is not the end (Ps. 16:10; 73:23f.; 49:15), that we will know some form of continued existence. Psalm 103:15–17 conveys the tension. There is death, with our life being as fleeting as the grass or flower in the field—"the wind blows over it and it is gone"—and yet there is hope, because the Lord's love is "from everlasting to everlasting" and there must be some meaningful state in which we can enjoy such everlasting divine love.

The author of Ecclesiastes hints at this:

> *And the dust returns to the ground it came from,*
> *and the spirit returns to God who gave it.*
> *(Eccl. 12:7)*

Similarly, Psalm 146:4 says that at death we turn to dust, but the spirit departs to God. God's revelation and self-declaration to Moses at the burning bush was that "I am the God of Abraham, Isaac and Jacob." The present tense implies that he continues to be the God of those who have died, who must exist somewhere in some form with him. Jesus made this very point when challenging the Sadducees (Luke 20:27–38).

In Psalm 23 we read of the faith of David: that after he has been "through the valley of the shadow of death," he expects to "dwell in the house of the LORD forever." Psalm 73:24 says that "afterward you will take me into glory." David believes that God reigns over the dead, and possibly suggests what our destination might be after death:

> *If I go up to the heavens, you are there;*
> *if I make my bed in the depths [Sheol], you are there.*
> *(Ps. 139:8)*

Although evacuated of hope by some theologians, the natural reading of Job 19:25f. is that he confidently expected to see his Redeemer in the end:

> *After my skin has been destroyed,*
> > *yet in my flesh I will see God;*
> *I myself will see him*
> > *with my own eyes—I, and not another.*

The Old Testament law forbade contact with the dead. It did not deny that the dead existed or were contactable (Lev. 19:31), and whatever we make of the extraordinary Witch of Endor, she seems to have been able to communicate with Samuel, even though he was dead, and he appeared to rebuke Saul (1 Sam. 28). Daniel 12:13 speaks of a rest after death for the righteous, followed by a general resurrection to receive an allotted inheritance. During the intertestamental period a clear understanding developed of the immortality of the soul and the resurrection of the dead (see Wisd. Sol. 3:4; 4:1; 15:3; 2 Esd. 7:88f.), when the martyrs are expected to be vindicated and rewarded in the afterlife (4 Macc. 10:1; 2 Macc. 6:31).

DEATH IN THE NEW TESTAMENT

The New Testament amplifies significantly the Old Testament reflections on death. Indeed, the whole New Testament is in a sense a reflection on God's dealing with death through Christ. The Old Testament barely gets going before the shadows of death darken paradise; the New Testament closes with the death of death and eternal life enjoyed in the new paradise. The Greek word for death, *thanatos*, occurs over 120 times in the New Testament, while its opposite, *athanasia* (meaning "immortality"), is much rarer, though widely implicit.[9] Death comes through Adam's sin (Rom. 5), but all die because all sin (Rom. 6:23). Death is not a natural process and therefore there is a groaning protest in the bowels of creation against death and decay (Rom. 8:19–22). Christ's death satisfies the law (Gal. 2:21), it overcomes the law of sin (Rom. 7:24), and it conquers our death (Rom. 5:9; 2 Tim. 1:10). The heart of the gospel is victory over death.

Death came through sin. Christ assumes sinful human nature and suffers in our place, taking the penalty of death for us. If we put our trust in him and are identified with him through faith and baptism, we become recipients of the merits of his death and, holding on to his glorious hem, accompany him through his resurrection into heaven. God gives life from death (Rom. 4:17), and life from death hinges on a right response to Jesus (John 5:24; 8:51; 11:25; 1 John 3:14). The breaking open of tombs and the resuscitations that occurred at the time of Jesus' crucifixion visually underline the fact that, in Christ's death, death is conquered for the saints (Matt. 27:52–53).

At death the soul divides from the body (Matt. 10:28; James 2:26).[10] Souls outlive bodies. Christ lived on immediately after his body was taken down at the cross—as he promised to be with the criminal in paradise that day. In the throes of death, Jesus committed his spirit to the Father (Luke 23:46), as did Stephen (Acts 7:59). The body decays in the grave, but the soul lives on, gathered to the spirits of the righteous in heaven (Heb. 12:23). Death means putting off the body's tent (2 Peter 1:14) and being "away from the body and at home with the Lord" (2 Cor. 5:8.). At death there is judgment (Heb. 9:27), whereupon some will be sent to a place of torment and some to a place of enjoyment (Luke 16:19–31).

At the resurrection God and Jesus will bring with them those who have fallen asleep, as the dead in Christ rise (1 Thess. 4:14–16). Souls will be enfleshed again in resurrected glorious flesh—not simply the flesh of our first ancestors before the fall,[11] but glorified bodies like Christ's, spiritual and incorruptible (1 Cor. 15:35–58; 1 Thess. 5:23; Phil. 3:21). All the dead will be made alive (Acts 24:15) and will bow their knees to Jesus. Judgment will take place and the saints will go to the new heaven and new earth, while those who rejected Christ will go to the lake of fire: This, says John, is the "second death" (Rev. 21:8).

WHERE NOW ARE THE GRATEFUL
AND UNGRATEFUL DEAD?

The so-called intermediate state (what happens to those who die before Christ's return) was not something that concerned the New Testament authors, nor the early church fathers. Their eschatological focus was primarily on the return of Christ, the resurrection of the dead, and the eternal reign of the King and kingdom. They were also generally more concerned with the corporate identity of the church than with individual destiny. However, Augustine's treatment of original sin raised questions about the state of grace of baptized or unbaptized individuals, and in the medieval period this developed into a greater focus on individual rather than corporate status, and so began the pragmatic baptizing of all infants in case of mortality, ensuring a divine welcome.

The early creeds, both apostolic and Nicene, simply stated that "he will come again to judge the living and the dead," saying nothing about the state of those who die before the return of Christ and general resurrection. I think Calvin was right when he cautioned us:

> *It is neither lawful nor expedient to enquire too consciously concerning our soul's intermediate state ... it is foolish and rash to enquire concerning unknown matters more deeply than God permits us to know. Scripture goes no further than to say that God is present with them and receives them into paradise ... what teacher or master will reveal to us what God has concealed?[12]*

These are wise words, and certainly the New Testament pays little attention to the experience after death and before the end times.[13] Nonetheless, because not everybody dies at the same time, it is natural to ask the question: "Where are the dead now?"

Purgatory

The word *purgatory* is related to "purge," from the Latin root for "purifying." The Catholic position holds to four possible states at death. There was a fifth called *Limbus Patrum*, the state of those Old Testament saints who died in faith and were held until Christ liberated them between his crucifixion and ascension (1 Peter 3:18–20). This is now redundant. The four remaining are as follows:

1. *Limbus Infantum*, a state of existence for infants who die unbaptized. In the condition of original sin (inherited

through Adam), but without having committed any actual sin, they have no possibility of attaining the beatific vision in God's presence.

2. *Hell*, for those who have died in a state of mortal sin (intentional sin that rejects grace) with no possibility of redemption. They will be punished proportionately for sins committed, and this punishment will intensify after the final resurrection and judgment.

3. *Heaven*, for the few who die in a state of grace and go directly to heaven, having attained perfection in this life.

4. *Purgatory*, where the majority go at death. Those who have venial sins (unintentional, lesser sins) are purged or purified of these sins and gradually progress toward a state of perfection when they may be elevated to heaven. Purgatory is temporary, and eventually all there will be perfected once their sins have been paid for.[14]

The church in the late Middle Ages built into the notion of purgatory the offering of indulgences to assist those in purgatory to move through the process more quickly. The church believed that she controlled the treasury of grace and merit.[15] These were released to the dead on the basis of indulgences offered—whether financial payment to the Vatican coffers, or spiritual intercession and sacramental offerings for the dead. While the Council of Trent put a stop to financial indulgences, the belief continued that the directed devotions of others through prayer, petition, offerings, and Masses could be beneficial in promoting the journey of those in purgatory.

The attempt to support this concept biblically hangs on an apocryphal text (2 Macc. 12:43f.) and is inferred from the words of Christ when he said that sin against the Holy Spirit cannot be forgiven, either in this age or the age to come (Matt. 12:32). It is suggested that this shows *some* sins may be forgiven in the age to come, a notion that even Augustine believed. This view is rather dismissed by the New Testament's rejection of salvation by "works," which is what such a notion amounts to (Gal. 3:1–14; Eph. 2:8f.), by the total absence of any evidence that someone other than Christ can by their own effort save another, and by the description of the judgment and division that occurs at death (Heb. 9:27; Luke 16:26).

Soul sleep

Technically termed *psychopannychism* (a conjunction of two Greek terms: *psyche*, meaning "soul," and *pannucizein*, meaning "to last the night"), this is a concept that is held by various groups from the Jehovah's Witnesses to the Seventh Day Adventists. Many very orthodox Christians have also championed it, including such worthies as John Milton, Martin Luther, and William Tyndale. John Donne wrote of death as sleep:

> *One short sleep past, we wake eternally,*
> *And death shall be no more: death, thou shalt die.*[16]

Luther actually advocated soul sleep in his famous polemic against the abuses by Rome when he nailed his ninety-five theses to the Wittenberg door. Against their notion and practice of indulgences and intercession for those in purgatory, Luther claimed that at death "all" sleep. There is no intermediate holding bay, thus all such practices are senseless, if not blasphemous. Luther asserted that, after death, the soul sleeps in a painless, unconscious state akin to natural sleep. He claimed that the dead are aware of nothing—not seeing, feeling, or understanding, with no comprehension of time. But at the sounding of the trumpet on the morning of resurrection and Christ's triumphant return, the dead souls who sleep shall rise and be enfleshed again. Luther wrote:

> *After death the soul goes to its bedchamber and its peace and while it is sleeping it does not realise it is asleep ... we shall all sleep until he comes and knocks on the little grave and says, "Dr Martin get up"—then I shall rise in a moment and be with him forever.*[17]

Where does this idea stem from? Clearly, in the case of such notable Protestants as Tyndale and Luther, it was their reading of Scripture that led them to this view. Scripture frequently speaks of the "sleep" of the dead (John 11:11; Acts 7:60; 13:36; 1 Cor. 15:6, 18, 20, 51; 1 Thess. 4:13–15), but is this a description of the post-death state, or is it simply a euphemism for death? The latter would be my understanding.

Against "soul sleep," we would point to Jesus' parable of the rich man and Lazarus, which speaks of a sentient state in torment or enjoyment while other brothers remained alive, and the rich man requests that Lazarus be allowed to go and warn them of their possible destinies (Luke 16:27). We can think of Paul's claim that he longed to "depart and be with Christ" (Phil. 1:23), implying that he could exchange his current existence for another without waiting through a period of sleep. Paul also stated that to be at home in the body is to be away from the Lord (2 Cor. 5:8), not away from sleep. Jesus said to the believing criminal on the cross, "Today you will be with me in paradise" (Luke 23:43), where "today" surely cannot mean after several millennia of soul sleep. Lastly, the visitation of Moses and Elijah, both long deceased, to encourage and witness to Jesus at the Mount of Transfiguration challenges the notion of soul sleep (Matt. 17:1–9).

It is important to note that some believe any treatment of the "intermediate state after death" fails to understand God's relationship with time and presupposes that eternity follows on a parallel space-time continuum. Consequently, it is conceived by some that, at death, in the twinkling of an eye, one is transported to the end of earth's time, to the resurrection day and the return of Christ. There may be something here, but the limits of my comprehension and the absence of clear scriptural help force me to leave it as an open question.

Scriptural principles

The parable of the rich man and Lazarus (Luke 16:19–31) provides important insights into what does and does not happen at the point of death. It may be a parable, a story, but it supplies some clear principles.

1. It rejects *annihilation*, the secular atheistic notion that at death our existence ceases completely, whether corporeally or spiritually. This parable presupposes that there is sentient, self-conscious existence after death (v. 22f.).
2. It rejects *reincarnation*, the Eastern notion that we continue to journey on, returning in some other life form, whether higher or lower (see also Heb. 9:27). In the parable the dead hold the same identity and are recognizable in that individuality just as they were before death (v. 24).
3. It rejects *purgation*, the Catholic idea (also found in some Greek mystic religions) that the afterlife is a preparation

for yet another location. In this parable there is no hint of improvement, or of an ability to cross over from the place of suffering to that of the blessed (v. 26).

4. It rejects *soul sleep*. The sentient experience of Lazarus and the rich man is occurring simultaneously, parallel to, but separate from, the living experience of the rich man's brothers (v. 27f.).

5. It presupposes a *judgment*: reward or punishment is meted out at death.

6. It challenges the *holding bay* notion that Hades is where *all* the dead go, subdivided into chambers for the righteous and unrighteous, for it clearly states that only the rich man went to Hades, while Lazarus went to Abraham's side (v. 23).

We need some caution here, for one cannot build a clear eschatology from one passage or parable. That said, other texts also seem to support the principles deduced from this passage, as will be shown in the summary below.

For the saints who die in Christ, the classic Protestant statement of faith, the Westminster Shorter Catechism, asks (Q. 37): "What benefits do believers receive from Christ at death?" The answer: "The souls of believers are at death made perfect in holiness and do immediately pass into glory and their bodies, being still united to Christ, do rest in the graves till the resurrection."[18] Fearfully, Calvin warned, "The lot of the reprobate is doubtless the same as that which Jude 6 assigns to the devils; to be held in chains until they are dragged to the punishment appointed for them."[19]

Let us tentatively summarize our teaching on the intermediate state, while acknowledging that biblical study has led the devout to disagree on some details.[20]

1. *Death is the separation of spirit and body* (Job 19:26; Eccl. 12:7; Matt. 27:50; Luke 23:46; Acts 7:59; 2 Cor. 5:8).

2. *The intermediate state of the believer's spirit is sentient and marked by enjoyment in heaven.* This world is seen as a gloomy shadow in comparison to heaven (Ps. 16; 73; Phil. 1:21f.; Heb. 12:22; Rev. 14:13).

3. *The intermediate state for the unregenerate is misery in hell/ Sheol/Hades* (Deut. 32:15, 22; Prov. 9:18; Matt. 11:23; Luke 16:19ff.; 2 Peter 2:9–10).

4. *The spirits of the dead will be resurrected prior to judgment, both for reprobates and believers.* Both will be clothed in bodies fit for eternity, judgment will be passed, and the saints will go to the new heaven and new earth, while the wicked will go to the lake of fire (Isa. 26:19; Dan. 12:2; John 5:28f.; 1 Cor. 15:35ff.; 1 Thess. 4:13–18; 2 Thess. 1:6f.; Rev. 20:12, 13; 21:8).

CONCLUSION

Let us not miss the hinge on which this eternal destiny hangs: Christ's death turns death into life. Michael Green (echoing John Donne's "Death, thou shalt die") wrote a wonderfully titled booklet about Easter called *The Day Death Died.* Christ's death puts death to death. Christians who trust in Christ's death have their own death annulled, and death for the believer is passing into glory. Jesus stated, "Everyone who looks to the Son and believes in him shall have eternal life, and I will raise him up at the last day" (John 6:40). This is not just a future hope, but something one mysteriously enters immediately: "Whoever believes in the Son has eternal life" (John 3:36).

Death for the believer is but the doorman at the gates to glory. Yes, we still go through the throes of death, but the eternal/spiritual consequence of punishment and separation from God is no more. The sting of death (sin) has been removed. Death becomes simply the wrapping of God's gift of life to us. Although none welcome the possible bodily pain and suffering of dying, death for the believer is no longer to be feared. Once death simply meant anxiety and agony, but, as Latourelle states, "Now that Christ has died, there is no event in the universe that is more important than death. If we die with him, the commonplace act of dying is taken up into the mystery of God."[21]

What response should we make to these biblical truths? We must make sure that we trust in Christ's death, so that we might be delivered from death. We can live a life of thankful praise to God for his gracious gift. We must refuse to worry about death, and instead live prepared and expectant to go to that far better place. We should no longer live materialistically, as if this world were the be-all and end-all. And we must take every opportunity to witness to the offer of life and warn of the final outcome at death for those who reject Christ. Surely, this has been the spirit of the multitude of Christians through two millennia, who have "loved not their lives even unto death" (Rev. 2:10; 12:11 RSV), martyrs throughout the centuries who willingly laid down their lives for Christ who laid down his life for them. Consider the faith of Dietrich Bonhoeffer, seen in his last words as he went to his execution by the Nazis on April 9, 1945: "This is the end, for me the beginning of life."[22]

FOUR

THE MILLENNIUM MAZE

They will be priests of God and of Christ
and will reign with him for a thousand years.
(Rev. 20:6b)

PARTIES AND PANIC ATTACKS

Mention the millennium, and many people will probably think of some of the Y2K projects, such as a new footbridge in London that wobbled in the wind, or the Docklands Dome, which is generally regarded as a wasteful white elephant. Both images are rather apposite for me: The doctrine of the millennium has been rather poorly presented, causing a lot of wobble, while great time and expense have been spent on it with little of significance to show. Some will be reminded of the neurotic fear that many felt, that on the dot of midnight 1999/2000 a bug, worm, or virus would cause all computers to crash and we would have apocalyptic scenarios of nuclear weapons launching, planes falling out of the sky, and financial markets crashing: The world would be thrown into chaos and even World War III.

Some on the lunatic fringe, obsessed with biblical number crunching, expected Jesus to come back to Jerusalem in the year 2000, not grasping that there is probably a discrepancy in the dating of Christ's birth—it was more likely 3 or 4 BC, and thus the Y2K celebrations may have been a bit late! Nevertheless, fifteen thousand police and security officers were drafted into Jerusalem just in case Christians went on the rampage, attempting to usher in the second coming and possibly assaulting the Al-Aqsa mosque while they were at it. For sports enthusiasts the millennium simply meant a new stadium in Cardiff; for the hedonists it meant a bigger New Year's party than usual; for the optimists it meant the hope of peace on earth; for the realists it meant just another date and business as usual. So, just what is the millennium?

DEFINING TERMS

The term *millennium* is a conjunction of two Latin words, *mille* ("thousand") and *anni* ("years"). In cultural terms it refers to a thousand-year era, usually the cusp of that era—ending one thousand-year period and beginning the next. As a religious concept it has usually been termed "chiliasm" (after the Greek *chilia*, meaning "a thousand"). The source for this is Revelation 20:1–7, where the term "a thousand years" is referred to six times, although the reference is unique and not repeated elsewhere in the New Testament. The rather modern terms "premillennialism," "postmillenialism," and "amillennialism" define the different theological positions taken on what the "thousand years" refers to:

- *Premillennialism* believes in the return of Christ before he establishes his thousand-year reign on earth.
- *Postmillennialism* believes that Jesus will return after the church has gloriously reigned for a thousand years (understood either literally or figuratively).
- *Amillennialism* believes that the thousand years is the era of the church advancing its rule, from its Pentecost conception to its end-time consummation when Jesus returns.

Generally speaking, the mention of the term outside the context of Y2K would probably be received with puzzlement. Mention the millennium in many church circles, however, and one soon finds oneself in the midst of a heated debate. Indeed, as a concept, its importance and interpretation have both defined and divided whole movements. James Garrett has rightly said, "The doctrine of the millennium has proved to be very obsessive and quite divisive among evangelical Protestants, especially in the United States." But he cautions:

> *It ought not to be an issue over which Christians should break fellowship and form antagonistic camps. If indeed there is only one biblical text and it is to be found in a highly symbolic book, some caution is to be desired.*[1]

Generally, that is the line this study will follow, although, as we shall see, many premillennialists believe that there are more texts than one to support the doctrine of millennium. They also observe that the book of Revelation, although highly symbolic, contains many plain and unambiguous statements.

MILLENNIUM NOTIONS IN HISTORY

Early understanding

The origins of a theological millennium, a thousand-year golden era, may be traced in Babylonian and Hellenistic cosmology, which influenced Hellenistic Judaism (e.g., 4 Ezra; 2 Bar.).[2] One notion derives from the six days of creation set out in Genesis 1. The psalmist says that each "day" is like a thousand years (Ps. 90:4), and thus some inferred that after six "days," representing a thousand years each, the seventh day of the Sabbath rest—i.e., the millennium—would come. In the intertestamental era it came to mean the hoped-for era of the physical reign of the Messiah from Jerusalem and the restoration of David's kingdom.

While millennial views, particularly premillennial, were evident in the first two centuries of the postapostolic era, they were virtually unknown in the apostolic era. In the second and third centuries, a non-figurative, literal view of Revelation 20 became apparent in the writings of the Montanists, Commodian, Irenaeus, and Justin Martyr. Tertullian claimed:

> *We confess that a kingdom is promised to us upon earth before the entry into heaven and in a different state of existence, but after the resurrection and for a period of 1000 years in the divinely built city of Jerusalem, a kingdom come down from heaven.*[3]

However, few of the ancient fathers accepted this view. It was not, for example, adopted by the great teachers of Alexandria or Rome.

Augustine

In the fourth century Augustine was initially attracted to a notion of the millennium as the seventh-day Sabbath rest of history, a literal thousand-year reign that would bring to an end the age of the church at the close of the first millennium AD. Later, with mature reflection on Scripture, he came to repudiate the concept, arriving at a very different interpretation. This is seen in his *City of God* (Book XX, Ch. 7), in which he presents the millennium as the consistent rule of God on earth through the course of the church's history.[4]

Augustine may well have been put off the premillennial view because it was held by the Donatist schismatics,[5] whose expectation of an imminent return of Christ led them to party enthusiastically, leading to extremes of sensuality and gluttony at their feasts. A further influence that whittled away at the literalist interpretation of Revelation 20 was the paradigm shift toward the Constantinian era, when the church was in ascendancy throughout the Roman Empire. Augustine was supported by Jerome and Tyconius in the belief that the millennium reign was not a future period, but covered the spiritual rule of Christ through the church militant, from the first advent of Christ to the second.[6] In other words, the millennium was the duration of the history of the church. Augustine held this view to the end, and in one of his last works, *De Civitate Dei*, he wrote that the thousand years of Christ's earthly kingdom stand in a symbolic way for "all the years of the Christian era." For him the first resurrection (Rev. 20:6) was the resurrection to spiritual life at conversion. Although the saints reign now with Christ, they will certainly reign with him differently in eternity. This rule of Christ through the church restrains evil and wickedness in the world.[7]

Augustine's spiritual view of the millennium as the reign of Christ through the church held the day. Although mention of the millennium was notably absent from all the major creeds, what has become known as amillennialism was declared orthodox eschatology at the ecumenical Council of Ephesus in AD 431.[8] Amillennialism dominated throughout the medieval period. Toward the end of the first millennium, hopes were high for the return and reign of Jesus, and this in part undergirded the Crusades. This approach continued on through the Reformation and up until the mid-nineteenth century. However, throughout church history, mystical and renewal groups have often been attracted to millennial expectations.

Changing views

The twelfth century saw the rise of the influential Joachim of Fiore, a prophetic abbot and founder of the Cistercian monastery in Fiore, Italy. He claimed that the world was divided into three epochs—the age of the Father, the age of the Son, and the age of the Spirit. His studies of John's Apocalypse led him to an optimistic view of history, and he believed that after the imminent crisis of the Antichrist, there would come a new monastic era of the church on earth, a contemplative utopia brought about by the Holy Spirit.

In the fifteenth century Savonarola envisaged a new Jerusalem descending on Florence, while the Dominican Giovanni Annio of Viterobo articulated a millennial model in which the pope defeated the Saracens, united the church, and inaugurated an era of the church's blessedness. However, officially, the Catholic Church, like the Orthodox Church, has always rejected chiliasm and taken an amillennial position.

The Reformers

In the sixteenth century the Reformers Luther and Calvin reckoned all millennialism to be a Jewish fantasy. The 1530 Lutheran Augsburg Confession stated:

> *Rejected too are certain opinions which are even now making an appearance and which teach that, before the resurrection of the dead, saints and godly men will possess a worldly kingdom and annihilate all the godless.*[9]

This in part was an attack on the likes of the peasant leader Thomas Muntzer and his prophetic followers, who believed in an imminent millennium preceded by a period of dominance by the antichrist Turks.

Calvin forcefully repudiated any millennial notion in his *Institutes*, with one chapter tellingly entitled "The Error of Chiliasm."[10] He states firmly:

> *Their fiction is too childish to need or to be worth refutation. And the Apocalypse (book of Revelation) from which they undoubtedly draw a pretext for their error does not support them. For the number "1000" does not apply to the eternal blessedness of the church but only to the various disturbances that awaited the church, while still toiling on earth. On the contrary, all scripture proclaims that there will be no end to the blessedness of the elect or the punishment of the wicked [Matt. 25:41–46] … even a blind man can see what stupid nonsense these people talk.… But let us pass over these triflers, lest, contrary to what we have previously said, we seem to judge their ravings worth refuting.*

Thomas Cranmer, in writing *The Book of Common Prayer* and defining English Protestant theology, in his first edition of 1553 had forty-one articles of Anglican faith, which were later reduced to thirty-nine by Elizabeth I's revision in 1563. One of the articles edited out was a refutation of chiliasm, dismissed as a "fable of Jewish dotage." The influential Henry Bullinger of Zurich wrote against what he thought was "the heresy of chiliastes and millennaries," supporting instead a spiritual interpretation of the millennial reign (Rev. 20) as the period between the two advents of Christ.

Notwithstanding the antichiliastic position of the major Reformers, many smaller European renewal movements such as the Bohemian Brethren, Taborites, Anabaptists, and Hugenots retained a millennial expectation. The Puritans and Nonconformists, having suffered much for their simple biblical faith, often held strongly to a postmillennial view, which contained ideas of the collapse of the papacy, the defeat of the Turks, the conversion of the Jews, and a reign of peace and gospel success. John Foxe (*The Book of Martyrs*) and John Milton (*Paradise Lost*) both anticipated a future millennium. In England an influential Puritan movement known as the Fifth Monarchists worked energetically for an imminent millennium, ushered in by politics and even military action.[11]

Eighteenth-century optimism

In the seventeenth and eighteenth centuries, the likes of Daniel Whitby in England, J. Albrecht Bengel in Germany, and Jonathan Edwards in America held to optimistic postmillennial views that included the notions that the papacy would decline, the Jewish nation would be established and converted, and worldwide evangelization would occur. These would usher in a millennial era of peace and thriving before the second coming. Edwards actually offered the date for the inauguration of the millennial reign as 1866, exactly 1,260 years after AD 606, when the Roman Church was universally recognized. Edwards believed the missionary fervor among the Indians was a sign that the millennium was dawning. A similar notion was held by the Jesuits, whose global evangelization was understood by some as an antecedent to the millennial reign.

Nineteenth-century positions

In the nineteenth century millennialism became a major feature of Nonconformist theology, with four main positions being taken: amillennialism, premillennialism, postmillennialism, and dispensationalism, although there are several subsets.[12]

Amillennialism has the longest and perhaps strongest church pedigree, as we have already noted, with the major fathers and Reformers subscribing to this view. It takes the thousand years as encompassing the period from Jesus' first advent to his last. The reign is understood either as that of the dead departed saints in heaven with Christ, or the reign of Christ through the church on earth. The second coming will be accompanied by the final defeat of Satan, now bound through Christ's work at Calvary and the church's kingdom advance and sacking of the demonic realm. The rapture, the return, the general resurrection, the day of judgment, and the establishing of a new eternal order are understood to occur at the same time. Liberal theologians tend toward a form of amillennialism in which the reign of Christ is understood merely through ethical, existential, or political categories. Many liberals, regrettably, reject the foundational biblical concepts of a literal historical end-time return and regard the rule of Christ as mythical.

Postmillennialism asserts that the millennial rule of Christ will be ushered in by the church, which establishes a platform for the return of Jesus. This will be the result of a passionate implementation of righteousness and peace on earth through tenacious engagement in political, social, economic, and secular spheres and aggressive global evangelism. The church, the glorious bride, will be perfected, triumphant, world-transforming, and after a period of great gospel fruitfulness, having taken over the world, will hand it over to Christ. Before the end the Enemy will briefly arise, only to be utterly defeated. This view became popular in nineteenth-century Latin America, China, Africa, and South Korea. It had heavyweight theological advocates such as Charles Hodge and A. H. Strong to propound it, and it influenced the great Scottish evangelical social activist Thomas Chalmers.[13] Such an optimistic outlook, however, suffered a serious blow on the battlefields of World War I, and today commands little support. It may, however, be found in the Restoration House Church movement, active since the late 1960s, and it underpins the theology of "Christian Reconstructionism" and "Kingdom Now Dominionists."[14] It is also undergoing a resurrection with scholars like Donald Bloesch and Lorranie Boettner. In essence it says, "God's cause triumphs through the church."

Premillennialism has, more than any other theory, dominated Nonconformist eschatology—supported by notable leaders like the Bonar brothers, Robert Murray McCheyne, and C. H. Spurgeon. In our day classic premillennialists include Carl Henry, Francis Schaeffer, and David Pawson. The charismatic Edward Irving, initially a postmillennialist, believed that only a glorious return of Christ could undo the world's evils, a view that directed him toward premillennialism. There is no consensus among premillennialists regarding the rapture and its relation to the tribulation: Dispensationalist premillennialists believe in a pretribulation rapture, while classic/historic premillennialists such as Pawson, Mounce, and Grudem believe in posttribulation rapture. Generally accepted is the conversion of Israel and the return of Christ, who will rule from Jerusalem for a literal thousand years. Finally, Satan will be destroyed, followed by the general resurrection and the last judgment, ushering in eternity. Ironically, this view is also held by less than orthodox groups like Irving's Catholic Apostolic Church, Seventh Day Adventists, Jehovah's Witnesses, and the Mormons.

What is the purpose of the millennial reign?[15] Premillennialists claim that the millennium reign of Christ as depicted in Revelation 20 manifests his reign to the world (a reign now hidden as he rules from heaven), making public his power and glory. The fact that sin and evil can continue during his reign on earth will show up the corruption of the human heart ,which still refuses to honor Christ, and will vindicate his justice in his later judgment on sin at the last judgment as the mil-

lennium epoch closes. Against this, some might say his reign is not all
that perfect, if demonic evil and sin in the human heart remain as the
alternative rule!

Dispensationalism[16] was a view developed in the nineteenth century,
associated with the Brethren founder, J. N. Darby, and the influential
Dr. Scofield. They interpreted the Bible to reveal seven dispensations
of God relating to the world. The final one of these was to be a literal,
earthly, thousand-year millennial kingdom, established at the end of
the church era when the church will be raptured to the new Jerusalem
that hovers over the earthly Jerusalem, where Christ reigns over a Davidic kingdom that rules over the entire world.[17] It has become a highly
influential view, notably in twentieth-century American evangelicalism.
The multimillion-seller Left Behind series has turned dispensationalism into both popular fiction and political commentary.

REVELATION 20:1–7: KEY TEXT OR PRETEXT?

As noted above, the Latin-based term *millennium* refers to the sixfold
mention of a thousand-year (*chilia ete*) period in this text. There is no
further reference in the New Testament to a millennial period in which
Satan is bound and Christ reigns. Most amillennialists infer from
this that other clear eschatological texts (Matt. 24; 2 Thess. 2:7–11;
2 Peter 3:7–13) must be the interpretative key for this single obscure
one. Premillennialists disagree and believe that the Revelation text
should be the interpretative key for other eschatological texts (Luke
1:32; 22:29f.; Acts 1:6f.; Rom. 11:29).[18] The amillennialist will point
out that the major eschatological texts do not refer to a millennium,
while the premillennialist will say that omission is not tantamount to
contradiction. New Testament scholar G. B. Caird rather dismisses this
text because of its notorious usage: "More than any other in the book,

[it] has been the paradise of cranks and fanatics on the one hand and literalists on the other."[19]

I don't want to be a crank, but being literalist may be the right thing in this context. In Revelation 20 we are dealing with a sacred text of canonical Scripture. We must read it with the dignity that inspired Scripture demands and decide whether it is to be taken literally. Please put this book down for a moment and take the time to **read Revelation 20:1–6**, as we'll be discussing it at length.

Musing over millennium[20]

To recapitulate on what we have already noted, interpretations of this passage from Revelation largely fall into four main theological camps: amillennialist, postmillennialist, premillennialist, and dispensationalist.[21] Each of these may have several subsets relating to the timing of the rapture and tribulation (see chapter 8). There is also a possible fifth group, the liberals, who sit loose to Scripture, reject the belief in a physical resurrection of Christ and his return to reign, and dismiss the millennium as myth. They do not believe that a millennium relates to any clear period of time, location, or relation to Satan. I will not be pursuing that theory further in this chapter. Set out below are thumbnail summaries of the four main strands of thought derived from this passage.

Interpretation

- Premillennialism generally sees the millennium as a literal thousand years following the return of Jesus.
- Postmillennialism sees the millennium as either a literal or symbolic thousand-year period of glory and prosperity precipitated by the church's righteous living and gospel work.

- Dispensationalism sees the millennium as a literal period following the era of the church, which has been raptured away.
- Amillennialism sees the millennium as figurative, the era of the church.

Occasion

- Premillennialism locates the millennium at the end of history after Christ returns.
- Postmillennialism locates the millennium at the end of history before Christ returns.
- Dispensationalism locates the millennium at the end of history after Christ returns.
- Amillennialism locates the millennium in history, initiated with Christ's first coming and consummated with his second coming.

Location

- Premillennialism generally sees Jesus reigning with the resurrected martyrs from Jerusalem.
- Postmillennialism generally sees the reign as that of the church over the world.
- Dispensationalism generally sees Jesus reigning with the Jews from Jerusalem.
- Amillennialism generally sees the millennial reign as the increasing influence of the church and kingdom advancement throughout the earth between the two comings of Christ.

Incarceration

- Premillennialism and dispensationalism understand this as the binding of Satan for a thousand years after Jesus' return, before his release and final destruction.
- Postmillennialism understands Satan as already bound and the ground open for taking by the church.
- Amillennialism understands this as the limiting of Satan's powers through the binding by Christ's earthly ministry that ushered in the kingdom, through the decisive blow dealt to the Devil at Calvary, and through the ongoing advance of the kingdom via the church.

Resurrection: Who are the resurrected saints?

- Premillennialism and dispensationalism generally understand this as the future raising of the martyrs to rule with Christ in the thousand years.
- Amillennialism and postmillennialism see this either as the resurrection from spiritual death to new life at conversion (following Augustine), or as the resurrection through death to eternal life in heaven.

Optimism or pessimism?

Stanley Grenz[22] suggests that postmillennialism is generally *optimistic*—the Evil One's attempt to thwart God's plans will fail and the church will grow and triumph, establishing a reign of peace and fruitfulness for a thousand years, followed by the Lord's return. Such a view typically leads to action and engagement in society at every level, seeking to bring in the reign of God. By contrast premillennialism is generally *pessimistic*—only the catastrophic intervention of Christ will establish the church in glorious worldwide influence and prevent the powers of evil from swamping it. However, this could lead to inaction, sitting back and awaiting the intervention of God. Amillennialism is generally *realistic*—understanding the history of the church through the parable of the wheat and the tares (Matt. 13:24f.)—there is victory and defeat, success and failure, and then Christ returns.

Amusingly, David Pawson has a similar analysis to Grenz, but reaches the opposite conclusion—that premillennialism is realistic while amillennialism is pessimistic.[23] You pay your money and take your choice!

Neville Jones believes that premillennialists, who expect Jesus to come and reign on earth for an extended period of time with the saints (as part of his administration), are perhaps more likely to look after the planet than those who think it will be trashed the minute he returns, and also to see their vocations as holy, since they may be called to exercise those vocations in his millennial administration. Jones says:

> *The optimism that the Premillennialists have (which the Amillennialists cannot share) is that Jesus has a glorious future for this earth which includes his followers. The pessimistic aspect of an Amillennialist is that they cannot see a greater future for the church on this earth.*[24]

Jürgen Moltmann believes that:

> *Without millenarian hope, the Christian ethic of resistance, and the consistent discipleship of Christ, lose their most powerful motivation ... without the expectation of an alternative kingdom of Christ, the community of Christ loses its character as "contrast community" to society.*[25]

While we might like to claim that obedience to the command of Christ, imitation of the person of Christ, and inspiration by the Spirit of Christ are powerful motivations for discipleship, Moltmann is right to suggest that a millennial vision is a powerful incentive for our discipleship now and for what we are working toward on earth.

Space does not permit me to go into all the details of the respective millennial positions. I have referred in the bibliography to balanced critiques from the various sides. I tend toward the amillennial position, interpreting the millennium as consistent with church history—although, following postmillennialism, I anticipate a glorious and global bride to greet Christ at his second coming and, following premillennialism and dispensationalism, I believe that God's end-time purposes involve the conversion of Israel.

MINING THE MILLENNIUM

Before we summarize what we have learned from Revelation 20, a few further considerations need to be borne in mind. Premillennialists take the thousand years to be literal. However, in numerous places in Scripture, "a thousand" is a figurative expression for a very long time or a very large number. Nontemporal figurative use includes Deuteronomy 1:10f.; Joshua 23:10; Job 9:3; 33:23; Psalm 50:10; 68:17; Isaiah 7:23; 30:17; and Song of Songs 4:4. Temporal figurative use includes Deuteronomy 7:9; Psalm 84:10; Ecclesiastes 6:6; 7:28; Psalm 90:4; and 2 Peter 3:8. There is no critical necessity to interpret the thousand years as literal, and traditional biblical usage suggests that it should not generally be read literally.[26] Most other numbers within Revelation—such as 666, 7, and 144,000—are normally understood to be figurative and symbolic rather than literal. I understand the thousand years to be a symbol of the timeless reign of God in Christ, with his saints, both reigning in heaven and extending his kingdom here on earth.

The book of Revelation is in the apocalyptic genre, which is rarely straightforward, clear, and propositional, but rather figurative, full of symbols, ciphers, codes, and often the bizarre,[27] with bowls, horned beasts, dragons, and the like. Revelation 20:1–7 is consistent with the style of the rest of the book, having numerous symbols, namely chains, keys, a pit, a serpent, and thrones. Obviously, we must tread carefully here and not assume that everything should be interpreted literally, as the premillennialists prefer to do.

The heart of the premillennial position is that Christ will return and reign on earth for a period (generally taken to be a literal thousand years), during which time Satan is chained and humankind remains free to respond to Christ and his rule. At the end of that period, Satan is let loose to deceive the nations (Rev. 20:7), who will rise up against Christ in war before finally being destroyed. However, I understand the "binding" of Satan (Rev. 20:2) to have been accomplished with the first coming of Christ, the appearance of the kingdom, the mission of the Twelve, the death and resurrection of Christ, the sending of the Spirit, and the advance of the church. While Satan remains alive and active, his powers are reduced and restrained and he has ultimately been dealt a deathblow. A number of passages elsewhere in Scripture (Matt. 12:29; 16:18f.; Mark 3:27; Luke 10:17f.; John 12:31; 16:11; Col. 2:15; Heb. 2:14; Rev. 12:7f.) detail the decisive defeat of Satan associated with the first advent of Christ—which could be seen to be paralleled here in Revelation 20.

Is it really credible, as the premillennialists believe, that Christ would literally reign for a thousand years on earth, exercising government over the nations while sickness, sin, death, and evil continue, and that at the end the Devil would be let loose to raise an army beyond number to march on Jerusalem? Surely Christ defeated all his enemies in Revelation 19! I find this interpretation inconsistent with the rest of Scripture's eschatology, at odds with the internal argument in Revelation, and therefore highly implausible.[28]

Robert Mounce makes the point that a careful reading of this millennial passage will show that it is perhaps limited to resurrected martyrs alone, and that it contains no specific indication that their reign with Christ takes place on earth, or that it necessarily follows the second advent.[29] Thus it could mean that the reigning of the martyrs in heaven with Christ runs consecutively with church history. Revelation 20:4 shifts from earth to heaven, not from heaven to earth. Other amillennialists see this first resurrection as the initial spiritual resurrection to eternal life, the awakening of the dead spirit at conversion. Still others see it as the resurrection at death to life in glory.[30]

Although it might seem natural, it is not necessary to read Revelation 19—21 in linear form, as the premillennialists do. That is, it is not necessary to see chapter 20 as a successive vision of a chronological, historical movement following the advent of Christ detailed in chapter 19, preceding chronologically to the establishment of the new heaven and new earth in chapters 21 and 22. I believe it may be read as reiterative, rather than progressive. The battle of Revelation 20:7–10 is thus not "another battle," but the same last battle as recorded in chapter 16.[31] It is quite plausible to think of 20:7–10 as a return to the vision in 12:7–11,[32] and some scholars have detected a "chiastic" structure (a literary styling) from chapter 17 to chapter 22, which presents the themes not in chronological succession but as a repeated mirror image: Thus themes ABCD are then mirrored back as DCBA. If this is right, it further calls into question the premillennialists' linear, consecutive reading of Revelation 20:1–7.[33]

MILLENNIUM MILEAGE?

Premillennialists will, of course, take issue with my brief commentary above and will suggest that it is not the most natural interpretation of the text, and that it reads other factors into it based on an *a priori* amillennialist view. They are probably right. Taken on its own in splendid isolation, I concede that the premillennial reading of Revelation 20:1–7 is highly plausible. But we do not read isolated Scriptures for doctrine; we allow Scripture to interpret Scripture to find the counsel of God. To my mind the premillennial view of Revelation 20 is not one that coheres easily with the rest of Revelation, let alone the rest of Scripture in its clearer presentation of eschatology. The Bible as a whole seems to envisage only one last battle, one return of Christ, one resurrection and one defeat of Satan (Matt. 24—25; 2 Thess. 2; 2 Peter 3:13). The premillennialists will say that other texts do support their view (Isa. 11:9; Dan. 7:27; 2 Tim. 2:12). However, their criticism that I bring an *a priori* amillennialism to my treatment of Revelation 20 could equally be levelled at their approach: They bring an *a priori* premillennial view to the treatment of these texts. Time will tell who is right.

While I respect the biblical integrity of premillennialism, I cannot say the same for dispensationalism. It seems to be a bizarre reading of Scripture, understanding the millennial kingdom reign as only Jewish, divorced from the church—while the church, a parenthesis in God's main dealings with the kingdom of Israel, is raptured away. The Bible does not describe two future peoples of God—Jews and the church, one in heaven and one on earth, but only one people—the Gentiles grafted onto the olive branch, the first covenant people (the Jews) becoming the second covenant people with the Gentiles (Eph. 2:11–22).

Postmillennialism offers a bold theology that not only spurs the church on to share the gospel actively with the world, but also to transform the world ethically and structurally through politics and ecology—driven by the vision and the hope that we, in the power of the Spirit, can make a difference and create a millennium, a reign of peace and righteousness that will be a platform for the returning Christ.

What we find in dispensationalism, premillennialism, and post-millennialism is a perspective in which Christ is involved in the drive of human history. This is something that can be rather lacking in amil-lennialism, which divorces the reign of Christ from history and culture and could therefore lead to a passive waiting for Jesus to end our his-tory and start eternity. The other views have a strong concept of Jesus not merely ending our history, but entering it at his return. Jesus does not simply come to rescue us from the world, but to reign within it. Althaus spoke of the Christian hope as having "this worldliness."[34] Postmillennialism and even premillennialism have an "anti-supernat-uralism,"[35] an earthly engagement by Christ with this world and with human history. This view is a challenge to the rather individualized and spiritualized amillennialist approach. Conversely, the dispensationalists have constructed a theology in which the church is whisked away from this world and from Christ, who reigns here with Israel. Alternatively, the premillennialists construct a thousand-year history in which Christ rules on earth and yet sickness, death, and sin still exist, and evil is allowed to rouse itself for a final assault on Christ and his reign. This seems to contradict other Scriptures and makes no logical sense.

Ultimately, I have concluded that *a single obscure text in one obscure book does not a doctrine make!* Now of course premillennialists claim support from other texts, generally late Old Testament prophecies, but I rather think these are distorted by their *a priori* view. One looks in vain for any clear statement from Jesus or the apostles to support such a view outside this single passage in Revelation. Premillennialism simply struggles to find a pedigree in the Gospels, Epistles, and apostolic teaching. Admittedly, it was a view held by some early church fathers, though not all, and by some of the great saints in the evangelical world. It was, however, rejected by both the Eastern and Western churches very early on; it finds no trace in the creeds and was dismissed by church luminaries from Augustine to Calvin, Luther, and Cranmer. Amillennialism has generally been the normative view of the historic major Protestant, Reformed, Lutheran, Catholic, and Orthodox churches.

I believe that the best reading of Revelation 20 concerning the millennium—though not without its own problems of interpretation—is to see it as a figurative symbol of a historical, present reign of Christ in the church promoting his kingdom in the world, spanning the whole era of the church until Christ returns. The saints, by virtue of all that baptism represents, have died and risen with Christ and are seated with him in the heavenly places, princes and princesses of Christ's kingdom on earth. The saints who have died in Christ worship and enjoy Christ in heaven. Prior to Jesus' return, the Enemy, whose powers have been restricted since the first advent, will be let loose and he will do his worst for a limited period. Christ will then return, destroy Satan, judge the world, re-create heaven and earth, and reign eternally.

I see myself, therefore, as a *composite millennialist!* While not agreeing totally with the postmillennialists' optimism—brought into question by the parable of the wheat and the tares—I believe that the gospel will advance to the nations and the whole "earth will be full of the knowledge of the LORD as the waters cover the sea" (Isa. 11:9). I do not believe that Christ will return to a disheveled remnant, but to a glorious global bride who will have salted and lighted the world. Although I reject much of the premillennial model, I do subscribe to their generally held belief in

the Jews' restoration to the land and conversion to Christ before the end
(Rom. 11:25f.).

CONCLUSION

Godly Christians, who hold the same high view of Scripture being
inspired by God, have nevertheless come to a varied and at times
contradictory interpretation of Revelation 20 and the millennium.
Consequently, all must be cautious in claiming that their interpretation
alone is right, gracious in their attitudes and careful about comments
concerning those with whom they disagree.

When all is said and done, doctrinal differences over such an issue
are secondary, not of the essence of faith and noncreedal. Consequently,
room for opposite views and respect for those who hold them are essential. Unity is a command from God; hostility and disunity over lesser
doctrine is a sin. I have benefited greatly from the teaching ministry and
godly witness of those who hold eschatological positions different from
my own. I rather like the quip by G. K. Chesterton in his *Charles Dick-
ens*: "We are to remove mountains and bring the millennium, because
then we can have a quiet moment to discuss whether the millennium is
desirable at all."

Whatever position one takes, the major inferences and consequences
are not so different: They generally boil down to timings and locations.
Whether amillennial, premillennial, postmillennial, or panmillennial (it
will all pan out in the end), all will generally agree that the main themes
from Revelation 20 include the following:

1. God is ultimately sovereign over human history.
2. God will intervene in human history when he determines
   to do so.

3. The Devil is active in human history.

4. The Devil is restrained by Christ from venting his full fury.

5. The Devil will mount a final attack and be decisively defeated.

6. The saints will suffer for their faith in Christ.

7. God has a corporate perspective on nations/saints, not just individuals.

8. The saints will overcome death through resurrection.

9. The saints will reign with Christ as princes and priests.

10. The end is not in doubt—Christ will have the last word.

Hans Schwarz notes that John's apocalyptic vision of a millennium was never intended to lead to triumphalism, but rather to be a pastoral comfort to those who, like him, and throughout the church since, suffer for following Christ.[36] We may take courage that, despite our suffering (and even martyrdom), saints in heaven rest and rule with Christ, who will return, resurrect the dead, rout the Enemy, and reign forever. As I have said before, "I've read the end of the book, and the Lamb wins."

FIVE

SIGNS OF THE END TIMES

When these things begin to take place, stand up and lift up
your heads, because your redemption is drawing near.
(Luke 21:28)

BIBLICAL BINGO

As a young boy I earned pocket money by helping to set up tables and
chairs for a bingo night. Occasionally, I also called out the numbers
and listened out for the shout of "Line!" or "House!" as a player ticked
the box and completed a line or card when their numbers were called.
Many Christians approach the question of "signs of the end times" a
little like bingo players. Listening and looking out for social, political,
economic, and cosmic events listed on their end-times signs card, they
tick them off one by one and wait expectantly for the card to be completed
and for the shout of triumph to come: "God in the house!"

The question we seek to tackle in this chapter is this: How accurate or complete is the end-times bingo card and how near are we to
completing it? Growing up, I remember the occasion when Britain
considered joining the Common Market—when government allowed
the people to vote on such things. Whispers went around my church
community that this was wrong, not because of conservative, even
xenophobic, attitudes by some British to the "Europeans," but because

such a move to a greater political union could be a potential instrument for the end-time manifestation of the Antichrist. They were "reasoning" from texts such as Revelation 13:11–18, which may hint at a demonically led, one-world economic, spiritual, and political system (see the latter part of chapter 6).

What are the indicators of the end of the age, the return of Christ and judgment on the world? The Active Bible Church of God lists forty-eight signs that they encourage readers to print out and apply as a template to the news, plotting the approaching Apocalypse.[1] They recognize that many of these events have occurred throughout history, but state that when such events "cluster together in a generation," the end is nigh. Among their forty-eight signs, they speculate wildly about a short-lived union of ten European nations led by a united Germany in a military alliance—not something one can immediately infer from the New Testament. Similarly, the Rapture Index lists forty-five indicators of the end-times return of Christ and the rapture of his bride.[2] Among its criteria are rises in oil prices, general inflation, arms proliferation, volcanoes, and nuclear expansion. Such factors may pragmatically be understood to exacerbate a political destabilization that could lead to an Armageddon, but they cannot be clearly identified in Scripture.

In every age the church has sought to interpret political, social, natural, and spiritual events through the grid of end-times prophetic fulfillment and the imminent return of Christ. The fact that this has happened for two millennia, and that the end has yet to come, must lead us to be cautious when we try to do the same today.[3] Many Christians pointed to the rise of fascism in the 1930s, to the rise of Communism in the 1950s, and to the rise of fundamentalist Islam in the 1990s as signifiers that we are living in the very end-time days. If our forefathers were wrong, prematurely announcing "House!" on their biblical bingo, we may make similar mistakes. Of course, objectively, we can at least say that we are nearer the end than they were.

IS THE END IN SIGHT?

We are, however, not left totally in the dark about the end times. A number of Scriptures directly or indirectly address the matter, even if the interpretation of them is less clear. The major text is the discourse given by Christ, recorded in the Synoptic Gospels in Matthew 24, Mark 13, and Luke 21. Many have noted the close structural parallel between Mark 13 and Revelation 6.[4] Other important texts are in the Epistles, namely 1 Timothy 4:1–3 and 2 Timothy 3:1–5, 7. There is also a long tradition of theological archaeological digs in obscure Old Testament prophetic texts, regarded as eschatological pointers to the restoration of Israel to the land, its conversion to God in the end times, and the full manifestation of the Antichrist before the return of the Lord. We shall examine these in chapters 6 and 7.

We must note that nearly all New Testament authors believed that they were already living at the end of the age. The signs of the end times were already evident to them (1 Cor. 10:11; 2 Tim. 3:1; Heb. 1:2; James 5:3; 1 Peter 1:5, 20; 2 Peter 3:3; 1 John 2:18). Particularly significant are 2 Thessalonians 1:1–12 and 1 John 2:18, which state that antichrists and lawlessness have already been unleashed. The first-century church was living in the end times and was experiencing the end-times manifestation of evil, a manifestation that we have now experienced for two millennia and will continue to experience until the return of Christ. Such texts adopt the eschatological framework of Judaism, a belief in the coming Messiah, end-time persecutions and deceptions from the Antichrist, the upheaval of evil and its titanic clash with God's people (Ezek. 38:2f.; Dan. 9:27; 11:31; 12:11; Zech. 14:2).

Jesus' end-time discourse (Matt. 24)

Rather than glean a perspective from numerous texts, many of which are contentious, we shall focus our attention on Jesus' teaching in Matthew 24, which remains the fullest treatment of end-time signs. The structure of this text has caused critics angst for centuries. As we will see, although Jesus places the signs in the future, they range from datable specifics, such as the siege of Jerusalem, through final date signs occurring on the day of the Lord's appearing, to more general occurrences, such as the persecution and deception against the church and her worldwide gospel proclamation.

The context is clear from the start. The disciples have commented on the impressive temple buildings, to which Jesus responds by prophesying that not one stone will remain on another (24:2). This draws out three questions from the disciples (v. 3): When will this destruction of the temple happen? What will be the sign of Christ's coming? What will be the sign of the end of the age? The single Greek definite article before the coming of Christ and the end of the age link these two events. Christ had not yet died, let alone ascended, so what the disciples understood by this is unclear. It is nonetheless significant that Matthew records Jesus coming with the end of the age. The sacking of Jerusalem and the destruction of the temple did take place in AD 70, as we now know, but although appalling, it did not usher in the end—it only signified what would occur leading up to the end. It may have been historically unconnected, but the destruction of the temple presented a prototype of the world's destruction at the end of time.

Unmistakable signs

Jesus replied to the disciples' questions by listing several signs that would serve as indicators of the drive of history toward the end. They do not signal the end as imminent, but they anticipate its coming (v. 6b), like the onset of the pains that precede birth (v. 8). Birth pains increase in intensity and occur more frequently as the actual birth draws closer. With one exception (v. 14), all the signs are negative. They are signs that can be traced across the various threads of human existence—political, spiritual, natural, and cosmological. They are not secret signs for the secretly initiated; they are public, observable, and unmistakable:

v. 5	False messiahs would lead many astray.
v. 6	Wars and rumors of wars would cause alarm.
v. 7a	Nation would rise against nation, kingdom against kingdom.
v. 7b	Famines and earthquakes would occur in various places.
v. 9	There would be hatred and persecution of Christ's disciples, even to death.
v. 10	Many would fall away from the faith and betray each other.
v. 11	False prophets would lead many astray.
v. 12a	Lawlessness would increase.
v. 12b	The love of many would grow cold.
v. 14a	The gospel would be preached throughout the world to all nations.

This global gospel witness will take place, and then the end will come. The Greek words *kai tote exei to telos* are clear. *Kai tote*, "and then," introduces what follows in time; *exei to telos*, "comes the end," refers to the cessation, completion, and climax of history.[5] Jesus informs the world that, following these signs, we may expect his glorious appearance.

Having spoken in future terms of signs on a general global scale, Jesus focuses on the specific future local sign of the defilement of the temple (prophesied in Dan. 9:27; 11:31; 12:11)—a repeat of what had happened previously in Israel's history:

v. 15   The abomination that causes desolation.

vv. 16–21 The tribulation of Israel.

This future sign event predicting Jerusalem's fall reflects the previous sign event of the manifestation and personification of evil, when for three and a half years around 170 BC, the Syrian king Antiochus Epiphanes (meaning "glorious"), who was nicknamed Epimanes ("crazy"), sought to crush Judaism. He blasphemously placed an altar to Zeus in the temple court, sacrificed swine on the altar, and turned the Levites' quarters into chambers for prostitution. He died insane after being defeated by the Maccabean revolt. But this historic event would act as a prophecy for what would happen again. Christ prophesies a similar tribulation for Israel—the defilement and destruction of the temple. This future event might also be a sign of the end-time manifestation of the Antichrist preceding Jesus' return.

Such an abomination was attempted by Caligula in AD 39 when he ordered that his statue be set up in the Holy of Holies, but public protest caused him to relent. Then in AD 70, Titus was dispatched to deal with the independent religious Jews. He brought an unparalleled time of evil to Israel, as recorded by Josephus (writing in the later AD 70s in his *War on the Jews*). Josephus explains how the siege of Jerusalem led to a famine, and describes how one woman killed, roasted, and then ate her suckling child (see "War" 6.3.4). Such barbaric and inhumane scenes were repeated widely. When the city finally fell to the Roman army, they found rooms piled high with the bodies of those who had starved to death (5.12.3). Some ninety-seven thousand Jews were taken into slavery, and 1.1 million were killed. Unlike the three and a half years of terror under Antiochus Epiphanes, which ended well for Israel with the Maccabean uprising, no such army would come to the rescue in AD 70. Titus ordered the complete flattening of the temple. Not one stone would be left on another, as Christ foretold.[6]

Then Jesus moves from the specifics of the fall of Jerusalem in AD 70 to the more general signs of the end times:

vv. 21–22 The great tribulation.

v. 23f.   The appearance of false Christs, false prophets.

v. 24   The deception of many through signs and wonders.

vv. 25–26 Further deception by the appearance of a mysterious Christ.

v. 27   A warning that disciples should not be deceived, for Christ will return instantaneously, unmistakably, universally.

v. 29a   The darkening of the sun and moon.

v. 29b   The stars falling to Earth and the heavenly bodies being shaken.

v. 30   The appearance of the Son of Man.

v. 31   The angels sounding their trumpets and gathering the elect.

Jesus says that "this generation" (*genea aute*) would not pass away before all these things were fulfilled (v. 34). Some interpreters think Jesus was simply mistaken, as the signs were not all fulfilled within the span of that generation. However, rather than interpreting the "things fulfilled" as all the signs, perhaps a better interpretation is that they refer more specifically to Christ's teaching about the Jerusalem tribulation and abomination as the answer to the disciples' first question about the end of the temple. This was fulfilled in AD 70, forty years after Jesus' teaching here around AD 30, well within one generation.[7]

Alternatively, some have rendered "generation" as "race," thus understanding the verse to mean that the Jewish people will not pass away until all the signs are fulfilled. Then Jesus will return. Although this lacks scholarly approval, it is not impossible, and the use of the word *genea* for "race" is as old as Homer. It certainly would remove the theological difficulties associated with this text, which C. S. Lewis has called "the most embarrassing in the New Testament," because of what he sees as its failure to be fulfilled.

Be alert

How should we respond to these signs? Jesus tells the parable of the fig tree (vv. 32–33) and reminds us that we know the summer season is near when the fig-tree leaves sprout. So when we see these signs, we know the season of Christ's return draws near. Then, in verses 36–39, Jesus informs us that no one, not the angels nor even he himself, but the Father alone, knows the exact hour and day of the end. But the coming of the Son of Man will be as "in the days of Noah." In those days most people were eating, drinking, marrying, going about their daily routine, oblivious to what was about to happen, while Noah and his family were preparing their ark, obeying the Lord, preaching the gospel. Noah and his family did not know the exact timing of God's impending visit in judgment, but they were going to be ready.

The floodwaters did not begin until the ark was completed; they did not overwhelm the land until all Noah's family and animals were aboard the ark (Gen. 7:7f.). I wonder whether the date of the end, known only by the Father (Matt. 24:36) and set by him (Acts 1:7), is not so much a specified time and date, but a fixed circumstance—that of our fulfillment of the only sign that we control, the preaching of the gospel to the nations. When all the elect have come in, then the end will come. Until that time the Father's preserving grace holds back the flood of evil and his flood of judgment against it. Of course, the omniscient Sovereign knows when that date is, but I am interested in whether it is fixed or movable depending on church commitment to worldwide evangelization.

In verses 40–51 we have the three parables: the two men in a field and two women at the mill where one of each is suddenly taken; the thief who comes by night; and the master who returns unexpectedly. Through these Jesus is encouraging his disciples to be awake, alert, and active so that they are not taken unawares at the coming of the Son of Man. The signs that Jesus offers indicate imminent eschatological activity.

Now—then—when?

The task of interpretation is not as easy as some might think and most would like. Ulrich Luz has posed the issue well:

> *In all ages its main question is: is our text to be interpreted historically or exegetically? Does it speak of the destruction of Jerusalem in 70 CE and of other experiences from the time of its composition? Or does it speak of the final tribulations, of the Antichrist and of the return of Christ? Or does it speak of both? If so, is there anywhere in the text a clear line between past history and anticipated end of history that brings God's final intervention?*[8]

We can identify five possible categories of interpretation:[9]

1. *Eschatological*—which understands this passage as referring
    specifically to the end times. This was the view generally held
    by the early church and repeated in the Apocalypse of Peter,
    Hippolytus, Hilary, Cyril, and Irenaeus, as well as in the
    classical later Reformed dogmatics.

2. *Historical*—understanding all these signs as relating to verses
    15–20 and the specific historical fall of Jerusalem. This view
    came to the fore in the Enlightenment, when the category of
    history became so important.

3. *Mixed*—Augustine believed this text had a threefold vista: the
    historical fall of Jerusalem in AD 70, the ongoing spiritual
    experience of the body of Christ the church, and the ultimate
    return of Jesus.

4. *Church historical*—this method was used historically by the
    Anabaptists and Pietists, and by many modern charismatics
    or dispensationalists (Left Behind types), who seek to
    interpret events of their day as particular fulfillments of these
    specific prophecies. The church has always put herself in
    this story. Church leaders claimed that false teachers like the
    Gnostics or Montanists were a fulfillment of Jesus' prophecies
    about false prophets. No doubt in times of persecution the
    Lord's prophecies were comforting to individuals who saw
    themselves as living out the text, ushering in the end. Of
    course there will come a point when it is directly relevant for
    the church on earth at the second coming.

5. *Spiritual*—Origen interpreted this text not in literal historical
    terms, but in an individual, personal, spiritual manner,

anticipating Rudolf Bultmann eighteen centuries later. This model understands the signs as personal experiences, not historical events.

The Lutheran Hans Schwarz states that the signs are "a theological evaluation of history in the light of the expected end and not a calendar by which one can calculate when the end will come."[10] For him this text conveys the demand for an immediate response. Similarly, the Dutch Reformed scholar G. C. Berkouwer argues that the signs may not be used as a "calculation of approximate temporal conclusions from certain selected phenomena."[11] He believes that the specific reference to the contemporary situation in Jerusalem "rids eschatology of any futurism."[12] John Hosier argues that these signs are to be taken not as end-time prophecy, but as an "overview of Christian history."[13] However, Berkouwer also argues for a "de-apocalypticising" and a "continuous historical contextual re-interpretation" of these signs. The church is called to live eschatologically now—not looking forward expectantly to the end, but living as if the end were nigh. The apocalyptic perspective, he says, is always a present perspective.[14]

Berkouwer rightly eschews attempts to calculate the date of the end by the signs of the present, but is it not possible both to live today as if it were the end, not knowing the exact time or date, and to recognize that there will be a literal historical end preceded by such signs, which therefore lead us to a greater awareness, eagerness, and preparedness? David Pawson takes these signs as being historically future, with any historical reference to the fall of Jerusalem and the desecrating abominations functioning merely as a foreshadowing— symbols and ciphers for a manifestation of the end-time Antichrist.[15] Joseph Ratzinger (now Pope Benedict), while cautioning against using such prophecies to calculate dates, understands them as referring to the end of time.[16]

In my view all the scholars above are correct in what they affirm, but wrong in what they deny. I believe it possible, like Augustine, to hold a mixed view, and to interpret this passage in a dynamic, prophetic way. Even as historic events become prophetic symbols for the future (e.g., the exodus as a prophetic type of God's deliverance of his people through Christ; the Davidic kingdom as a prophetic type of the kingdom reign of Christ; the birth of a king in Isaiah 7:10f. as a prophetic type of the incarnation of Christ), so the fall of Jerusalem may point beyond its particular historic event and have layers of historic prophetic engagement.

The "abomination that causes desolation" may be a useful interpretative key for the whole discourse on the signs, combining as it does several legitimate perspectives. It is a *retrospective motif*, looking back two hundred years to 170–168 BC and the immoral desecration of the temple by Antiochus Epiphanes, who set up an idol to Zeus and offered pigs' blood on the altar. It is a *prospective motif*, looking forward forty years to when Titus's Roman army would besiege and destroy Jerusalem and notably blaspheme God and defile God's temple. It is a *figurative motif*, of the incessant work of the Enemy to defile God's temple, the church, and the believer, and perhaps also of God's judgment against a rebellious people. It may also be a *proleptic motif*, anticipating a demonic manifestation toward the end of time, be it person or regime, that sets itself up as the object of worship, that seeks to defile and destroy God's domain of church and kingdom. Some indeed believe that the Antichrist will be like Antiochus and Titus, blaspheming God, attacking Israel, and desecrating a rebuilt temple (see chapter 6).

Similarly, church persecutions, deceptions, natural disasters of famines and earthquakes, and social conflicts in war have always happened. God's people have been instructed here by Christ not to take fright, but to take hope, for such events are birth pangs, prophetic pointers to the return of Christ. The references to astral phenomena, especially the darkening of the sun and moon, seem yet to be fulfilled, although we might interpret these as ongoing eclipses, or even as symbolic apocalyptic language pointing to an "earth-shattering event." As the rainbow is a promise that God will never destroy the earth again by flood, so such natural, social, and spiritual events, although negative, speak positively of Christ's return. As well as constant current indicators that time is marching toward its end, it is possible that Jesus wanted us to understand that such signs will intensify and cluster toward the end of the age.

ACCELERATION OF END-TIMES SIGNS?

I have suggested that the Matthew 24 signs may be understood from three vantage points: as historically specific (the fall of Jerusalem); as the ongoing narrative of the groaning church awaiting redemption (persecutions, deceptions, gospel proclamations) and the groaning world awaiting redemption (earthquakes, famines, lawlessness, wars); and perhaps also as a clustering of these to signify the very end of the age and the coming of Christ. Is there any evidence for this last view?

False messiahs

"False messiahs" are not just those who claim to be Christ, but any who claim to be a divine world savior. Numerous people have actually claimed to be Jesus Christ. Many have been treated for psychosis. One even stormed my church pulpit once to declare himself! Numerous others have proffered themselves as messianic figures, from erstwhile sports presenter David Ike to rock musician Jim Jones. If one reads a certain American city telephone directory, dozens claim to be God or Christ.[17]

False prophets

These are more prevalent than false messiahs, and less obvious. It is their stock-in-trade, by word or remarkable deed, to distract people from the truth contained in Scripture and revealed in Christ. Moses declared that any prophet who incites the people to follow any God other than Yahweh is a false prophet (Deut. 13:1–5). In the early church, false prophets and false teachers undermined the work of the apostles and were challenged and warned against (Acts 13:6–12; 2 Peter 2:1–3). We live in an age when, increasingly, self-appointed prophetic figures claim divinely inspired spirituality and charismatic authority. But these claims are no proof of a genuine inspiration and calling. Jesus himself said that remarkable signs and prophecies offered in his name were no test for authenticity (Matt. 7:15f.). John offers the test for the false prophet: He is one who cannot acknowledge that Jesus Christ is God "come in the flesh" (1 John 4:1–3).

Wars

A survey of wars shows that there have been many more in the last five hundred years than there were in the previous five millennia. Unquestionably, more people were involved in war and were victims of war in the twentieth century than in the previous nineteen hundred years put together. At the time of writing, there are ongoing wars in Colombia, the Philippines, Tamil, Turkey, Kurdistan, Iraq, Western New Guinea, Uganda, Senegal, Somalia/Ethiopia, Kashmir, Nagaland, India, Congo, Laos, Afghanistan, Puttani, Côte d'Ivoire, Pakistan,

Chad/Sudan, Sahara, Mexico, and Israel. Technological advances and population increase have caused an exponential rise in the number of deaths through war. Rumors of wars also abound: The whole Middle East seems poised for conflict, while the former Soviet Union is destabilized and volatile.

Famines

Famines are nothing new. We see them throughout Scripture in the experience of Abraham, Joseph, Ruth, and the early church. In Europe famines wreaked havoc in Finland in the seventeenth century, in Iceland in the eighteenth century, and in Ireland and France in the nineteenth century. During the twentieth century, a total of seventy million people died from famine, thirty million of those in China between 1958 and 1961. Famine struck the Netherlands in the 1940s, killing thirty thousand—it is remembered as *Hongerwinter* ("hunger winter"). As I write, there are famines in Cambodia, China, the former Soviet Union, Ethiopia, and North Korea. Although at present we have enough food resources to feed the world, albeit hindered in places by political or economic factors, in time global warming will affect the production of crops detrimentally and the rapid population increase will perhaps double the number of mouths to feed (twelve billion) by 2050. This signals trouble ahead.[18]

Earthquakes

Earthquakes have always occurred. It is difficult to evaluate whether they have increased. Some believe that the data supports an exponential growth in earthquakes, but others challenge this. The proliferation of seismic centers from 350 in 1931 to over eight thousand today could simply mean that we are far more accurate in receiving and analyzing data. The National Earthquake Information Center records twenty thousand earthquakes a year, over fifty a day, of which up to twenty exceed 7.0 on the Richter Scale and cause serious collateral damage and loss of life.[19]

Persecutions

Christians have always been persecuted. The book of Acts may be read as an account of church expansion amidst persecution, whether from Judaism or Rome. Let us not forget that much of the New Testament was written by believers in jail, and several of its main authors died for their faith. Only when Constantine converted his empire to Christianity did such systemic persecutions cease. But whenever the gospel has pioneered new inroads across the globe, suffering has accompanied it. Today it is estimated that, in the 250 or so nations of the world, Christians are under pressure in all but thirty, and that number of "safe" countries is shrinking. Some two hundred million Christians do not have full human rights and face everything from harassment to rape, torture, and murder. The fiercest persecution is found in Islamicist- or Communist-ruled countries.[20] There has certainly been an increase in persecution in recent times, with more martyrs in the twentieth century than in the previous nineteen centuries put together.

Lawlessnes

Lawlessness is a term depicting departure from God's moral decree. Paul declared that in his day the end times were in evidence through the prevalence of evil:

> *People will be lovers of themselves, lovers of money, boastful,*
> *proud, abusive, disobedient to their parents, ungrateful, unholy,*

without love, unforgiving, slanderous, without self-control,
brutal, not lovers of the good, treacherous, rash, conceited, lovers
of pleasure rather than lovers of God—having a form of godliness
but denying its power. (2 Tim. 3:2–5)

So actually nothing has changed. In the "civilized" United Kingdom, we hear of people being kicked to death by gangs while others film it on their phones to send to their friends. We have seen a staggering 2,054 percent increase in syphilis between 1996 and 2005. Television chat shows celebrate everything from promiscuity to bestiality. In 2000 there were 7,617 pregnancies among girls under the age of sixteen, of which 54.5 percent ended in legalized abortion. Two in three marriages end in divorce, with all the social and psychological trauma that involves.[21] Crime statistics claim 10,912,000 incidents in 2005–2006 in England and Wales alone, with 23 percent of the population being victims of crime and 2.4 million people being victims of violence.[22]

So is the end imminent?

The question remains whether such signs are accelerating, and thus indicating that history is hurtling toward the end times. Do we really live in a society that is more immoral than Caligula's Rome, or more oppressive than under Hitler's Nazi regime? Is life more tenuous today than it was in the medieval period? My own view is that, obviously, after two millennia, we are nearer "the end of the end" than when Christ spoke. But whether there has been a proliferation or conglomeration of such signs, indicating an imminent end, is open to question. We must not lose sight of the fact that the New Testament authors announced they were already in the last days, and that many of the signs have remained consistent throughout the ages.

Most significant is Christ's reference to the sign of gospel proclamation to the world. This seems to me to be the crucial criterion indicating the proximity of the Lord's return. It is also the only sign that we have an active role in fulfilling. Jesus is clear that the gospel witness must go worldwide before the end and his return. We know we have yet to get anywhere near such a fulfillment. Statistics vary about how many remain unevangelized, but one estimate is that 27 percent of the world's population have yet to hear the gospel and, despite missionary endeavor, this number is set to increase due to population growth.[23] The task is made more difficult by increasing ethnic fragmentation and migration of the world's population, so Christian mission means trying to connect to moving targets.[24] There is still much gospel work to be done before the trumpets sound and the saints are gathered up to meet Christ in the air. Also still to be fulfilled is the last sign, the conversion of all Israel (Rom. 11:26), after which Christ will return. We will return to this in chapter 7.

CONCLUSION

How do we respond to these signs? Perhaps there are four groups, each with a different approach.

First, there are those who are *fearful*—paralyzed by a belief that prophetic predictions have been laid out, that antichrists are rising, that disasters are imminent. As Eugen Weber notes, "Dreadful apprehensions of the approaching end were an integral part of medieval minds."[25] He records one event in 793 when, following a prophecy that the end was nigh, "in terror the people fasted all night until the 9th hour on Sunday when [one] feeling hungry declared, 'let us eat and drink for if we are to die we might as well die fit.'"[26] In the eighteenth century peasants fearing the rise of the Antichrist offered sacrifices of young calves to the Virgin Mary, to ward off disease from the herds. But Jesus foretold us the signs specifically so that we would *not* be afraid (Matt. 24:6).

Then there are the *fatalists*—recognizing that if indeed the end times and signs are being played out, little can be done to change things. Thus the atheist Voltaire, writing against the backdrop of heightened religious anxiety caused by the mid-eighteenth-century earthquake in Lisbon, wrote his "Poem on Natural Law" stating that the world was incomprehensible, the Eternal either deaf or nonexistent and humanity the helpless football of fate.[27] But Jesus gave us the signs specifically so that we would *not* be indifferent and fatalistic (Matt. 24:42f.).

Some others are *fanatics*. Believing the end is nigh, they seek to precipitate or partake in it, preparing themselves or their religious communities often in extreme paranoid pietism. One thinks of the Montanist movement in the early second century, which followed a ruthless asceticism and encouraged its followers to await the return of Christ and the descent of the New Jerusalem in the desert of Pepuza. A modern equivalent can be seen in the cultish Waco community in Texas led by David Koresh in the 1990s. But Jesus gave us the signs to warn us and make us *discerning* in the face of such false claims (Matt. 24:4f., 23f.).

Finally, some are *faithful and faith-filled*. Noah knew that God had spoken. Judgment was coming. For 120 years he lived obediently to God's command, building the ark and preaching righteousness, not knowing the exact timings or details, but trusting that God would visit in fulfillment of his promise. Jesus answered his disciples' request for signs of the temple's destruction, Christ's return, and the end of the age, not so that they could play biblical end-times bingo, but so that they might be *encouraged*. Yes, his words are theological and eschatological, but they are also pastoral and practical. Facing false prophets, they should be unsurprised. Facing betrayal and persecution, they should be strengthened. Living amidst the increase of wickedness and natural or cosmic upheavals, they should be buoyed up by faithfulness to Christ. The parallel passage in Luke has this glorious call in the face of such signs: "When these things begin to take place, stand up and lift up your heads, because your redemption is drawing near" (Luke 21:28).

The catalogue of prophetic end-time signs in Matthew 24 includes experiences and evidences that range from natural to supernatural, spanning the breadth of the world and the depth of history since the time of Christ. They may yet be intensified further as we accelerate to Christ's second coming, but that remains supposition and speculation. The specific historic event of the "abomination that causes desolation" and the destruction of the temple originally fulfilled in AD 70 may be repeated literally with a personality defiling a rebuilt temple in Jerusalem, or—more likely—with a political personality blasphemously setting himself up as the object of worship and by a brutalizing of God's holy people. Regardless of whether we see such signs as historic, current, or future, the promised return of Christ has pastoral and practical implications: Jesus' illustrations of the budding fig tree, the days of Noah, the homeowner's alertness to the thief in the night, and the servant's alertness to the master who returns unexpectedly all encourage us to be awake and watchful—not alarmed—and ready to meet our Maker whenever he comes.

Doomsday or Glory Day?

On the day I wrote this, the Doomsday clock was set forward. This symbolic clock face, set up sixty years ago and managed by atomic scientists at the University of Chicago, routinely guestimates humanity's nearness to a thermonuclear war, on the basis of current international political, social, economic, and natural events. The clock has now been set at five minutes to midnight—with midnight representing the end of the world. This is, claim the scientists, the nearest to destruction that we have ever come.

Should we be scared? Is the Doomsday clock accurate in foretelling the end? We should surely be concerned about the things that have led the Chicago scientists to this conclusion, and we should certainly want to be responsible about issues such as nuclear proliferation and climate change—but Jesus gave us a glimpse of the end-time signs so that we might be faith-filled in expectation, faithful in preparation, and engaged in far-afield gospel proclamation. He called us not to focus primarily on the signs or to be gazing into the heavens, but to look prayerfully on the nations where we must preach the gospel until he comes. Let us not start playing end-time-signs bingo. Rather let us play our part in the end-time signs by preaching the gospel to the nations.

SIX

ANTICHRISTS, BEASTS, AND THE MAN OF LAWLESSNESS

Dear children, this is the last hour; and as you have heard
that the antichrist is coming, even now many antichrists
have come. This is how we know it is the last hour.
(1 John 2:18)

In the last chapter we considered the so-called signs of the times that would precede the return of the Lord and the end of the age, focusing on the discourse in Matthew 24. Jesus spoke of natural disasters, conflicts, false messiahs, and false prophets who perform false signs and wonders, terrible persecutions on the church, and the manifestation of "the abomination that causes desolation"—the demonic demigod who would defile God's temple. We concluded that all of these signs have always been a part of church history, but the "abomination" had a historic prefiguring in 170 BC when Antiochus Epiphanes defiled the temple, and a prophetic historic fulfillment in AD 70 when Titus destroyed the temple. However, we suggested that all of these signs may well cluster together and be intensified at the end of time. Indeed, I believe that the abomination that causes desolation will find its final manifestation in the figure described as "the Antichrist" by John (1 John 2:18–26; 4:3–6; 2 John 7), titled "the man of lawlessness" by Paul (2 Thess. 2), and depicted as "the beast" in Revelation 13.

ANTICHRISTS NAMED AND SHAMED

If you Google the word *Antichrist*, more than four million sites lead you into a labyrinth of possibilities for identifying this elusive beast. First up as contenders are President George W. Bush, then *Baywatch* star David Hasselhoff. Other early contenders include Microsoft maestro Bill Gates, Russian president Vladimir Putin, and rock star Marilyn Manson, though quite why they are chosen is not entirely clear.

In every age of the church, personalities and powers have risen and been regarded as the Antichrist.[1] The title "Antichrist" describes a movement, idea, or personality that sets itself up in opposition to Christ. The early church fathers generally identified the Antichrist as being personified in the oppressing Roman Emperors who viciously persecuted the church—notably Caligula, Nero, and Domitian. In the early second century, Polycarp believed the Antichrist was the spirit of heresy, while Irenaeus identified it as Rome, as did Hippolytus in the third century. Perhaps the greatest Western church father, Augustine, living after Emperor Constantine's conversion to Christianity and Rome's embrace of it, preferred not to label any system or personality, so he wrote in generalities of "heretics, schismatics, perjurers, cheaters, evil doers, soothsayers, adulterers, drunkards, usurers, slave dealers—whatsoever is contrary to the Word of God is antichrist."[2]

In a Christian-tolerant Roman Empire, Rome could no longer be identified as the Antichrist and so, not surprisingly, Rome's enemies the Goths, Huns, and Tartars became vilified as Satan's right arm. Meanwhile, increasing theological disagreement between the Western and Eastern churches caused the power-loving Roman Church to flex her muscles and claim that iconography, a core aid to Orthodox spirituality, was the Antichrist, relying on poor exegesis to support this view (Rev. 13:15). Internecine conflict caused Pope Gregory IX to denounce emperors such as Frederick II, and Innocent IV was declared "the Dragon of the Apocalypse." In the fourteenth century, power plays within Catholicism led some cardinals to set up a parallel papacy in Avignon for thirty-one years, with the respective popes of Avignon and the Holy City accusing each other of being the Antichrist.[3]

From Roman Empire to Roman Catholicism

The dawning of the Reformation led prophets like John Huss, John Wycliffe, Martin Luther, and John Calvin[4] to regard the Roman Church as the Antichrist. Predictably, Rome retaliated by denouncing these Protestant accusers themselves as the Antichrist. Bolstered by Calvin's *Institutes of the Christian Religion* and the Geneva Bible, the growing Protestant body became convinced that the Antichrist formerly manifested as the Roman Empire was now the Roman Catholic Church. Congregationalists, Lutherans, and Baptists all declared the pope as Antichrist in their declarations of faith.

The great English Protestant authors John Bunyan and John Milton readily identified Rome as the Antichrist. The important Calvinist statement of faith, the Westminster Confession (ch. 25, sect. VI), unequivocally declared, "The Pope is the Antichrist," and to this day many Presbyterians would concur. Even as recently as 1959, the Wisconsin Evangelical Lutheran Synod reaffirmed this historic view.[5] Bizarrely, the antagonistic atheist Friedrich Nietzsche was keen to take the title for himself and his work, often signing his letters "Dionysius against the Crucified." In the Orthodox Church, Tsar Peter the Great was given the title of Antichrist for separating church and state and making priests conform to state laws and taxes.

Ironically, disagreements and divisions within Protestantism caused even notable figures such as John Wesley to gain the title! It seems that anyone who is a threat or in disagreement with you might qualify. The title is even given by some Muslims to Paul of Tarsus for corrupting the truth as they see it. Since the Middle Ages demonic conspiracies have been assigned to Templar, Illuminati, or Masonic orders. Numerous leaders who amassed great power, built great empires, and attracted almost spiritual adoration have received the label from their enemies—including Napoleon, Stalin, Hitler, and Mussolini. Even the Russian monk Rasputin earned the label for his religio-political machinations—and, having survived a stabbing in the chest and attempts at drowning, was depicted as the beast of Revelation.

Big Brother watching you

In the technological revolution of the twentieth century, end-time angst coupled with Luddite tendencies led to numerous technologies being named as potential tools for the Antichrist. Surveillance, after all, is the most powerful tool in George Orwell's *1984* vision, in which we are not simply watched but controlled. Weber notes, "TVs, computers, credit cards, ATMs, satellites, micro-chips, fibre optics all established new levels of social control that Antichrist could use."[6] In 1981, Mary Stewart Relfe wrote a book that sold three hundred thousand copies in three months. It was called *The 666 System is Here*, and it identified the number of the beast with product barcodes. At the close of the twentieth century, the Internet and Bill Gates's Microsoft empire were held by some to be preparing the ground for the Antichrist.

WWW, or one-world worship

A one-world religious, political, and economic system could qualify as a mark of the beast in Revelation 13—the beast who exercises authority over every tribe and people (v. 7b), who commands all to worship his image (v. 15), and who controls all economic transactions (v. 17).

Consequently, any political movement toward this end has aroused suspicion, whether it be the League of Nations after World War I, the United Nations (UN) after World War II, the European Economic Community (EEC), or latterly the ambitious twenty-first-century UN's Alliance of Civilizations.[7] The Left Behind series overtly identifies the UN's treaties and alliances as paving the way for the coming of the one-world government headed by the Antichrist.[8] The latest contenders for the office are former Soviet president Mikhail Gorbachev and former U.S. president Bill Clinton, whom some still see as having global ambitions.[9] The Antichrist spirit is seen by many in the homogenous religious drift of the (modestly sized) Christian Ecumenical Movement, or in the more worrying Interfaith Movement with its overt syncretism.[10]

Right-wing? Homophobic? Anti-Semitic?

The late Jerry Falwell, an outspoken fundamentalist, told pastors at a conference in 1999 that the Antichrist was probably alive and was certainly Jewish. He was drawing on an ancient Christian tradition interpreting Daniel 11:37, which speaks of an end-time pseudodivine king showing "no regard for the gods of his fathers"—understood by some to be a Jew rejecting the God of Abraham, Isaac, and Jacob. Since the time of John Chrysostom, some have seen the reference in Revelation 7 that omits Dan in the list of tribes at the sealing of the 144,000 as an indication that the Antichrist will come from the tribe of Dan. This ascription of the Antichrist as Jewish has fueled anti-Semitism for centuries. The verse in Daniel 11 continues by referring to this individual rejecting the desire of women. From this it is suggested that the Antichrist is unmarried, child-hating, or perhaps even homosexual.[11] It is essential that we are directed by sound interpretation of Scripture, and not by paranoia, homophobia, or xenophobia.[12]

So what do we make of this proliferation of personalities and possibilities that have the name "Antichrist" ascribed to them? It is clear
from history that the identification of someone or something as the
Antichrist is often projected from people's fear, assumed of people's enemies, and suggested of anyone, any group, or anything that threatens
us or disagrees with us. How careful we must be in our interpretation
of Scripture, and how cautious in coming to any firm conclusions. It is
noteworthy that nowhere in the New Testament does the divine Spirit
of prophecy specifically name and shame the Antichrist.

ANTICHRISTS, DRAGONS, BEASTS, AND LAWLESSNESS IN SCRIPTURE

The word "Antichrist" is not found in the Old Testament, presumably
because it would have been anachronistic to speak of such until the
Messiah had appeared.[13] However, the type is foreshadowed in Daniel's
demonic beast, the "abomination that causes desolation" (Dan. 7:7–8,
23–27; 8:25; 11:36f.). In the three centuries preceding Christ, an
eschatological scenario developed that understood that there would be
a mighty end-time cataclysmic confrontation between the forces of evil
and the reign of God in the person of the Messiah. The actual term
"Antichrist" is found only in John's epistles (1 John 2:18, 22; 4:3; 2
John 7), and the writer himself may have coined the term.[14] It occurs
five times—four in the plural, one in the singular. John thus appears
to suggest that the spirit of Antichrist has multiple manifestations in
this stage of history. However, the concept does occur elsewhere and,
as noted earlier, is widely regarded as synonymous with the "man of
lawlessness" in Paul (2 Thess. 2) and the "beast" in John's Apocalypse
(Rev. 13). All three draw on Old Testament apocalyptic motifs and
the possibility of an end-time "abomination that causes desolation."[15]

Semantically, the Greek term *antichristos* does not convey the Latin sense of *anti* as "against," but rather the Greek sense of *anti* as "in the place of." This personality or system will seek to stand, rule, and operate *in the place of* the Anointed One of God.

Hans Schwarz somewhat pessimistically claims that "the diversity of the concept of the antichrist shows us that the NT has no clear doctrine of the antichrist."[16] I disagree. I believe it is possible to synthesize the New Testament's teaching on this. The three main texts can cohere without resorting to exegetical gymnastics.

The Antichrist in John's epistles

Take a moment to read the following Scriptures: 1 John 2:18–19, 22; 4:3; and 2 John 7. John's purpose in writing is to encourage the church to be faithful and not to be alarmed or taken in by former members who have proved to be deceptive and demonic, undermining the gospel. Drawing on the Jewish apocalyptic understanding of the manifestation of evil in the last days, John claims that his readers are in fact in the last hour (1 John 2:18), the closing scenes of history: The evil time and evil manifestation are upon us. This so-called Antichrist is defined as:

1. both plural and singular;
2. both a spirit and persons;
3. secessionist from the church;
4. not just deceived, but deceivers;
5. denying that Jesus came in the flesh, and denying that he is from God.

John describes "antichrist" as a spirit that works in a person who rejects Jesus Christ as the eternal Son of God. John may well have in mind the Docetists who aligned themselves with the church. They rejected the belief that Jesus was fully human, claiming that he only appeared as such (the Greek *dokeo* means "to seem"). Or he may have been thinking of an early Gnostic group who rejected the coequality and shared divinity of the Son with the Father, regarding the Son as a created subordinate.

Because John speaks of the close of history as already current and the manifestation of antichrists as already present, did he also expect a future personified manifestation? I think so. Smalley says:

> *Spirit from antichrist ... might be interpreted in an abstract, impersonal timeless sense; but equally it might imply that John regarded the current situation as pointing toward a future coming of antichrist himself, while sharing even now in the general character (or spirit) of that moment.*[17]

John's distinction between the one and the many, the future and the present in the same sentence appears to support this: "the antichrist is coming, even now many antichrists have come" (1 John 2:18). Already he is abroad in the world and the church, but we await his final disclosure. Such a view finds further support in a parallel passage in Paul.

THE POWER OF LAWLESSNESS AND
THE MAN OF LAWLESSNESS (2 THESS. 2:1–11)

John accepts that there is a present manifestation of the spirit of antichrist, but expects a future coming of the Antichrist. Similarly, Paul states that while "the secret power of lawlessness is already at work" (2 Thess. 2:7), nevertheless "the man of lawlessness" has yet to be revealed (vv. 3, 8, 9).[18] The evil advance force is already at work, but the commander is still to come. The Greek expression *o anthropos tes anomias* is sometimes translated as "the man of sin," although the words literally mean "the man against the law."

Paul's designation of "the man of lawlessness" may well be his own construct, even as "antichrist" may be John's. We have every reason to think they are one and the same. Writing in the early AD 50s, Paul is drawing on the composite picture in Daniel (7:25; 8:25; 11:36) and is no doubt aware of Jesus' teaching on the signs of the end and the hallmarks of the "abomination that causes desolation." The power of this is already present, but Paul expects it to be personified and intensified. As with John's pastoral letter, Paul's purpose is to correct the false teaching that the end has already come and that the second coming has already happened (2 Thess. 2:1–2).

v. 3a	The second coming of Christ will not come until the man of lawlessness has been revealed, when the final "rebellion" has occurred.
v. 3b	The man of lawlessness is doomed to destruction.
v. 4	He is marked by opposition to God; he will seek to take the place of God, to occupy the temple of God, to declare himself as God, to receive worship due to God.
v. 6f.	The power of lawlessness is already at work, but the man of lawlessness is currently being restrained, held back until the proper time.
v. 7f.	Restraints will eventually be removed, and the man of lawlessness will be revealed.
v. 8	Christ will return and overthrow him.
v. 9	The lawless one is the executive of Satan.

v. 9–10   He will dazzle and deceive through counterfeit
          miracles, signs, and wonders.

v. 10f.   People who refuse to love the truth and be saved will be
          deceived and will be handed over to condemnation by
          God.

To sum up, then, Paul's "man of lawlessness" is presumably a man, promoted by Satan, violently jealous of God, blasphemous in his pretensions, and capable of deceiving people about the gospel through his miraculous powers. He will become manifest when Christ's restraining hand permits, and he will be destroyed when Christ returns.

DRAGONS AND BEASTS IN REVELATION

Of the making of many interpretations of the Apocalypse there is no end! The prophetic has been the special preserve of the religious lunatic fringe for centuries.[19] On the other hand, ignoring and discounting the prophetic has long been the approach of the liberals. We must tread cautiously and not throw the baby out with the bathwater. The passage in Revelation 13 is rich in apocalyptic imagery and layered in ciphers and symbols. G. C. Berkouwer rightly notes that "the passages in the Bible that talk of the antichrist do not readily lend themselves to doing away with mysteriousness."[20] We must resist the temptation to press for an interpretation that is not readily forthcoming, but we need to pray for wisdom and discernment to unravel it and apply it.

Revelation 13—unlucky for some

The Dragon, Satan, brings forth a beast from the sea (Rev. 13:1) and later a beast from the earth. Ancient traditions spoke of two primeval monsters, Leviathan from the sea and Behemoth from the ground

(1 Enoch 60:7–10). To the ancients the sea was evil. As Mounce says, "For the last great enemy of God's people to arise from the reservoir of chaos would be entirely appropriate."[21] Some suggest that the sea represented the Gentiles, and the land represented Israel (Ps. 65; Isa. 17:12; 60:5; Ezek. 32:2).

The beast that comes out of the sea has seven heads and ten crowns on ten horns (Rev. 13:2). The number seven in Revelation represents completeness, and this may well be speaking of complete power. Some, however, see here a symbol for Rome, built on seven hills and ruled over by ten emperors wearing their crowns. The beast's form has features of a leopard, a bear, and a lion (v. 2). These are all symbols of former historic dynasties (Dan. 7:25f.) and may suggest the rising power of Rome, which succeeded from and even surpassed the place and power of former empires. Throughout the Bible, horns symbolically represent strength, power, and authority, whether negative or positive (Ps. 18:2; Luke 1:69), and the exercise of this demonic authority is described in verses 5, 7, 12, 14, and 15. These beasts are not cuddly pets; they are dangerous and vicious.

One of the heads of the beast has a fatal wound that has healed (v. 3). Some think this is a reference to Nero, who took his own life by slashing his throat with a sword, but was still reported to be alive and awaiting a return to power. Perhaps Caligula was also a candidate, as he became very ill but then recovered. The Protestant tradition has suggested that this represented the Roman Church, possibly suffering a wound through the collapse of the Roman Empire, only for the antichrist spirit to reassert itself with the Roman Catholic Church, or perhaps suffering a wound through the Protestant Reformation, but ready to rise again in the end times.

The whole world was "astonished" and worshipped the beast and the

Dragon who had given authority to this beast (vv. 3–4). This speaks of a personality, behind a world power, who receives worldwide worship— and knowingly or unknowingly, the worship that flows to the beast goes to the Dragon, Satan. Worship is God's due, but this beast establishes himself as a blasphemous counterpart to God, uttering "proud words and blasphemies," opening his mouth "to blaspheme God, and to slander his name and his dwelling place" and those who dwell with him (v. 5–6). The Roman emperors increasingly claimed divinity, leading to the development of the cult of the emperor in which all under Rome's power were forced to swear to Caesar as Lord. Refusal brought torture and death. Nero was referred to as "saviour of the world," and Domitian was addressed as *Dominus et Deus Noster*, "our Lord and our God."[22]

This beast's power seems unassailable (v. 4b): "Who can make war against him?" Only an end-time visitation of God can overcome him. And it will. His power is directed against the church: He makes war "against the saints" (v. 7). Presumably there is no pretribulation rapture here. Until Emperor Constantine in the early fourth century, the Roman state systematically persecuted Christians, most viciously in the first century under Nero and Domitian.

Verse 7 also says, "He was given authority over every tribe, people, language and nation"—the desire of every totalitarian regime from the Greek Alexander and the Roman Caesars to the Russian Stalin and the German Hitler. While the world worships the beast (v. 8), the faithful saints resist. They only worship "the Lamb," Jesus Christ, in whose Book of Life their names are recorded (v. 11).

Then a second beast comes up from the earth: "He had two horns like a lamb." This is a parody of Jesus the Lamb, who alone is worthy of worship (v. 8). We have an imitation motif here. The first beast had a fatal wound from which he recovered, and the second beast is described as being like a lamb. But appearances are deceiving. This is no gentle lamb: "He spoke like a dragon" (v. 11b).

The second beast, sometimes called the false prophet (Rev. 20:10), is the first beast's executor, even as the first beast is the Dragon's executor. "He exercised all the authority of the first beast" (v. 12), forcing people to worship the beast. Some have seen in this second beast the emperor cult that forced worship to the first beast, the emperor himself. Many have observed the "trinity of evil," which parodies the Holy Trinity.[23] The Holy Trinity is Father, Son, and Spirit; the unholy trinity here is dragon, beast, and false prophet. F. F. Bruce observes that as Jesus received authority from the Father (Matt. 11:27), so the beast receives authority from the Dragon, Satan (Rev. 13:4). As the Holy Spirit glorifies Christ (John 16:14), so the false prophet glorifies the beast (Rev. 13:12).[24]

This second beast is a false prophet given powers to perform "great and miraculous signs" (vv. 13–14) that bolster his commands to lead people to worship the beast. By the Spirit, Jesus came to life. By the Spirit the Eucharistic bread and wine become life to us. Yet here, in another demonic parody, this second beast causes an image of the wounded first beast to come to life (v. 15). Whereas Jesus invites us to worship him, the second beast coerces people to worship the first beast or face death (v. 15b). This was something that the emperor cult forced on the church: Christians had the choice to declare that "Caesar is lord" or die.

At the end of John's description, we read that this beast forces everyone, "small and great, rich and poor, free and slave," to receive a mark on their right hand or forehead, "so that no one could buy or sell unless he had the mark" (vv. 16–17). The beast thus orchestrates not only the one-world worship, but also the one-world economy. All trade is in his hands. Some see this "mark" as Roman coinage that was itself blasphemous, depicting the heads of emperors who claimed divinity. This mark is "the name of the beast or the number of his name" (v. 17). John says, finally, "This calls for wisdom … the number of the beast … is man's number. His number is 666" (v. 18).

The number of the beast: 666

This has been variously ascribed, from Nero to Hitler and even John Wesley, as well as to barcodes and American zip codes.[25] We saw previously that a mark of the beast, numbered 666, was for global trade and economic control. In the Old Testament, 2 Chronicles 9:13 and 1 Kings 10:14 refer to the weight of gold brought annually to Solomon, weighing 666 talents, and it is conceivable that this number merely corresponded to materialism in general. More commentators have observed that letters in the ancient languages often had corresponding numbers. In Greek the first nine letters of the alphabet represented the numbers one to nine. "Gematria" was the practice of representing words and names by the sums of their numerical equivalents. Interestingly, the ancient Sibylline Oracles Book 1.325 offers the number 888 for Christ.[26] In Hebrew the transliteration of the Greek name *Nero Kaisar* yields the number 666. The fact is, getting someone's name to add up to 666 involves what is known as a Diophantine equation, and critics of numerology point out that any name can be made to add up to 666—indeed, any name can be made into any number given enough mathematical variables.[27]

While John may well have intended to refer to the blasphemous Roman Emperor Nero, an archetypal church-persecuting antichrist, perhaps we may better understand 666 as that evil trinity that apes but always falls short of God's number. Both three and seven represent perfection in Jewish thought, and thus "three sevens," 777, represent the three absolute perfect persons within the Godhead, the Holy Trinity. The unholy trinity, 666, is the number of the beast, who consistently aspires to be seven, but is only six, falling short of God. William Hendrikson speaks of it as "failure, failure, failure."[28]

Given the biblical material we have reviewed, we may tentatively put forward the following scenario.

- The mark of the end-time Antichrist, the man of lawlessness, the empire of the beast, will be a one-world economic, political, and spiritual regime.

- The references in Revelation 13:3, 7, and 12 to his influence over the whole world and his authority over all tribes, peoples, languages, and nations underscore the global one-world nature of this manifestation.

- The emphasis in Revelation 13:4, 15 on the compulsory worship of the beast underscores the one-world religious nature of this demonic system.

- The emphasis in Revelation 13:16f. on the beast's control of all financial transactions underscores the unified global economy that marks this manifestation.

- This one-world global, spiritual, and political system is controlled by Satan, who is fronted by the masked personalities of the beast and the false prophet—who are probably "men."

- By brutal might or mysterious magic, the inhabitants of the whole world (Rev. 13:3, 4, 7, and 8) will be compelled to worship this beast of the sea, a figurehead of the Dragon Satan.

- This one-world system will be marked by totalitarianism, with no room for Christian freedom; by blasphemous imitation and a direct parodying of Christ; and by fierce persecution against Christians.
- A single world leader figurehead (the beast), publicly promoted by an assistant (the false prophet), a single worship, and a single currency all mark this demonic manifestation.

Dragons and beasts are no match for the Lamb

Revelation 13, with its demonic depiction, is not the end. This regime will be short-lived: It will last forty-two months (v. 5), or three and a half years—half of the complete number seven. Revelation 13 (an unlucky number for some, namely the Antichrist) is followed by Revelation 14, which offers a vision of the Lamb of God standing on Mount Zion surrounded by his faithful 144,000. Revelation subsequently depicts the return of Christ, the battle at Armageddon, and the final destruction of the Devil, the beast, and his false prophet, who are thrown in the lake of fire and tormented forever (Rev. 20:10).

The apostolic authors were inspired by the Spirit to write 2 Thessalonians, 1 and 2 John, and Revelation 13 so that we might be aware of and alert to the Enemy's end-time manifestation of evil, deception, oppression, and suppression of truth. We are to be strengthened in our resolve to discern deception and to stand firm in persecution. When we see these things, we may lift up our heads, for our redemption draws near. The Evil One has disclosed himself and Christ will soon return to destroy him "with the breath of his mouth." Paul's and John's epistles exhort us *not to be deceived* by the secret power of lawlessness or the spirit of antichrists already at work. Revelation 13 encourages us to *stand in faithfulness and patient endurance* (v. 10) and to *exercise wisdom* in calculating the number of the beast, "man's number," 666 (v. 18). It is important to note that, apart from this code, which remains unclear, *nowhere* does Scripture name or unequivocally identify the Antichrist.

We cannot prevent the appearance of the Antichrist, for God destined this end-time manifestation. Nor should we want to, for it signals the Enemy's ultimate defeat and our ultimate redemption. While I encourage caution in concluding too readily that this person or that movement is the Antichrist, we are called to be *primed* to the rise of his system, which will be identified by a unified global economic, spiritual, and political hegemony—ruled with a vicious rod of iron, holding the threat of death over any who object. Even as Christians stood against evil, stood up for Christ, and stood alongside the victims of such antichrist regimes as Hitler's Nazism and Stalin's Communism, so we, too, must be *prophetic* in our denunciations of any antichrist spirit, unflinchingly preaching Christ; *passionately* worshipping the Lamb alone (no demonic substitute); and *pastorally* assisting the many who are victims of evil.[29]

SEVEN

ISRAEL—PAST, PRESENT, OR FUTURE?

And so all Israel will be saved.
(Rom. 11:26a)

A HOT POTATO

In this chapter we continue our study on "signs of the end times." Many students of Scripture believe its prophecies and promises indicate that among the crucial end-time signs will be the reestablishment of ethnic Israel to "the Land" and the conversion of ethnic Israel to the Lord. Theologically, there is no consensus on the matter. Over two millennia Christians have become polarized on various theologies, such as divine sovereignty versus human free will, but the question of God's ongoing relationship with ethnic and geographic Israel may well be the hottest potato of them all. I am middle aged (just), middle class (just), middle English (just), and Anglican—historically taking the *via media*, the middle way. I believe that a middle way may—indeed, must—be found between the two poles of Christian Zionism (the conviction that the Jewish people have a divine, political, or moral right to the land of Israel/Palestine) and Christian successionism (or "replacement theology," the conviction that the Jewish people and the land of Israel/Palestine have served their purpose in the economy of God and have been succeeded, or replaced, by the spiritual geography of the church).

In writing this, I am aware that some of my Christian friends and colleagues, whom I profoundly respect and who have a strong commitment to Scripture's authority, come down on opposite sides regarding the theology of Israel. We must remember that any biblical interpretation on this issue is neither obvious nor unambiguous. I trust that, despite my conclusions, and despite any divergence of opinion, our friendship and respect will be maintained. The issue of Israel in God's plans has never been a gospel, creedal, or confessional issue, and therefore doctrinal disagreement here should not lead to disunity.

Culturally and politically, we exist in a time when there appears to be an almost universal loathing for the nation-state of Israel.[1] Israel has become the world's whipping boy, and not for the first time. Prelates, politicians, and professors gain immediate brownie points by pointing accusing fingers at what they deem to be Israel's human rights violations. English establishment figures such as Cherie Blair, wife of the former prime minister, came close to justifying suicide bombings in Israel on the grounds that they were the only recourse available to an oppressed, powerless Palestinian people. The increasing radicalization of Western Islamic youth is seen as a justifiable response to Anglo/American foreign policy in the Middle East, but Israeli/Palestinian tensions are often cited as the cause. *The Shorter Oxford English Dictionary* defines Zionism as "a movement for the re-establishment of a Jewish nation in Palestine (and since 1948 the development of the State of Israel)."[2] In 1975 the UN passed resolution 3379 declaring that Zionism "is a form of racism and racial discrimination." Meanwhile, anti-Israel rhetoric, with an underlying anti-Semitic value judgment, appears to be politically correct. The UN resolution was bizarre considering that it was they who actually established Israel as an independent nation state in 1948, only twenty-seven years previously. Fortunately, recognizing that resolution 3379 was inconsistent, if not itself possibly racist and discriminating, they revoked it in 1991 with resolution 4686—without commentary![3] It is not my intention here to engage in cultural, political, or historical debate, but to try to tease out what Scripture has to say about the people of Israel and the land of Israel in God's purposes both today and in the future. Whatever the current political rights and wrongs of Israel's policies, we must try to read Scripture on its own terms—noting that it does indeed have something to say about current ethics and politics.

A PERSONAL JOURNEY

My own beloved father has taught and lived the Bible for forty-five years. He is learned in Scripture's original languages, its overall geography, narrative, and theological structures. And he is a Christian Zionist. He is not militant about this, but it is a deep current within him that influences his prayers, his spirituality, and his eschatological hope. Growing up, I was accustomed to rooms in our home being taken over by strangers who had traveled to learn biblical Hebrew from my father. They were not the regular church members. They seemed to me to have, or at least think they had, something extra. Whatever that might have been, I was not interested: Middle-aged women with head-coverings excitedly muttering occasional words in Hebrew hardly seemed like a divine epiphany!

When I became freed from the constraints of my Strict Baptist upbringing, I embraced the life in the Spirit. I encountered another group in a charismatic church who were passionate about the future of Israel, but here was an expression of Christianity that felt like a retreat to the heavy legalism I had left behind. It was not for me, and I decided that I would never again attend this group.

At seminary I met and shared a study with Joseph Steinberg, who has become a lifelong friend. He is a Jewish Christian, whose coming to faith in Christ as a teenager cost him dearly. Called by God, he trained in Jewish studies at the Moody Bible Institute and embraced evangelism with missions to Jews in America and England. God wonderfully called him to be ordained in the Church of England. When Archbishop Carey stepped down from being patron of CMJ (what is now called the Church's Mission among Jewish people), Joseph was pained. To this Jewish Christian, committed to bringing other Jewish people to believe in Jesus as Messiah, and training for ordination by the Church of England, Carey's action appeared to suggest that evangelism to Jews was no longer necessary.[4] In the end Joseph remained committed to his calling in the Church of England and exercised a faithful and fruitful parish ministry before returning to full-time evangelism among his Jewish brethren. He is now a director of the Church Mission Society. Joseph was so conscious of his Jewish identity and God's call to Abraham that he had his son circumcised on the eighth day. But what impressed me about Joe was his absolute scriptural clarity. As he would often remind me, "Jesus said to a Jewish leader, 'You must be born again —the gospel of salvation is for the Jew first.'"

Two years ago I took a group of Oxford students on a pilgrimage to Israel, led by a dear colleague who had lived and worked there for ten years. My overall impression was mixed. I went prayerfully with an open mind; I came back with a troubled mind. What I saw of the place and the people did not impact me as much as the growing spiritual sense of oppression. This did not seem like a Holy Land. It seemed like a very unholy land. Jerusalem itself particularly troubled me. Its streets had run with blood for nearly three millennia. That blood cried out to me. At the Wailing Wall, I wailed. My heart cried out for these Jewish worshippers who stood as near to God as they thought they could get, face-to-face with a stone wall, yards from where the Holy of Holies may have been in Solomon's temple. I wrote out prayers and pressed them into the wall, praying that God might save Israel—removing their veil, their blindness, their wall. The weather was mild, but the spiritual clouds were thick and oppressive. No open heaven—I sensed only warfare in the heavenlies. Why was this place so oppressive? Others in my party said they felt scared. Me, too. I had visited European Nazi concentration camps that simply felt "void." But this felt like a place over which there was a very present darkness. My growing discernment was that the Enemy was abroad in this place. But why? On returning home and reflecting, my deduction was that the Enemy has a vested interest in Jerusalem—and if he did, then might God also? Did this place have a strategic part to play in his end-time plans? Was it the case, as some Christian Zionists claim, that Jerusalem would be the place of God's glorious end-time manifestation and the Evil One's final, ignominious downfall?

I am well aware that these different experiences have influenced me and overshadowed my reading and reflecting on this issue. A frustrating brush with zealous Zionist Christians, a powerful impression made by a messianic Jew who has lived to preach the gospel to Jews, and a disturbing experience of oppression in Israel that led me to believe that the Enemy had a vested interest here. Readers will have to judge whether my interpretation of Scripture has been biased by these experiences.

THE GREAT DIVORCE

The history of Christian reflections on and relations with Judaism is not among our proudest moments. Anti-Semitism, while evident in other contexts, seems to have been a tragic but often familiar attitude of the church. In some respects the New Testament itself, written by Jews, sets the tone that would intensify in later years. Douglas Moo rightly says:

> *The NT can justly be said to be anti-Judaic in the sense that it claims to leave no room for the claims of Judaism to mediate salvation through the Torah. But the NT is not anti-Semitic.*[5]

Jesus himself told the Pharisees, who were priding themselves on their Abrahamic ancestry, that they were of their father the Devil (John 8:39f.). In Philippians, Paul recites his Jewish credentials almost dismissively.

Speaking against the backdrop of persecution in the church, Paul can refer to "the Jews, who killed both the Lord Jesus and the prophets, and drove us out, and displease God and oppose all mankind by hindering us from speaking to the Gentiles that they might be saved" (1 Thess. 2:14–16 ESV). In Peter's Pentecost sermon he addresses the gathered onlookers, religious Jews, and speaks accusingly of "this Jesus, whom you crucified" (Acts 2:36). The vicious anti-Semitic accusation that has echoed through two millennia, "Christ killers," was placed first on the lips of the Jewish apostles Peter and Paul. But theirs was merely an honest historical observation and experience. Of course, Peter and Paul loved their people, but this term would be taken up by the church, twisted, and used by later generations as justification for great abuse.

The Jewish Christians believed that Jesus was the Messiah, but temple Judaism rejected Jesus as a false prophet. In John's Apocalypse, Christ himself speaks of the "synagogue of Satan" (Rev. 3:9). Are we to infer from this a generic understanding of the demonic nature of synagogues *per se?* In both Romans and Galatians, Paul writes that a Jew is not one outwardly, genetically, and ancestrally, but inwardly and spiritually through the circumcision of the heart (Rom. 2:28; 9:6–8; Gal. 3:29). What, then, of those who were Jews "after the flesh" (an expression used in the King James Version of the Bible)? Paul seems clear: What matters is not Abraham's ancestry, but his exemplary faith. Indeed, John the Baptist dismissed the Pharisees' attempt to claim spiritual position through sharing DNA with Abraham, arguing that God could raise up children of Abraham from the stones if he wished (Luke 3:8).

When Jewish apostles welcomed Gentiles into the family fold and seemed to dismiss Torah observance (Acts 10:15), a wedge was driven further in between Judaism and the church, fueling the tensions. The book of Acts clearly presents official Judaism as persecuting the embryonic church and resisting every attempt at mission (Acts 7; 8; 9:23f.; 12:1f.; 14:19f.; 21:27f.). One new man was developed (Eph. 2:11–22) and a new community, a new people of God, emerged (1 Peter 2:9f.), in which old distinctions were removed in baptism and there was neither Jew nor Gentile, slave nor free, male nor female (Gal. 3:28). God's temple becomes the believer and the church (1 Cor. 3:16; 6:19). The law, the sacrifices, the priestly duties are merely shadows that, when cleared, have made way for the light of the high priest of a new covenant, Jesus Christ (Heb. 8).

Was it any wonder that a chasm opened up between historic-ethnic Torah and temple-centered Judaism and the Spirit-filled people of God in Christ? It was inevitable. The developing theology of the church, with its increasing detachment from Torah Judaism, came to see the church not simply as fulfilling Old Testament law and promise, but as annulling it, replacing it, cutting free from the limitations of historic Judaism (Eph. 2:15 *katargesas*=annul). The destruction of the temple in AD 70 and the Diaspora (scattering) of the Jews seemed symbolic, not only of God making Judaism redundant, but also of Judaism being under divine judgment. In the postapostolic era, Marcion, the son of a Christian bishop, headed a religious movement that attempted to exorcise every trace of the Old Testament and Judaism out of Christianity, even rejecting Matthew's gospel as too Jewish!

THE GREAT ABUSE[6]

Following the conversion of Emperor Constantine and the formal embrace of Christianity by Rome in the early fourth century, the persecuted became persecutors. Constantine himself issued legislative measures against the Jews, pointedly changing the date of Easter, which was no longer to coincide with the Passover. The church, now in the office of state, turned against the Jews who had earlier turned against them. Augustine (in his *City of God*, Book 18, Ch. 46) claimed that the Jews were terribly mistreated by the Romans, evicted from their land because they slew Christ. Their ill treatment, he believed, actually demonstrated the truth of Scripture! Jerome wrote of "Judaic serpents of whom Judas is the model." Chrysostom, in his work "Against the Jews," characterized them as plundering cheats and thieves who abandoned the poor.

For many Christians the Jew took on the antichrist persona. This was reinforced through reference to the absence of the tribe of Dan in the list of tribes gathered before the Lamb in heaven (Rev. 7) and through the manifestation of the Antichrist in Daniel 11:37, who is said to have "no regard for the gods of his [Jewish] fathers." Luther made an infamous attack on the Jews in his shamefully titled work, *On the Jews and their Lies*. He wrote of them as "venomous beasts, vipers, disgusting scum, devils incarnate." He reckoned that their houses should be destroyed, their lodgings should be in stables, their synagogues should be burned down, and they should be used as forced labor.

Throughout the world the Jews wandered and were often ghettoized. In England, Edward I expelled all Jews, though not without exacting ransom payments from three thousand of the wealthiest. Jews were even hanged from cathedral spires. In 1492 they were expelled from Spain, though many converted to Catholicism in order to remain. But a decade later their blood betrayed them, and the Inquisition burned alive thousands.

Nazi Germany epitomized Jewish persecution by annihilating over six million. Its "Final Solution" policy merely followed a Christian trajectory two millennia old. Every legislative decree of the Nazis against the Jews between 1935 and 1939—from insisting that Jews wear yellow markers, to burning down synagogues, defiling the Talmud, and restricting Jews from the professions—all had an exact parallel decreed by church councils from Clermont in 535 to the Fourth Lateran Council in 1215. The German Christians knew well what the attitude and intentions of the burgeoning Nazi party were toward the Jews. The Nazis were voted into power with Christian votes, and subsequent claims of the populace's general ignorance of their anti-Semitic policies simply belie the facts.[7] Hitler once said, "There is no room for two chosen people," and he inspired many to believe that the title of "divine elect" was the preserve of the Aryan Christian.[8]

Today, ironically, the political left wing and the fascist right find one thing around which to unite: suspicion, loathing, and accusing of the Jews. In some places such rhetoric leads to violence. Political sensitivities and sympathies for the Palestinians have once again stirred the undercurrent of anti-Semitism. Whatever the facts, Israel and her supporters are blamed for the Middle East's instability.

THE GREAT EMBRACE

By no means have all Christians in every church period contributed to
this narrative of abuse. While Luther and Calvin understood the church
to have succeeded or fulfilled Israel, their contemporaries, including
Martin Bucer, Peter Martyr, and Beza, Calvin's successor at Geneva,
increasingly envisaged a future for Israel, both the people and the land.[9]
The theology that informed this was a literal reading of texts such as
Romans 11:26, which speaks of an end-time conversion of all Israel, and
Revelation 16:16, which speaks of God's end-time purposes centering
on Armageddon in Israel. The Geneva Bible, the theological rampart of
Puritanism, stated in its marginal notes on Romans 11: "He sheweth
that the time shall come that the whole nation of the Jews, though not
everyone, particularly, shall be joined to the church of Christ."

In the sixteenth century the Dutch were moved to welcome a large
population of the wandering Jewish people into their land. They were
influenced by the developing Puritan doctrines, which recognized Israel
as having a key role in the end times. This Puritan biblical eschatological
concept was also felt in England, and from the days of Queen Elizabeth
I to Cromwell's protectorate, Jews were increasingly welcomed to set
up home in England.[10] In 1621, Sir Henry Finch caused a great stir
with his utopian theocratic vision of "The Restoration of the Jews." He
wrote, "Out of all the places of thy dispersion, East, West, North and
South, His purpose is to bring thee home again and to marry thee to
Himself by faith for evermore."[11]

Throughout the seventeenth century numerous sermons were
preached, presentations were made to parliament, and books and tracts
were produced on the theme of the Jews' purpose in God's end-time
plans and the church's and England's necessary penance for their historic mistreatment of them. Every notable Puritan for more than a

hundred years held the view that there would be a future conversion of all the Jews to Christ. In Scotland whole days of prayer were called to this end.

Cotton Mather recalls how he lay in the dust prostrate before the Lord, lifting up his cries for the conversion of the Jewish nation.[12] The greatest Puritan theologian, John Owen, in a sermon to the House of Commons, encouraged "the bringing home of His ancient people to be one fold with the fullness of the Gentiles … in answer to millions of prayers put up at the throne of grace for this very glory in all generations."[13]

The great missionary expansion was fueled by the belief that the Lord would return after Israel was restored to the land and the Lord, and after the fullness of the Gentiles had come in. Scholars began translating the New Testament into Hebrew in readiness. Evangelical leaders such as William Carey, Johann Albrecht Bengel, John Wesley, Jonathan Edwards, Charles Simeon, Martyn Henry, and Charles Spurgeon all embraced this view. John Wesley wrote in his notes on Romans 11, "So many prophesies refer to this grand event [the restoration of Israel] that it is surprising any Christian can doubt it."[14]

Two early nineteenth-century ministers, Edward Irving and J. N. Darby, made an influential contribution. Irving was a Scottish minister who founded the Catholic Apostolic Church, its marked features including belief in the charismata and the imminent return of Christ. He came across a work by a seventeenth-century Chilean Jesuit, Emmanuel Lacunza, titled *The Coming of the Messiah in Glory and Majesty* and published posthumously in 1812 under the pseudonym Rabbi Juan Jehosophat Ben Ezra. It put forward the novel view that there would be two returns of Christ, first for the church, then for Israel, who was expected to convert to Christ and be restored to the land.[15] Irving was so taken by this work that he learned Spanish in order to translate it himself, publishing it as the work of a "converted Jew." This book fueled the expectation of the restoration of Israel.

J. N. Darby, a former Anglican who founded the Plymouth Brethren and was initially associated with Irving, held "prophetic" conferences in the 1830s at which a theological view developed known as dispensationalism (see chapter 4). This asserted that there are seven dispensations—distinct theological periods—of God's dealing with humankind. Since the time of the apostles, we have been in the "age of grace"—the church age. When this age closes, the church will be raptured and the final age—that of the Jews restored to the land and to the Lord—will occur. The church is merely a "parenthesis," a side step, in God's dealings with Israel. Dispensationalism became influential through the work of Cyrus Scofield and Charles Ryrie, especially in the United States.

The British commitment to the restoration of Israel was a topic widely discussed in Victorian England—in the House of Commons, in pulpits, and in national newspapers. This groundswell of opinion culminated in England's drafting of the Balfour Declaration, which pronounced on November 2, 1917, that the British government favored,

> *the establishment in Palestine of a national home for the*
> *Jewish people and will use their best endeavours to facilitate*
> *the achievement of that object, it being clearly understood that*
> *nothing shall be done which may prejudice the civil and religious*
> *rights of existing non-Jewish communities in Palestine.*[16]

Some, however, suggest that Balfour tied Britain in knots because the country had earlier promised the land to the Arabs in the 1915

Hussein/McMahon correspondence, for their assistance in dismantling the Ottoman Empire during the so-called Arab Revolt of Lawrence of Arabia fame.[17] No formal treaty was ever signed, and the exact extent of the promise made is debated, but certainly the Arabs believed that Palestine would be theirs.

International governments and Jewish communities believed that Britain would now follow through on her declared intentions in the Balfour Declaration. Indeed, many believed Britain was granted the mandate for that end. Political machinations meant that England failed to deliver on her promises, however, even when she was handed the Israel mandate from 1917.[18] Sadly, in a murky political muddle, she pragmatically looked to her own best interests rather than those of the people she had vowed to repatriate.[19] Several bloody and futile postwar years ensued, when Jewish terrorism flared up, incensed as they were by British intransigence. Finally, Britain washed her hands of it all and, thirty-one years after receiving the mandate, relinquished Palestinian control.[20] The state of Israel was reestablished, and within hours a bloodbath ensued as the five neighboring Arab nations marched on Israel, seeking to annihilate this infant before she could walk. In the weeks that followed, there were indisputable injustices and atrocities on both sides. Israel, against all odds, won the day.

Old Testament promises

God promised the land to Abraham and his heirs (Gen. 12:1–3; 15:7; 17:8f.; 22:15–18). He repeated this promise to Isaac (Gen. 26:1–6) and to Jacob (Gen. 28:3–5, 10–15). The promise was particular to Abraham, Isaac, and Jacob—not to Abraham's brothers, not to Isaac's brother, and not to Jacob's brother. Whenever God repeats that he is "the God of Abraham, Isaac and Jacob," he is reaffirming that he is the covenant-making God who has made a covenant with Abraham's descendants, a covenant to multiply their number, to bless the world through them, to establish them in the land. God declared this to Moses (Ex. 6:2–4) and repeated it over Israel in the desert (Deut. 1:7f.).[21]

God swore on oath to give Abraham and his heirs this land, and a promise is a promise (Deut. 11:24). There is never any hint that this promise was partial, temporal, or revocable. Israel was warned that exile would be the result of covenant unfaithfulness (Deut. 28:36; 30:1–4; Ezek. 36:16–20), but return was promised to the repentant. Incidentally, this land belongs to neither the Jews nor the Palestinians. God says that it is *his* (2 Chron. 7:20). As Neville Jones says, "God holds the freehold and title deeds—Israel has only a long-term lease, and often in her chequered history has failed to keep the terms of the lease."[22]

Psalm 105:8–11 is crucially important:

> *He remembers his covenant for ever,*
> > *the word he commanded, for a thousand generations,*
> > *the covenant he made with Abraham,*
> > *the oath he swore to Isaac.*
> *He confirmed it to Jacob as a decree,*
> > *to Israel as an everlasting covenant:*
> *To you I will give the land of Canaan*
> > *as the portion you will inherit.*

Unless words are meaningless, this Spirit-scribed psalm surely settles the matter. The land is given to a particular people permanently. The belief in Israel's restoration to the land and conversion to the Lord is predicated on what is understood as God's eternal covenant with Abraham to give him and his descendants the land.

Zionists take these Scriptures at face value. Those who seek to interpret the covenant with Israel and the land "spiritually" must reread specific statements about a physical place as being about a spiritual kingdom, and must transfer specific promises for an ethnic people to a global "spiritual" people. While Christians take Old Testament promises to themselves, they seem less keen to take Old Testament commands, and even more reluctant to appropriate the warnings of judgment and the consequent punishments! The theological question that confronts us is whether certain Old Testament promises are specific for a generic Israel—both people and place—or whether they are to be spiritually subsumed into Christianity, having become redundant or annulled in Christ.

Christian Zionists would assert that "replacement/fulfillment" theology removes the promises and prophecies in Scripture from their context and robs them of their divine intent. I believe that successionists make a simple mistake in interpretation by conflating and confusing the Abrahamic covenant with Christ's fulfilling and annulling of the Mosaic covenant. While Jesus fulfilled the Mosaic covenant of law, I believe that Abraham's covenant of land remains intact—just as Noah's covenant remains in place for all people (Gen. 9:4; Acts 15:20, 29).

OLD TESTAMENT PROPHECIES

Because of their faithlessness to the covenant, Israel was taken from the land as God warned. Following the division of the land under Rehoboam, the northern tribes of Israel were dispersed in 722 BC, and the southern tribes in Judah were exiled between 606 and 586 BC. The return of the southern tribes following the Babylonian captivity took place under Zerubbabel, and a second contingent went up with Ezra (Ezra 2:1; 8:1; Neh. 7:6). Scholars estimate that perhaps less than fifty thousand returned to the land. However, the prophetic promises of return point not to a partial remnant of the northern tribes, but to "all the clans," "the whole house of Israel" (Jer. 31:1; Ezek. 36:10). While the return in 538 BC from Babylon certainly involved representation from other tribes, by no means could it be said to fulfill the prophecies in depth and breadth—Jeremiah having likened the return to the exodus, when two million people were brought into the land (Jer. 23:3–8).

Both the major and minor prophets are saturated with the promise of a return to the land and an existence in the land that simply was not fulfilled in the meager return from Babylon (see Isa. 14:1–2; 49:19–22; 60:1–21; 65; 66:8; Jer. 16:14, 29:14; 30:3–24; 31:8–40; 32:37–42; Ezek. 36—39; Zeph. 3:19f.; Amos 9:9–15; Zech. 1:17; 2:10–12; 8:1–8). Fred Wright summarizes the ordered pattern of biblical prophecy as follows:[23]

- rescue of the land;
- regathering to the land;
- fruitfulness of the land;
- raging of the nations;
- cleansing of the people;
- return of Christ.

Prophetic particulars include a nation born in a day (Isa. 66:8), which was actually fulfilled by the UN mandate in 1948, and a single language spoken (Zeph. 3:9; Jer. 31:23), which was fulfilled by Israel's adoption of the Hebrew tongue as its official language in 1948. In the previous two millennia, various languages had been spoken by the dispersed Israel, from Aramaic to north European-based Yiddish and Latin-based Ladino. Other prophecies relating to Israel remain unfulfilled as yet, notably an end-time conflict with the nations gathered in

Israel at Armageddon (Zeph. 3:8; Zech. 14:1f.), but political and military analysts think such a scenario is still very plausible!

One of the most remarkable prophecies comes in Ezekiel 36:16f., where God makes repeated promises concerning the end of Israel's abuse among the nations, where they had been scattered by God because of their idolatry. God intervenes: He declares that he will act on behalf of the scattered Israel, not for their sake, but to honor and magnify his name (vv. 22–23; 32).

> *I will take you out of the nations; I will gather you from all the countries and bring you back into your own land. I will sprinkle clean water on you … I will cleanse you.… I will give you a new heart and put a new spirit in you; I will remove from you your heart of stone … I will put my Spirit in you and move you to follow my decrees … You will live in the land I gave your forefathers; you will be my people, and I will be your God. I will save you from all your uncleanness. I will call for the grain and make it plentiful … I will increase the fruit of the trees and crops of the field … You will remember your evil ways … and you will loathe yourselves for your sins.… (Ezek. 36:24–31)*

Clearly such a text has been only partially fulfilled. There has been restoration to the land and restoration of the land, but we still await their sprinkling and cleansing of heart and turning to God. Currently, Israel is officially a secular state, whose morals are unscriptural and who has aborted over two million babies since 1948. Successionists, of course, would suggest that Ezekiel 36 has already been fulfilled in other ways, initially by a return to the land from Babylon and subsequently in a sprinkling of the heart by the Spirit begun at Pentecost.

While a reference to the new heart and new spirit may be appro-
priated as the experience of all believers in Christ at regeneration, it is
difficult to see how unequivocal references to being restored to the land
may be incorporated into the Christian experience. Daniel Block, in his
exhaustive commentary on Ezekiel, summarizes the prophecies in chapters 36—39 and comments that "to reduce these oracles to symbolic
language and to restrict their fulfilment to the NT church is to annul
the hope that the prophet was attempting to restore."[24]

Before we leave these Old Testament prophecies, three things must
be noted. First, Israel in the land must live in the land righteously as
God declared in the law or prophets, or they, too, will be judged. Gary
Burge has clearly shown in narrative form how Israel today is guilty of
violating human rights. One wonders, has David become a Goliath?[25]
If God will not ignore injustice, then neither may the church.[26] Israel
was formerly removed or ruined on more than one occasion because
of her sin. The land and covenant fidelity are inextricably linked. It is
not inconceivable that Israel could be exiled again. Indeed, Zechariah
14:2f. indicates that, immediately prior to the great day of the Lord, the
Messiah will gather to Jerusalem armies who will wage war against her,
wreaking great destruction, and taking half the city into exile. Could
God be using these foreign armies to bring judgment on an unjust and
ungodly nation? Historically, God always used the nations to judge
Israel (1 Kings 8:33). Before God judges the nations at the return of
Christ, will he use them first as a rod against Israel?

Second, the Jews are not the only ones in the land. The Zionist
notion of "a land without a people and a people without a land" was
never wholly true, although Joan Peter's study "From Time Immemorial"
repays careful study on exactly who was and wasn't resident in the land.[27]
What of the existing Arab residents? Legally, the Balfour Declaration

and UN treaty also recognized their rights to a home and, indeed, Israel's declaration of independence stated:

> *We appeal—in the very midst of the onslaught launched against us now for months—to the Arab inhabitants of the State of Israel to preserve peace and participate in the up-building of the State on the basis of full and equal citizenship and due representation in all its provisional and permanent institutions.*[28]

The nations surrounding Israel made war on this fledgling state because they refused to recognize Israel's right to be a nation-state—although Israel then recognized the rights of Palestinians to coexist in this state.[29]

I believe that Scripture offers a way through this impasse of whose land it is. In Ezekiel 47:21f., God states:

> *You are to distribute this land among yourselves according to the tribes of Israel. You are to allot it as an inheritance for yourselves and for the aliens who have settled among you and who have children. You are to consider them as native-born Israelites; along with you they are to be allotted an inheritance among the tribes of Israel. In whatever tribe the alien settles, there you are to give him his inheritance. (vv. 21–23)*

And in Jeremiah 22:3b, he commands, "Do what is just and right.... Do no wrong or violence to the alien." Of course, no Palestinian would like to be thought of as an alien in the land, but theologically this is not a pejorative term, but refers to one who is not an Israelite in the land.

Burge claims that Christian Zionism is "unqualified endorsement of Israel's politics based on biblical principles."[30] I question Burge's use of the word "unqualified" in his definition. But if one accepts this, then I am no Christian Zionist, for I believe that anyone who holds to the Zionist position on biblical principles must agree that life in the land should also be lived on biblical principles, namely righteousness and justice, especially for the alien or settler. Certainly, those who were in the land when Israel was established have a right for themselves and their families to remain in their homeland, if they themselves will live justly and peaceably in it.

Finally, Isaiah 60:12f. indicates that, because of his peculiar love for this particular people, God will judge those who refuse to honor Israel. This reiterates the promise made to Abraham at the beginning, in Genesis 12:3: "I will bless those who bless you, and whoever curses you I will curse." Currently, Israel is loathed among the nations. Although we must not be shy to support those who may be victims of Israel's internal politics when they speak up for justice and against abuse, a note of caution must be sounded. While we may want to bless Israel, as stated above, we can never bless her injustices. But would Israel listen more readily to those who challenge her on her international politics if they have also been the first to speak blessing over her?

NEW TESTAMENT HOPE

The claim above is passionately dismissed by many Christian theologians. Leek says, "The NT not only reinterprets the OT, it also de-Zionises it."[31] Consequently, says N. T. Wright, "Any attempt to give a Christian gloss to the Middle-Eastern political events since 1947 and thereafter is without exegetical foundations."[32] Colin Chapman says that Christian Zionism is based "on a profoundly flawed method of interpreting the

Bible, it seems to read the NT through the eyes of the OT, rather than reading the OT through the eyes of the NT.... [Such Christians] are supporting something that has led to some disastrous consequences."[33]

This opinion, however, is held among those who understand the church to have succeeded, replaced, or fulfilled the Old Testament role of Israel—where the promises and prophecies of the Old Testament are transferred from Israel to the church and generally applied spiritually. What matters is no longer the land, but the spiritual kingdom; no longer the Old Testament covenants, but the new covenant; no longer Israel, but the church. Such a view appeals to those who make distinctions between Israel "after the flesh" and "the Israel of God" (1 Cor. 10:18 KJV; Gal. 6:16 KJV), who consider "the seed of Abraham" to be those who share his faith, not his genes (Gal. 3:16, 29; Rom. 3).

There are clear statements that not all Israel is Israel (Rom. 9:6); that the Israel who receives the promise of the Spirit by faith in Christ is the Israel after Isaac who inherits the promise (Gal. 3:29; 4:28; 6:14f.), while those who reject Christ are Ishmael (Gal. 3:14).[34] Replacement teaching would have us believe that the "convert to Christ" is speaking in Isaiah 44:5:

> *One will say, "I belong to the LORD";*
> *another will call himself by the name of Jacob;*
> *still another will write on his hand, "The LORD's,"*
> *and will take the name Israel.*

One significant theological challenge to any form of Zionism is the argument that true Israel is neither the Jews nor the church *per se*, but Jesus Christ. The church and the Jews are only Israel in their relationship with and inclusion in Christ.[35] This is a Christological rather than geographical or racial reading: Abraham was looking to the day of Jesus (John 8:56) and the city whose architect and builder is God (Heb. 11:10). This is true, of course, although between Abraham's vision of Christ and the eternal city built by God, the land certainly had a central part to play in God's economy.

In *The Church and Israel*, David Blangren claims that "the Church not only receives the blessings of Israel but by being grafted in, the church becomes the Israel of God to the extent that unbelieving national Israel no longer is."[36]

Burge states:

> *The Kingdom was fundamentally God's reign over the lives of men and women—not an empire, not a political kingdom with borders and armies ... fundamentally a spiritual idea, a spiritual experience that transcended any particular place, time or land.*[37]

Burge is clearly right in what he affirms, but I believe wrong in what he denies, for he presents an either/or when the kingdom is both/and. Yes, the kingdom is spiritual and global and nonpolitical, but to affirm this, one must acknowledge God's historic giving of land and involvement with Israel's politics; and one must not negate the promise and prophecy of an end-time kingdom given to a particular people in a particular place to serve God's end-time purposes.

It is my understanding that God's Old Testament promises cannot be so easily decontextualized, overspiritualized, and accommodated to the church. The observation that the New Testament says little about the land does not negate what the Old Testament said about it. How many times does God need to repeat that the covenant of land for Abraham's descendants is permanent? I believe that the successionists are right in highlighting the texts cited above, but not to the negation of the other texts concerning the eternal Abrahamic covenant. God speaks through Jeremiah in terms that allow for *no* replacement, abandonment, or fulfilment of Israel's unique relation to God. God's promises are promises, sworn on oath. He does not change his mind, and he keeps his word. The same word that sustains the universe is the word of promise that sustains the relationship with Israel.

> *This is what the LORD says,*
>> *he who appoints the sun*
>> *to shine by day,*
>> *who decrees the moon and stars*
>> *to shine by night,*
>> *who stirs up the sea*
>> *so that its waves roar—*
>> *the LORD Almighty is his name:*
> *"Only if these decrees vanish from my sight,"*
>> *declares the LORD,*
>> *"will the descendants of Israel ever cease*
>> *to be a nation before me....*
> *Only if the heavens above can be measured*
>> *and the foundation of the earth below be searched out*
>> *will I reject all the descendants of Israel."*
> *(Jer. 31:35–37)*

ISRAEL'S RESTORATION TO THE LAND

It is obvious that the New Testament authors had little to say about the land, because they were all writing at a time when the land was still the home of Israel, albeit a province of the Roman Empire. The lack of clear argument in the New Testament of a Zionist nature does not itself undermine the position. The teaching of the Old Testament does not have to be repeated in the New Testament for it still to stand. As I asked above, how many times does God actually need to say that the land—literally and geographically, not spiritually—is given as an everlasting covenant before he is heard and believed? That said, there are clear indications in the New Testament of an end-time restoration of Israel to the land and to the Lord before God wraps up human history.

Luke 21:24

> *Jerusalem will be trampled on by the Gentiles until the times of the Gentiles are fulfilled.*

From the time of the exile of Judah's southern tribes in 586 BC, Israel was trodden down by Gentiles. After the Babylonians came the Persians, then the Greeks, then the Romans, who ultimately expelled her after the failed Jewish uprising in AD 134. Until 1948, when the nations of the world made Israel a nation-state and her peoples returned, the land was under Gentile rule—Roman, Catholic, Saracen, Ottoman, British. This prophecy of Christ given in Luke is most naturally read as implying an ending of Gentile (i.e., non-Jewish) rule of the land, prior to his return.

Acts 1:6—7

> *"Lord, are you at this time going to restore the kingdom to Israel?" He said to them, "It is not for you to know the times or dates the Father has set by his own authority."*

Jesus was the Messiah, vindicated by his resurrection. The apostles, following prevalent Jewish belief, were expecting the Messiah to overthrow Israel's enemies and establish her kingdom through David's throne. Their question was, "Has the time now come for this free, political, powerful kingdom to arrive?" Significantly, Jesus does not say, "You've got it all wrong—we're about a spiritual kingdom here, not a physical, national, political state." His answer suggests that such a concept is not wrong, but rather not for now: The Father has indeed set a time and a date for that to happen, a date that coincides with the gospel reaching the ends of the earth. They are to concern themselves not with dates or Israel's status, but with preaching the gospel to the nations. Some people believe that the kingdom of Israel that Jesus spoke about here was reestablished in 1948, partially the time and the date set by the Father, but awaiting the King to rule it.[37]

Revelation 16:16

> *Then they gathered the kings together to the place that in Hebrew is called Armageddon.*

Clearly, countless names, numbers, and places function as symbols in Revelation. Armageddon is understood by many to be another such symbol (see chapter 9). While a New Jerusalem is envisaged coming down from heaven (Rev. 21), before that appearance the old Jerusalem and her lands take center stage in world politics and become the decisive context for determining world history. With the exception of the period during the medieval Crusades, Israel and Jerusalem have proved insignificant in world politics until this present time. We live in an age now when Jerusalem has become, arguably, the most significant city in the world.

ISRAEL'S RESTORATION TO THE LORD

The definitive text that promotes this hope is Romans 11:25–26: When "the full number of the Gentiles has come in," then "all Israel will be saved." Ignored by almost every commentator for the first few centuries of the church, this text went on to become foundational to evangelical eschatology and missiology, from the Puritans to the great Victorian evangelicals. Taking this text at face value, believing in an end-time revival among the Jews, they sought to make a home for Israel and engaged in tenacious worldwide evangelism, seeking to bring in the fullness of the Gentiles, so that Israel might be saved, so that the Lord might then return.

Not everyone, however, understands the text in this way. G. C. Berkouwer suggests that to take it this way is to miss the whole flow of Romans, which is to isolate it as a mystery and admit it as a novelty in Paul's thinking.[39] Like successive notable scholars from Augustine and Calvin to N. T. Wright today,[40] Berkouwer understands "saved Israel" here as referring to the elect of God, both Jew and Gentile, who have become the spiritual Israel of God. A few scholars, balking at the implications of this verse, have even suggested that it is an interpolation, a later gloss.[41] Modern scholarship, however, has almost universally moved away from this view, and for good reason. The massive commentaries by Cranfield, Dunn, Fitzmyer, Moo, and Jewett all take Paul to be referring to an end-time conversion to Christ and the salvation of ethnic Israel.

Romans 1:16 speaks of the gospel coming to the Jew first and then the Gentile. Chronologically, this was the case, as those who were first saved by the gospel went abroad to the nations, bringing the Gentiles to the Messiah. Romans 11:26 inverts this order, as a literary "inclusio," or bracket, which brings the whole to an end. When the gospel, which has gone from the Jews to the Gentiles has achieved its end, when the fullness of the Gentiles has come in, then Israel will be saved—the first covenant people becoming the second covenant people. Could Jesus have been partly alluding to this when he said, "Some are last who will be first, and some are first who will be last" (Luke 13:30 ESV)? The broken-off branches will be grafted in through Christ, the descendants of Jacob and Israel will say, "I belong to the LORD" (Isa. 44:5).

Paul says he does not want the Roman Church "to be ignorant of this mystery." There is a divine mystery here, a term that speaks not of something hidden, because they are to know it, but of a secret from God now revealed. Yet this mystery still remains a mystery to many Christians! The mystery is that "Israel has experienced a hardening [to the gospel] in part [a remnant always remained, e.g., Paul] until the full number of the Gentiles has come in [then that hardening will soften to the gospel]. And so all Israel will be saved" (Rom. 11:25–26). The Jewish hostility and hardening to the gospel was part of God's doing—it was pragmatic, enabling the Gentiles to come in (11:11–15, 25b, 30). This hardening was *partial* (there was always a remnant) and *temporal* (only until the Gentiles come in), and then Paul expected its *removal* (when all Israel will be saved). Although hardened, although broken off from the olive tree, she will be grafted back in.

What do we mean by "saved"?

Paul began his letter by speaking of the gospel of salvation (Rom. 1:16). That theme of salvation is expounded throughout the letter and is understood to be a removal of God's divine judgment and wrath (3:9f.), an establishing as righteous (3:21f.), a restoration of divine glory, peace, and love (5:1f.), an ending of condemnation (8:1), a new life joined to Christ (6—7), and a resurrected body in eternal glory (8:18f.).

Who will be saved?

All Israel will be saved. "Israel" means Israel, not the church. To argue that "Israel means church" would render this text as saying, "All the church will be saved," surely a pointless tautology and certainly no mystery of which they were ignorant, for we have never had a problem believing that the church will be saved. Against those who want to interpret Israel in this text as "all the elect, all Christians," Paul is clearly juxtaposing Gentiles with Jews here. All bar one of the references to Israel in the New Testament and every reference in Romans (clearly in this immediate context, 11:25) refer directly and uniquely to ethnic Israel. Paul's immediate citation of Isaiah referring to Jacob (11:26) proves the point: The Israel of verse 26a is the Jacob of verse 26b. And Jacob was named Israel by God. The church has never been named Jacob! The only possible reference to Israel as the total elect community comes in Galatians 6:16, and there Israel is uniquely qualified by the predicate "of God," distinguishing it from the historic, geographic, and ethnic Israel.

"All Israel" is a frequent Hebraism, *Kol Yisrael*, which occurs 148 times in the Old Testament and always designates historic, ethnic Israel.[42] Dunn says, "There is strong consensus that all Israel must mean Israel as a whole."[43] Cranfield states, "Paul was thinking of a restoration of the nation of Israel as a whole to God at the end, an eschatological event."[44] All Israel being saved does not necessarily mean every Israelite throughout history, though some take it to mean this. More likely it refers to a general ethnic turning to Christ before his return.

When will they be saved?

The Greek conjunction *kai houtos*, "and then," means "after such, in this way, as follows." Israel's saving is more than just consecutive to the fullness of the Gentiles coming in, but almost a consequence, as if the saving of the Gentiles spurs the Jews to Christ. "The fullness of the Gentiles," as Cranfield says, "is probably to be explained as meaning the full number of the elect among the Gentiles."[45] This poses a problem for those who lean toward an Arminian doctrine—rejecting the Calvinist concept of the sovereignty of God in determining a fixed time for the eschaton and a fixed number for salvation. Nonetheless, the obvious reading is that there is a fixed, finite group of Gentiles who will be saved before Israel is. "Have come in" refers to entering the kingdom, being grafted into the olive tree, being welcomed into the people of God.

How will they be saved?

Some have suggested that they will be saved according to their election under Abraham or their adherence to the Torah. But this is a nonsense. There is no *Sonderweg*, no "separate path."[46] There is only one way to salvation for the Jew, as for the Gentile, namely being grafted onto the olive tree through faith in Christ. Paul's citation from Isaiah of a deliverer from Zion who will turn away Jacob's godlessness and remove her sins can only be a reference to Jesus—not Judaism, obedience to the Torah, or Abrahamic descent. As noted earlier, Jesus said to a devout Jew, "You must be born again" (John 3:7). Israel will be saved by accepting Jesus as Messiah, as deliverer, through embracing the gospel by faith and thus entering the church. Romans 1:16 is clear that salvation is by faith, and Romans 10:9 states that such a faith must be placed in Jesus as Lord.

Some have suggested that the Jews will be saved on the basis of their DNA, their Abrahamic ancestry, and covenant. No! That would nullify the whole of the argument in Romans 1—5. They are saved by Jesus' blood, not Abraham's. They are saved by faith like Abraham's, not faith in Abraham. As Millard J. Erickson says, "There is no statement anywhere in the NT that there is any other basis of salvation."[47] Lance Lambert, a messianic Jew, says, "Those who constitute 'all Israel' are those who have turned from transgression in Jacob and have been saved through the finished work of the Messiah."[48]

Why will they be saved?

They will be saved because God keeps his covenant (Rom. 11:27); because God has elected them (11:28b); because God has loved them (11:28c); because God has gifted and promised them (11:29); and because these covenants and gifts are irrevocable. It is not because of Israel's faithfulness, holiness, or worthiness—their general salvation is based exclusively on God's grace and God's commitment to honor his word and his name. Their existence, their perseverance, is due to God's faithfulness as the covenant keeper.

This scandal of particularity offends the mind of many who object to the idea that there is a fixed number of Gentiles who will be saved, and who object that *all* Israel, despite her long-term rejection of Christ, will be reconciled. But God's love is a love that cannot be requited, an election that cannot be annulled, a promise that cannot be countermanded, a covenant that must be kept. Romans 9—11 is an illustration of the point Paul makes at the end of Romans 8 that nothing can "separate us from the love of God," saying at the start of Romans 12, "in view of God's mercy," God's dealings with Israel are about God's inseparable love and incomparable mercy.

Where will they be saved?

Romans 11:27 states, "This is my covenant with them." Verse 29 reminds us that "God's gifts and his call are irrevocable." We saw above that God gave the land by gift and through his eternal covenant to Israel. This gifting cannot be reversed.

Where will it all end?

Israel's rejection of the gospel resulted in the Gentiles being welcomed to it and finding salvation. Israel's final acceptance of the gospel will usher in the return of the Lord, the resurrection of the dead, and all Israel's entry into glorious eternity: "For if their rejection is the reconciliation of the world, what will their acceptance be but life from the dead?" (Rom. 11:15). This chapter has been concerned with Israel's role in the end times. Rodman Williams has summarized the interpretation I have adopted on this issue, by speaking of the conversion of Israel to Christ as the "climactic sign," claiming that "the end will not occur without Israel's coming to salvation."[49] Pragmatically, and according to the prophetic promise, that will take place when the people of Israel are back in the land of Israel.

CONCLUSION: A HOPE AND A FUTURE

There are five reasons why I believe God has a future for the nation of Israel:

1. *I believe God has a future for the Jews because of Scripture.* This has to be the starting point. Many of the prophecies and promises in the Bible remain only partially fulfilled, and cannot easily be emptied of their obvious relevance to the people in the land today.

2. *I believe God has a future for the Jews because of the nature of God. He does not lie, he stands by his word, and his promises are sure.* If Israel has no future, that would make God a liar. Conversely, I would suggest that the return to the land after two millennia and the establishment of the nation-state is

more of a miracle and proof of God, given the Holocaust. If God did not exist, there could never have been a 1948 restoration of Israel to the land, nor a sixty-year prosperity in the land despite numerous efforts to remove them from it.

3. *I believe God has a future for the Jews because they still exist as a distinct people group with Abraham's DNA.* It is a miracle in human history that an identifiable people group who have wandered among the nations for twenty-five hundred years can still trace themselves back to Abraham, Isaac, and Jacob. Friedrich the Great once asked the pious statesman Ziethen for proof of the existence of God. He replied, "Your majesty—the Jews!"[50]

4. *I believe God has a future for the Jews because of modern history, which is being sucked powerfully into the Middle East.* Who would have thought that the wasteland scrub of Israel/Palestine would be regarded as the key to political stability in the world? Whatever the rights or wrongs of Israel in the land, she nevertheless seems to have taken center stage in world politics—as Scripture foretells.

5. *I believe God has a future for the Jews because of the interest Satan has shown in them throughout history,* seeking to wipe their memory off the face of the earth—from Pharaoh to Hitler to many others today. Whatever Satan rages against has a special purpose in God's plan.

What is our response?

Our first response should be *appreciation*—gratitude, not conceit (Rom. 11:25a). We are in debt to the Jews, because theirs are the covenants, the promises, the patriarchs, and through them we received Christ, the gospel, the Scriptures. Their rejection of Jesus was for our benefit and in accordance with God's decree. Sadly, conceit is exactly what the church has exhibited since the early church fathers! In churches all around, there is a conceited and almost sinister tone among many who deem themselves to have replaced Israel in God's affection.

Our next response must be *confession*. The Jewish people have long memories. Understandably, they do not pass lightly over two millennia of persecution at the hands of Christians. We must repent for atrocities committed in the name of our Lord and our church. For fifteen years after World War II, Basilea Schlink's community in Germany stood in silence at breakfast—identifying and repenting of the Nazi crime against the Jews—while blessing Israel.

Another response is *intercession*. We need to discern prayerfully what God is doing in the world and also what the Enemy is doing. Politics is the field that plays out what is happening in the heavenlies. We need to be aware and in prayer. But let the Bible and not the political pundits be the filter for our theology. We are still in a position to obey the injunction of Psalm 122:6 to "pray for the peace of Jerusalem."

We should also offer *provocation*: For the kindest of reasons, we make Israel jealous (Rom. 11:14). Hosier says, "If we have a concern for the Jews, the best way to reach them is to build a glorious church to provoke them to envy and to hasten the coming of the full number of Gentiles."[51]

Finally, we should respond with *mission*—we should witness to them appropriately. Derek Prince says that it is the Christian duty to love the Jews, not to attempt overt forms of evangelism.[52] Here I take issue with him. If we love the Jews, we must seek to share the Messiah with them. I look for an end-time conversion, but throughout there has always been a remnant saved through gospel work. As Douglas Moo says, refusal to preach the gospel to Jews is anti-Semitic.[53]

In Genesis 39—45 we follow the story of Joseph, rejected by his brothers, sold into slavery, raised to power as a lord of all Egypt, saving them in famine, and then being the savior of his people Jacob, who eventually come to him for aid and then to acknowledge him. He declares, "Do not be angry with yourselves for selling me here, because it was to save lives that God sent me ahead of you" (45:5). He tells his brothers, "God has made me lord of all Egypt" (45:9). When Joseph's father hears what has happened, Jacob/Israel says, "I'm convinced! My son Joseph is still alive" (45:28). Joseph later reassures his brothers and speaks kindly to them, saying, "You intended to harm me, but God intended it for good" (Gen. 50:20). Israel's sons sent Jesus to his death. They intended to harm him, but God intended it for good. For he would become the Gentile Lord, a Savior in spiritual famine, gloriously back from the dead. One day Israel will receive their Brother, Savior, and Lord when Jesus reveals himself again.

EIGHT

TRIBULATION AND RAPTURE

At that time the sign of the Son of Man will appear
in the sky, and all the nations of the earth will
mourn. They will see the Son of Man coming on the
clouds of the sky, with power and great glory. And
he will send his angels with a loud trumpet call, and
they will gather his elect from the four winds, from
one end of the heavens to the other.
(Matt. 24:30–31)

SIGNS AND SIGHS

In the last three chapters we have been considering Scripture's
treatment of and the church's reflection on the so-called end-time
signs that will precede the return of Christ. We explored the numerous
indicators mentioned in Jesus' end-time discourse in Matthew 24,
including persecution of God's people, false messiahs, natural disasters,
international conflicts, wars and rumors of wars, darkened heavenly
bodies, the manifestation of "the abomination that causes desolation,"
and the proclamation of the gospel to the nations. Luke comments
on the response to such signs: people fainting with fear at the cosmic
upheavals (Luke 1:26) and hearts weighed down with dissipation,
drunkenness, and the anxieties of life (Luke 21:34).

The discourse was Christ's answer to three specific questions from the disciples (Matt. 24:3): When will the destruction of the temple happen? What will be the sign of Christ's coming? What will be the sign of the end of the age? In the disciples' minds all three questions may have been understood to relate to a specific single event, the day of the Lord. However, Jesus' composite answer has been seen to be fulfilled in three ways: *historic specific* (AD 70 and the destruction of Jerusalem), *historic continuous* (such signs in part have always been evident in the church and the world), and *historic future* (such signs may be expected to increase, like labor pangs at the approach of a birth, immediately prior to the return of Christ).

We then considered the Antichrist. We understood "the abomination that causes desolation" manifested in AD 70 to be a prototype of this person, while the "spirit of antichrist" has been abroad since the founding of the church (1 John 4) and is synonymous with the man (or power) of lawlessness of which Paul spoke in 2 Thessalonians 2. We suggested that the power of lawlessness and the spirit of antichrist would take personified manifestation in the end times as the man of lawlessness, the human Antichrist depicted in Revelation as the beast who establishes and controls a global, financial, and political regime directing worship to Satan (Rev. 13).

Lastly, we examined the major unmistakable sign, the prophesied return of all the tribes of Israel from all corners of the earth to the land, and, more remarkably, what Ratzinger has called "the necessary preliminary" before the ending of time: ethnic Israel's conversion to the Lord.[1] We suggested that the first stage of this sign was partially fulfilled in the establishment of the nation-state of Israel in May 1948. Nonetheless, we still await the conversion of the nation to Christ, which Scripture says will occur when "the full number of the

Gentiles has come in" (Rom. 11:25). This will presumably not occur until the gospel has been preached to the nations (Matt. 24:14). We are some way off from this, and it is the only sign in which the church has any part to play—and perhaps could accelerate by her own faithfulness to the Great Commission.

Jesus informed the church of these signs so that we might be aware, active, and not alarmed. Indeed, even though such awesome signs will cause many to be gripped with fear, when we see these things happening, we are to lift up our heads in expectation, for our redemption draws near (Luke 21:28).

Fixing a time line is elusive. Jesus said it was prohibited. Consequently, any attempt at ordering such signs and creating an "eschatological map," though increasingly popular among some church groups, seems to me misguided as it presupposes that we have clear biblical templates. I do not believe we have them. Such signs have *always* been featured in the trajectory of history, although such signs as the return of Israel to the land, the proclamation of the gospel to the world, the conversion of the Jews to the Messiah, and the rise of the Antichrist are significant indicators that the end is drawing near.

In this chapter I want to pull together some of the signs—notably the persecution of the church, the rise of the Antichrist, and the restoration of Israel—and see how they relate to what has been termed the *tribulation*. This has become an increasingly important theme in the modern church, along with its (rather ugly) sister the *pretribulation rapture*. Such a statement doubtless betrays in advance what my conclusions will be. For those who want a detailed, evenhanded examination of the relationship between the tribulation and the rapture, I recommend the work of Erickson and Gundry.[2]

THE GREAT TRIBULATION

The nature of the tribulation

In the Old Testament and intertestamental material, the day of the Lord—the coming of the messianic kingdom—was always understood to be marked by apocalyptic signs in the cosmos as well as fiery tribulation. "Messianic woes" were expected to prefigure the welcome of the Messiah.[3] Clearly, the Messiah himself would endure tribulation as the "suffering servant." Jesus endured his own holocaust, and he indicated that his followers would endure great suffering by association (John 15:18–25; 16:33). He also made it clear that his return would be prefaced by a period of great suffering for the church especially and the world generally (Matt. 24). The New Testament church is destined to endure a fiery furnace. Most of the New Testament was written by men who were martyred. It is full of exhortations to persevere under trials (1 Thess. 1—3; Heb. 12; Rev. 1:9; 2—3). Erickson calls tribulation "the normal, typical experience of the saints."[4] Tribulation is business as usual for the church (1 Thess. 1:6; 2 Tim. 3:12; Acts 20:23; Heb. 10:33).

Some have seen a semantic change between the general tribulation of Matthew 24:9 (*thlipsin*, which the NIV translates as "persecuted") and the great tribulation of Matthew 24:21 (*thlipsis megale*, which the NIV translates as "great distress"). Certainly, Jesus' statement that there will be distress unequaled since the beginning of the world would seem to indicate an unimaginable nightmare, only cut short by God's mercy for the sake of the elect. There is a general consensus that Scripture foretells an experience of great suffering before Christ returns. What biblical scholars cannot agree on is the nature this will take, who is the victim, and who is the perpetrator.

The major issue is whether the tribulation refers to what Christians experience at the hands of the Antichrist (Rev. 13) or what the reprobate world experiences at the hands of God (Rev. 6:16f.). Is it targeted at Christians by the Antichrist, or at the world by God? Will the church endure it or escape it? If she endures it, will she endure all of it, or just part of it? Such views are not necessarily polarities. It is possible to see the sovereignty of God over the Antichrist's persecution of the church and to understand God to be using this to perfect and test his church. Equally, one might see the judgment as God pouring out tribulation wrath on the world, as a similar means of perfecting the saints. Such views may not be generally palatable to the church, but they are not without biblical warrant.[5] There is more than a hint of this in the great eschatological and apocalyptic passages of Zechariah 13—14, which speak of two-thirds of those in the City of God being cut off and the surviving third being refined as silver and tested as gold through fire, before the return of the Lord and the final display of his glory and majesty.

Erickson notes that of the fifty-five uses of *thlipsis* (the New Testament term used to speak of affliction/tribulation/trials), forty-seven of them refer to the church's experience. Consequently, he concludes that the tribulation "is not God's wrath against sinners but the wrath of Satan/antichrist and the wicked against the saints."[6] This great tribulation will be met by a great apostasy (unbelief) as persecution and betrayal cause the love of many to grow cold and the falling away of many on account of Christ (Matt. 24:9–14). Revelation 13:7 and its prophetic anticipation in Daniel 7:25 are clear: The Antichrist will "make war against the saints," and many will give way. In Revelation 7:14, we have a glimpse of heaven and are told of the saints who came out of the "great tribulation" (*thlipsios tes megales*). Revelation 8 continues by speaking of angels offering up the prayers of the saints—such prayers prayed by those still on earth. There is no sense that the saints escape. However, we must note that in the Septuagint, Daniel 12:1 uses the term *thlipsis* in the context of the end-time suffering of God's people. Here we are informed that those whose names are written in the book of life are delivered; they do escape. Is this a pretrib rapture? I am inclined to think not. I believe it relates either to the end-time wrath of God against the nations, which the saints escape, or the end-time raging of the nations, which God will bring the saints through at the resurrection.

I find that the most convincing support for the thesis that the church endures the tribulation comes from Christ's own words in Matthew 24:29f., where he states that "immediately" after the tribulation, there will be various cosmic and fearful signs in the sky and then he will return in the clouds (v. 30). After that the angels will summon and gather his elect from the four winds (north, south, east, and west). The elect are Christ's saints, his church, his chosen ones—those who have endured the great tribulation and survived the great apostasy, who are still on earth, awaiting his return and this gathering of themselves to him.

Others, however, understand the tribulation to be directed at the world in judgment by God, rather than at the church in malice by the Devil. Rodman Williams asserts, "In the matter of the great tribulation, which is not persecution suffered by believers but God's wrath on the world, there will be total protection." And again, "God will shield his own from the judgments that are to be poured out upon the oppressors."[7] This view is drawn from the prophecies of the seven seals (Rev. 6, 8), the seven trumpets (Rev. 8:6—9:20), and the seven bowls (Rev. 15—16). However we interpret them—figuratively, factually, consecutively, or consistently—they are seen as manifestations of divine wrath against a demonized world that culminate in the final judgment (Luke 21:23).

George Eldon Ladd attempts to hold together the whole of Scripture's counsel on this matter by understanding the twofold nature of the tribulation—as divine judgment on the world and demonic assault on the saints:

> *Although the church will be on earth in these final and terrible days, and will suffer fierce persecution and martyrdom at the hands of the beast, she will be kept from the hour of trial which is coming on the pagan world. God's wrath poured out on the kingdom of antichrist will not afflict God's people.*[8]

To a certain extent he must be right, but I suspect there is a third form of tribulation, besides persecution and judgment on the Antichrist: namely a general suffering experienced by fallen humankind in the decaying world as a consequence of sin, which all creation must endure, groaning, while awaiting the day of redemption.

The duration of the tribulation

We have already noted that tribulation has been a feature throughout the history of the church in terms of persecution, and throughout the course of the world's history in terms of suffering, disease, and death. But the end-time great tribulation associated with the manifestation of the "abomination that causes desolation"—the Antichrist, the man of lawlessness—is often given specific timings. On the basis of mathematical massaging of texts, with a week representing seven years, it is argued that the time of the Antichrist will be a seven-year period (Dan. 9:24–27). The tribulation will be the second half of that time, with the first half promising peace as the Antichrist comes to power by establishing a false utopia. Daniel anticipates this lull before the storm:

He will confirm a covenant with many for one "seven" [week].
In the middle of the "seven" [week] he will put an end to sacrifice
and offering. And on a wing of the temple he will set up an
abomination that causes desolation, until the end that is decreed
is poured out on him. (Dan. 9:27)

The exact period of the great tribulation is held by many to be the second half of the seven-year period—three and a half years, forty-two months, or 1,290 days:

He [the Antichrist] will speak against the Most High and oppress
his saints and try to change the set times and the laws. The saints
will be handed over to him for a time, times and half a time.
(Dan. 7:25)

From the time that the daily sacrifice is abolished and the
abomination that causes desolation is set up, there will be 1,290
days. Blessed is the one who waits for and reaches the end of the
1,335 days. (Dan. 12:11–12)

The beast was given a mouth to utter proud words and
blasphemies and to exercise his authority for forty-two months.
(Rev. 13:5)

I personally believe the focus here is not so much on "literal time" as on "limited time." His authority is partial—it is given to him, and it is temporary—and lasts only three and a half years. Seven is the perfect number in Scripture and speaks of completeness. To speak of his time as seven years is to speak symbolically of the fullness of the exercise of his reign. To speak of three and a half years is to underline that for only part of his time will he exercise his blasphemous ways, and then only partially. Jesus promises that "those days will be shortened" (Matt. 24:22): The Lord will not allow Satan to have his way totally, and the period of tribulation will be interrupted sovereignly by Christ's return.

That the church will be snatched away/raptured is not in dispute. What is in dispute, is the when, who, and why.[9]

Troubled by a trifle of tribs?

We have already touched on some theological understandings of the church's place in the tribulation. There are two major views—pretribulationism (hereafter pretrib) and posttribulationism (hereafter posttrib). Lesser-known views include midtrib, partial pretrib, and late trib.

Midtrib rapture claims that the church is snatched away halfway through the great tribulation, after which the full force of God's wrath in judgment on the world is meted out, three and a half years into the seven-year manifestation of the Antichrist. Holders of this view cite texts such as Daniel 7:25, with its "time, times and half a time," and Revelation 12:14 where the mother and child are snatched away to the desert. The midtrib understanding, as with the pretrib, is that the rapture is distinct from the second coming, which thus becomes a third coming!

Partial pretrib rapture claims that only the spiritual and faithful church will be raptured. The unfaithful, carnal, and compromised church will remain as a remnant to be purified by the great tribulation.

Late trib rapture[10] is deduced from Revelation 14, which speaks of "two harvests"—the first when the Son of Man comes in the clouds with a sickle to reap the harvest of his saints (14:14–16); the second when the grim reaper angel reaps the grapes of God's wrath in judgment (14:17–20). The question is whether this is a simultaneous event at the second coming, or whether this is an event in time with history still running its course. The narrative continues in Revelation 15—19, detailing the final pouring out of divine wrath (the seven plagues in 15:1; the seven bowls in 16:1), the battle at Armageddon, and the fall of the beast and Babylon, while making no reference to the saints' continued perseverance or persecution, but only to their rejoicing in heaven. Thus, if Revelation 15 is understood as continuing historically after the reaping of Revelation 14, then such a notion as a late trib rapture could be plausible. However, if we understand Revelation to be more cyclic or repetitive in its presentation, it is possible that the two harvests are simultaneous with the end-time visitation. Chapters 15—19 are intended merely to flesh out more fully the end-time scenario on earth and in heaven preceding the second coming.[11]

The major alternative to pretrib rapture (see below) is *posttrib rapture*, which equates the second coming of Christ (the *Parousia*) with the rapture at the end of time following the tribulation. This is the traditional historic view held by the church fathers, Reformers, and mainline Catholic and Protestant denominations. The church is understood to go through an end-time tribulation of persecution at the hands of the Antichrist, though some suggest she is protected from the tribulation of God's end-time wrath on the world. One feature of Christ's return will be the rapture of the saints, the welcome party, who meet their Beloved returning in the air, but this is concurrent with the end of history and the new beginning. The rapture will be immediately followed by the day of judgment, the destruction of evil, the reward of the faithful, the re-creation of the new heaven and new earth, and the reign of Christ.[12]

Rapture rescue ready!

The theological position of *pretrib rapture* has developed only in the last 170 years through the so-called dispensationalists (see chapter 4). They claim that Christ will come secretly for the church and "rapture" her away to heaven. This return of Christ is *not* to be confused with the second coming, which for them, technically speaking, will be his third coming (advent, rapture, final return). After the church is raptured, judged, rewarded, and taken to heaven, the history of the world will continue briefly. The Antichrist will rise to power, Israel will be restored and take her destined place on the world stage, the two witnesses left on earth (see Rev. 11:3) will preach the gospel, and many will respond. God will pour out his wrath on the earth and the demonic powers in what is known as the great tribulation, and the nations will rush to Armageddon, when Christ will return publicly for a third time to destroy his enemies and establish his millennial eternal reign.

Dispensational pretrib rapture has no theological antecedents before the early nineteenth century, although its adherents have ransacked ancient authorities in attempting to locate a pedigree for their notions. The first hints of such a view are found in Edward Irving in the 1830s. It has been suggested by some that it stemmed from a prophecy given in 1830 by a young Scottish charismatic, Margaret MacDonald, which had an impact on Irving and also J. N. Darby.[13] The actual term "pretrib rapture" is credited to Darby, whose Plymouth Brethren movement adopted the view. This was picked up in the late Victorian era by Scofield, who incorporated it into his overall biblical outline and whose Bible notes on the dispensation proved widely popular. Indeed, Scofield's work was influential in shaping the twentieth-century eschatology of large sections of American Christianity.

It was given theological support particularly through Dallas Theological Seminary and others, whose founding fathers were passionate advocates of pretrib dispensationalism.[14] Some scholarly attempts to present this view have been offered. Lewis Sperry Chafer wrote a well-received seven-volume systematic theology that promoted the notion. A notable attempt at a biblical theology was written by J. F. Walvoord.[15]

Pretribs like to emphasize the "surprise" element of the secret rapture (Matt. 24:40–43; 1 Thess. 5:1–5), and more popular works in this vein include that of J. Dwight Pentecost, whose book *Things to Come—A Study in Biblical Eschatology* sold 215,000 copies. Hal Lindsey's phenomenally successful best-seller *The Late Great Planet Earth* has sold upwards of fifteen million copies, and the recent narrative series by Tim LaHaye and Jerry Jenkins, *Left Behind*, has sold sixty-five million copies so far.[16] Movies such as *A Thief in the Night* in the 1970s, *The Rapture* in the 1990s, and the Left Behind series in the last few years have all added grist to the mill. The Left Behind series offers a typical presentation of full-blown pretribulationalism:

> *Our senior pastor loved to preach about the coming of Christ to rapture his church, to take believers dead and alive to heaven before a period of tribulation on the earth. He was particularly inspired once a couple of years ago....*
>
> *"Well," Barnes said, "the pastor used that sermon and had himself videotaped in this office speaking directly to the people who were left behind. He put it in the church library with instructions to get it out and play it if most everyone seemed to have disappeared."[17]*

David Pawson, himself a "posttrib rapturist," suggests that there are two positives to the idea of pretrib rapture: First, it gives great comfort to the church as they hope that they will be removed from the tribulation; and second, it challenges the saints to evangelize because the time is short and at any moment the church could be snatched away.[18] Many of those who subscribe to this view are very sincere, biblical evangelicals who are passionate in serving Christ. As we have noted, however, it has little historic pedigree. Can it be found clearly in Scripture?

IS THE RAPTURE BIBLICAL?

The term *rapture* first appeared in the Victorian era, referring to the church being taken up into the air to meet Christ. It comes from the Latin *rapere/rapio*, which broadly means "to carry off," and was used in the Latin Vulgate (the principal Latin version of the Bible) to translate the Greek verb *harpazo* in 1 Thessalonians 4:17, which the NIV renders "caught up." In context it speaks of those who are dead in Christ, along with those who are still alive in Christ at his return, being gathered together in the clouds to meet the Lord in the air. The Greek term literally means "to steal away" or "to carry off" and is actually related to the word for theft.[19] These verses in 1 Thessalonians 4:13–18 have a "great capacity for spectacular enlargement by creative imagination."[20] It is one of the linchpin texts in support of the dispensationalist pretrib rapture position. But, as close examination shows, there is no hint here that this is anything other than a description of the second coming of Christ.

WE WILL MEET HIM IN THE AIR

Jesus is coming to collect the church, but there is no "secret rapture": it is a noisy public event, heralded by angelic trumpets and "a loud command" (1 Thess. 4:16). Paul's reference to being "caught up … in the clouds" (v. 17) appears to match what Daniel foresaw of the Son of Man coming "with the clouds of heaven," being given dominion and glory and a kingdom over all the world that will never be destroyed (Dan. 7:13f.). The same event was recorded by John in Revelation 1:7 and 14:14, where he says that Jesus will come in the clouds to collect his church. This will be plainly visible, with every eye beholding him, and will be synonymous with that hope of a second coming promised by the angels in Acts 1:11. Can there really be any doubt that what Paul is speaking of in 1 Thessalonians 4 is no secret rapture at all, but the second coming of Christ prophesied in Matthew 24?

> *Immediately after the distress of those days … all the nations of the earth will mourn. They will see the Son of Man coming on the clouds … he will send his angels with a loud trumpet call, and they will gather his elect from the four winds, from one end of the heavens to the other. (vv. 29–31)*

Yes, the rapture is biblical—but it is far from being some secret exodus of the elect, while history continues its course until a third coming of Christ. The second and final coming of Christ will be in the clouds, summoning the dead in Christ, gathering the universal church to himself, and then enacting final judgment against the world.

LIKE A THIEF IN THE NIGHT

Jesus said he would come like a thief in the night (Matt. 24:43) and exhorted his church to be ready for this event. In 1 Thessalonians, immediately following the reference to the rapture, Paul uses the very phrase "thief in the night" twice (5:2, 4) to speak, not of the sudden unexpected rapture when Christ returns secretly to collect the church, but of the sudden inescapable destruction that Christ ushers in with his second coming (v. 3). That the church is still here at this judgment event is secured by the fact that Paul says, "But you, brothers [i.e., the church], are not in darkness so that this day should surprise you like a thief [i.e., that you would be unprepared for this day].… For God did not appoint us to suffer wrath but to receive salvation" (vv. 4, 9). This refers not to escaping the tribulation, but to escaping the wrath of God at the final judgment. This motif is also found in Revelation 16:15, speaking of the return of Christ to defeat the Antichrist's armies at Armageddon.

It seems unlikely that there will be several returns like a thief in the night, and therefore it is reasonable to believe that Jesus' return to collect the church (Matt.24:43) is concurrent with his destroying of the enemies of God (Rev. 16:15) and with his judgment on the world (1 Thess. 5:2, 4). A parallel passage to this is Matthew 24:37, which exhorts the church to be prepared, so it will not to be taken by surprise, as with the thief in the night. Likewise Jesus will come to bring sudden deliverance for his church along with destruction upon an unprepared world.

AS IN THE DAYS OF NOAH

Jesus also said that his coming would be just as "in the days of Noah" (Matt. 24:37). Jesus here is primarily indicating that most were surprised by and unprepared for the floods, except Noah and his family. God's visitation by flood was judgment and destruction on the world, but the deliverance and rescue of Noah and his family in the ark was concurrent with that event. In saying that his coming will be as in the days of Noah, surely Jesus is suggesting that it will be a surprise to those who will perish in that day of judgment, but it will be unsurprising for those who have long anticipated and prepared for his visitation.

In the days of Noah, God's visitation was a singular event of both judgment and deliverance. Noah was not delivered, nor raptured, nor given an escape *before* the judgment, but *amidst* the judgment: At the very moment that the world was being destroyed, Noah was being saved. Similarly, Christ's return will be as "in the days of Noah," bringing destruction (1 Thess. 5:3) and deliverance (1 Thess. 5:9), the two hand in hand. As with Noah the righteous will not have been raptured away beforehand, but will join Christ in the clouds before the world is judged. Jesus' final coming will be like a thief in the night, as in the days of Noah: His church will be alert, awake, and prepared. They will not be swept away by the flood of judgment, nor overtaken by darkness, but they will be rescued from destruction, raptured into the air, and reunited with Christ forever.

In his commentary on Thessalonians, Joel Green helpfully summarizes what is really happening in this passage:

> *This teaching was presented to comfort those in grief by connecting the confession of the creed (Jesus died and rose again) with the reality of the resurrection of the dead in Christ. This is not the stuff of speculative prophecy or best sellers on the end times. The text is located at the funeral home, the memorial service and the graveside. It is placed in the hands of each believer to comfort others in their time of great sorrow. The decidedly bizarre pictures of airplanes dropping out of the sky and cars careening out of control as the rapture happens detract from the hope that this passage is designed to teach. The picture presented here is of the royal home-coming of Jesus Christ. The Church as the official delegation goes out to meet him, with the dead heading up the procession as those most honoured.[21]*

TRIBULATION NOT TRANSPORTATION

There are a number of points to make as we try to draw the threads of this chapter together.

The treatment of Scripture

Aside from the passages mentioned above, dispensationalist pretribs marshal other texts (e.g., John 14:1–3; Titus 2:13), which they claim speak of two separate events. So, for example, Titus 2:13 is deemed to read, "The blessed hope *[and]* the glorious appearing of our great God and Savior, Jesus Christ," rather than the more obvious sense, "The blessed hope *that is* the glorious appearing of our great Savior" Matthew 24:40f. is often cited by pretrib rapturists. It speaks of two men in a field, one of whom is taken while the other is left behind; and of two women grinding at a mill, one of whom is taken while the other is left. But the focus of Christ's teaching is not on the rapture so much as on the distinction Jesus will make between those who are his, who will be with him, and those who are not his, who will be rejected at his coming.

The rapture is also identified by some in Revelation 4:1f. when John is suddenly called up in a vision to heaven. Some choose to present him as a type of the church raptured at this juncture.[22] Another passage cited is 2 Thessalonians 2:3, which speaks of an "apostasy," a falling away (in Greek *apostasia*), and is translated by some pretribs as a "carrying away," meaning the rapture. Neither of these interpretations carries much weight. Fundamental to pretribs is their understanding that God has promised to protect the saints from wrath (1 Thess. 1:10; Rev. 3:10). Rather than see this as deliverance from God's end-time consuming wrath on judgment day, they mistakenly take it to mean the church's deliverance out of the great tribulation, which they believe God will send as judgment on the world before Christ returns.

Generally speaking, I believe that pretribs take clear statements and details about the final day of general resurrection and apply them to a private, secret rapture of the church. I agree with David Pawson, who concludes that "there is not one single clear statement in the NT that there will be a secret rapture of the church before the great tribulation."[23] This, of course, is challenged by the pretribs, who seek to secure their view scripturally and deconstruct any posttrib interpretation.[24] Readers must weigh the texts and judge for themselves.

No escape for the church

Pretrib rapture is seen as necessary to rescue the church from enduring the wrath of God in the tribulation. However, the tribulation has been shown to be a period of both divine wrath on the world and demonic wrath against God's elect. The end-time church is not called to escape suffering, but to have comfort and courage to endure suffering. If God were to rapture the church before the manifestation of the Antichrist and the tribulation in order to keep them out of harm's way, he would at the very least be acting inconsistently, having not acted to rescue those Christians who suffered from Nero to Mao, from Domitian to Stalin. Will the end-time tribulation conceivably be worse than that suffered for two millennia by the church family?

Corrie ten Boom, survivor of Belsen and wonderful advocate for Christ and encourager of the church, tells of the disastrous pastoral implications of the false hope in a pretrib rapture.

> *I have been in countries where the saints are already suffering terrible persecution. In China the Christians were told: "Don't worry, before the tribulation comes, you will be translated,*

raptured." Then came a terrible persecution. Millions of
Christians were tortured to death. Later I heard a Bishop from
China say, sadly: "We have failed. We should have made the
people strong for persecution, rather than telling them Jesus would
come first." Turning to me, he said: "Tell the people how to be
strong in times of persecution, how to stand when tribulation
comes—to stand and not faint."[25]

We have already demonstrated earlier (in the section on the tribulation) that it is against the *saints* that the Antichrist wages war (Rev.
13:7). We saw in Matthew 24:22 that the tribulation is cut short for
the sake of the *elect*, and in 24:29–31 that the elect are gathered to
Christ *after* the tribulation. To escape the obvious interpretation that
the church must go through the tribulation until the end, dispensationalists suggest that the elect and the saints in this text must refer to those
who have turned to Christ after the church's rapture and before his second coming. Walvoord makes much of the fact that Scripture speaks of
the "saints" or the "elect" and not of the "church," suggesting that they
are either Jews or post-church-rapture converts. However, such a distinction will simply not stand up to critical scrutiny. The terms "saints"
and "elect" are clearly used throughout the New Testament to refer to
the church (Eph. 1:1; 1 Peter 1:1–2; Rev. 5:8f.).

Israel

Pretrib rapture is based on a model of the end times that requires
the church to leave the scene in order to make way for God's end-time
program focused on Israel. Because the church and end-time-restored
Israel are two very distinct eras in dispensational theology, it is deemed
necessary to remove the church before Israel can come to the fore and

fulfill her prophetic destiny. The church in this scheme is a so-called "grace parenthesis" to God's main focus on establishing his kingdom with Israel.

Rodman Williams is right to say that this division "is biblically and theologically out of the question."[26] I believe it is a classic example of eisegesis (reading into the text) rather than exegesis (reading out of the text). My understanding of Scripture is that Israel will be saved in the end by accepting the Messiah (Rom. 11:26), but only when the first covenant people join the second covenant people (i.e., the church)—all saved by the mercy of God (Eph. 2:14–21).

A more trustworthy view

By contrast, *post*tribulationism has been accepted by most of the church for most of her history, because it is the most faithful in handling the Scriptures that address the matter of the tribulation, the rapture, and the return of Christ. Erickson notes:

> *Post-tribulationism displays less of a tendency than its competitor to read preconceived ideas into a text. It seldom finds in a text special ideas that one would find only if he came to the text with a preconceived system.*[27]

Hans Schwarz says of pretrib dispensationalism: "Most of these speculations do not stand up to historically informed exegesis of the biblical texts … they often rest on dangerous theological presuppositions."[28]

The creed simply states, "He will come again to judge the living and the dead"—not, "He will come to collect the church and then come again at a later point to judge the world"! Article 4 of the so-called 39 Articles of the Protestant Church of England states, "He

ascended into heaven and there sitteth until he return to judge all men
at the last day." No notion here of a double return. I am unaware of any
historic Catholic or Protestant advocacy of the notion of rapture, apart
from the final second coming of Christ. That view, as we have seen, is
very much a latecomer to theology, with no historical support before
the early nineteenth century and no clear biblical support at all.

Conclusion

As with every other subject in this book so far, we have wrestled with
difficult texts, difficult concepts, and diverging interpretations to try
to make sense of the so-called rapture and tribulation. Tribulations
range from natural disasters and violent revolutions to persecutions
against the church. The former may be understood as the indirect
wrath of God on a world of sin (Rom. 1:18f.; Rev. 6); the latter is
directly the manifestation of the Antichrist. Tribulations have always
marked the church, but even as the Nazis, knowing the Allies were
advancing, gave orders to speed up the demonic annihilation of the
Jews, so immediately prior to the return of Christ the tribulations will
increase against God's elect as the blasphemous Antichrist seeks to do
his worst before his ultimate destruction. We reject the increasingly
dominant view in the evangelical West of a pretrib rapture, that we
believe offers a false hope of escape to the church—a vain hope which
we believe wrongly divides Scripture.

The tribulation will last for a limited period within the sovereignty
of God, who allows it as a judgment against the world and as a purification of the church. There is no secret rapture of the church by Christ
and then a subsequent public return of Christ with the church. Scripture knows of only one second coming. At the appointed time the
trumpet will sound, the dead in Christ will rise, and the saints who

remain alive will gather with them in the air to welcome their coming King. We have already argued in chapter 4 against a literal millennial reign followed by a final end-time conflict. Consequently, we believe there is one return, when the sinful are judged the faithful saints are rewarded; Satan, the Antichrist, and his cohorts are consumed by fire; a new heaven and new earth are established; and the righteous reign of God for eternity begins.

Tribulation then rapture, rapture then tribulation—whatever view we take, all students of Scripture will conclude that the final state of our God-forsaking world will be tribulation from the judgment seat of Christ, while the final state of the church will be rapture in the sense of unbridled bliss, flowing from eternal union with Christ.

NINE

ARMAGEDDON

Then they gathered the kings together to the
place that in Hebrew is called Armageddon.
(Rev. 16:16)

We have come to our final sign, the last scene before the curtain on human history closes and the lights of eternity come on as Christ returns to reign. *Armageddon* is a term that represents an end-time, decisive, cosmic, cataclysmic conflict between good and evil—the kind of thing portrayed in Tolkien's *Lord of the Rings* and C. S. Lewis's *The Last Battle*. As a literary motif it has been found in many of the major writers from Shelley and Kipling to Joyce.[1] It was a theme in poetry to describe the horrors of World War I,[2] and more recently Hurricane Katrina's devastation of New Orleans.[3] Similarly, it has been a theme creatively explored by artists.[4] In modern slang it can mean to bring retribution on someone, to get even, to beat up, to push around, or in the worst case to kill.[5] It is more generally used to describe a potential global crisis caused by technological, or ecological disasters.[6]

HISTORY IN THE MAKING?

In its biblical setting (Rev. 16:16), Armageddon represents an occasion and a location for the grand, decisive, and final conflagration between God and Satan, played out in a world war to end all wars. Many have suggested that we are living in the end times and are therefore moving toward the final battle that defines the end times. Hal Lindsey, writing thirty years ago, claimed that the rebirth of the nation-state of Israel was "the fuse of Armageddon,"[7] and evidently a literalist understanding of the associated texts concerning Armageddon places it as happening somewhere in Israel.

Lindsey's highly influential work claimed to predict from Scripture a full-blown narrative of the Apocalypse. By prophetic jigsaw assembly, he asserted that the end will climax with four power blocks confronting each other. The Arab-African confederacy headed up by Egypt ("the king of the South," see Dan. 11) will launch an invasion on Israel. Russia and her allies will use the occasion to launch an attack on the Middle East. For a brief while Russia will conquer and establish a command headquarters in Jerusalem on the Temple Mount. Then the ten-nation alliance of the revived Roman Empire will destroy Russia, and the remaining two power blocks of the West and the Orient (Red China) will go toe-to-toe at Armageddon. As the battle reaches its climax in the valley of Jezreel—as all life hangs in the balance—Christ gloriously appears to defeat his enemies and establish his millennium reign.[8]

Lindsey's presentation has received widespread popular acceptance, particularly in America. However, as Hans Schwarz rightly muses, "We wonder about the appropriateness of Lindsey's highly imaginative but entirely unhistorical approach to the scriptures."[9] We will consider the scriptural jigsaw pieces more fully below.

WRITE ME IN THE STORY

The Puritans thought they were writing their own part in Armageddon. Some, like Thomas Brightman in his early seventeenth-century *Apocalypsis Apocalypses—A Revelation of the Revelation*,[10] believed the end-time conflict would be between the Catholic Church and the Protestants, perhaps centered around the holy city of Geneva. Other Puritans, such as Edward Holyoke, understood Armageddon not as a literal end-time battle, but as a symbol for every conflict past, present, and future between the saints and their enemies. Intriguingly, Roger Williams, founder of Rhode Island, believed Armageddon was indeed an end-time international battle, but one to be fought with words not weapons. More typical of Puritan thought was the approach of American Increase Mather, who wrote of it as "the most terrible day of battle that ever was." He claimed that Asia would be aflame with war between Turks and Israelites, while in Europe war would be waged between the followers of the Lamb and the followers of the beast. The victorious Protestant and Israelite armies would vanquish the Roman Catholic and Ottoman Empires, the Jews would be converted and restored to the land, and the reign of Christ would begin.[11]

The Puritans were not the only ones to place themselves in the story and interpret Scripture in their own context. During the Cold War, Armageddon was seen in terms of nuclear war between the Communist Soviet Union and the NATO (North Atlantic Treaty Organization) alliance. When the Cold War thawed, prophetic pundits shifted their end-time speculations to a clash between American-led coalition forces and the fundamentalist Islamic nations. Some now fear that a fundamentalist, literalist end-time scenario is not simply reflecting the current situation, but actually driving politics. President Bush's foreign policy, his wars in Iraq and Afghanistan, and his posturing at Iran are regarded by some political pundits as an attempt by Bush and his administration to write themselves into the end-time scheme of events, initiating a political/military scenario that will culminate in Armageddon.

Whatever the truth or untruth behind Bush's messianic mind-set and the relationship between his policies and Scripture's prophecies, many sincerely believe that Armageddon is imminent. Some fundamentalist Christians have already bought land in the vicinity of the claimed site of Armageddon, some fifty miles outside Jerusalem, so that they can get a ringside seat for the final showdown. Well, time will surely tell.

In the tragedy of Waco, we saw how David Koresh and his followers, known as the Branch Davidians, believed themselves to be taking part in the end-time Armageddon narrative.[12] When the agents of the Bureau of Alcohol, Tobacco, and Firearms came to search for unlicensed weapons on February 28, 1993, they were regarded by Koresh as the Antichrist's envoys and met with a hail of bullets. A fifty-one-day siege ensued that culminated in the storming of the ranch by federal agents, whereupon the Davidians set themselves and the ranch on fire. Schwarz says, "The fiery inferno of Waco for the Branch Davidians was the battle of Armageddon."[13] Sadly for them, they died needlessly—and the history of the world continued without their expected epiphany of Christ.

THE WAR TO END ALL WARS?

> *Then I saw three evil spirits that looked like frogs; they came out of the mouth of the dragon, out of the mouth of the beast and out of the mouth of the false prophet. They are spirits of demons performing miraculous signs, and they go out to the kings of the whole world, to gather them for the battle on the great day of God Almighty.*

> *"Behold, I come like a thief! Blessed is he who stays awake and keeps his clothes with him, so that he may not go naked and be shamefully exposed."*

> *Then they gathered the kings together to the place that in*
> *Hebrew is called Armageddon. (Rev. 16:13–16)*

The NIV captures the sense of the Greek in Revelation 16:14 when it speaks of *the* "battle." In Revelation 19:19 and 20:8, it similarly speaks of "the war," "the battle" (*ton polemon*)—there being a definite article in the Greek here. This suggests not some generic rolling conflict, but a final, ultimate, decisive battle, the well-known, long-anticipated war to end all wars.[14]

The conflict described in Revelation between chapters 16 and 20 is probably one and the same event. Premillennialists believe Armageddon is a penultimate conflict, with the final battle coming after a literal millennium rule (20:8), but I prefer to see in Scripture just one final decisive battle that manifests Christ and conquers his foes. In this view, Revelation 20:8 is a *reiteration* of this conflict, which is set in place in chapter 16 and described in chapter 19. It makes little sense to me to believe in a decisive battle at Armageddon in which Christ finally overthrows and kills his enemies and hurls the beast and false prophet into the lake of fire (19:20f.), only for that scenario to be repeated a thousand years later with a new enemy.[15] That the battle of Armageddon in Rev. 16f is reiterated in Rev. 20:7f is supported by the fact both share the same themes of nations demonically deceived and summoned for battle—indeed they share the very same Greek sentence: *sunagagein autous eis ton polemon*—"to gather them to the war" (16:14, 20:8). These nations drawn to ultimate conflict are defined as Gog and Magog in Revelation 20, prophesied in Ezekiel 38—39, which shares motifs with the great day of the Lord depicted in Zechariah 12—14, of the ultimate conflict ushering in God's eternal and glorious reign.

Armageddon is a battle precipitated by the unholy trinity—the Dragon, the beast, and the false prophet. They in turn inspire demonic spirits deceitfully to summon kings and their armies to Israel. The frogs in verse 13 are used symbolically, perhaps because they were one of the curses on Egypt, or because they were replicated by Pharaoh's magicians (see Ex. 8). Their croak is characteristically loud and meaningless.[16] The nations are deceived into thinking that they are gathering to exterminate the saints, but they are gathered together ultimately by God only in order to meet their own judgment at the hands of Jesus (Rev. 19:11–21).[17]

It is a battle long anticipated by the prophets. Ezekiel 38 and 39 prophesy that Gog and Magog, whose identities remain uncertain, will be brought up to make war on Israel, whereupon God will intervene in jealousy and zeal for his people. Accompanied by apocalyptic signs of earthquakes and hailstones, judgment will then fall on Israel's enemies (see Ezek. 38:7–10, 15–16).

The minor prophets also predict that God will gather the nations to Jerusalem. She will be besieged, some will be exiled, and appalling distress will fall on her (Zeph. 3; Zech. 13:8; 14:2).

The battle will climax with the visitation of Christ, coming like a thief (Matt. 24:42f.; 1 Thess. 5:4) as he gathers the elect to himself in the air (Zech. 14:5b; Rev. 17:14). He himself will go out and fight against the assembled nations (Zech. 14:2–5).

This is the day of the Lord Almighty, because he will be manifested and vindicated, and his enemies will be defeated. The unholy trinity and their unholy military alliance of nations will lose this final battle. The outcome is determined and described in Revelation 17:14, 19:14–21, and 20:7–10: Armageddon spells defeat for the Devil.

I saw heaven standing open and there before me was a white horse, whose rider is called Faithful and True. With justice he judges and makes war. His eyes are like blazing fire, and on his head are many crowns. He has a name written on him that no one knows but he himself. He is dressed in a robe dipped in blood, and his name is the Word of God. The armies of heaven were following him, riding on white horses and dressed in fine linen, white and clean. Out of his mouth comes a sharp sword with which to strike down the nations. "He will rule them with an iron sceptre." He treads the winepress of the fury of the wrath of God Almighty. On his robe and on his thigh he has this name written:

KING OF KINGS AND LORD OF LORDS.

And I saw an angel standing in the sun, who cried in a loud voice to all the birds flying in midair, "Come, gather together for the great supper of God, so that you may eat the flesh of kings, generals, and mighty men, of horses and their riders, and the flesh of all people, free and slave, small and great."

Then I saw the beast and the kings of the earth and their armies gathered together to make war against the rider on the horse and his army. But the beast was captured, and with him the false prophet who had performed the miraculous signs on his behalf. With these signs he had deluded those who had received the mark of the beast and worshiped his image. The two of them were thrown alive into the fiery lake of burning sulfur. The rest of them were killed with the sword that came out of the mouth of the rider on the horse, and all the birds gorged themselves on their flesh. (Rev. 19:11–21)

REAL LOCATION OR SYMBOLIC OCCASION?

Much in John's Revelation and the other prophetic texts is symbolic, including place names. Babylon (Rev. 18) clearly represents the demonic countersymbol to Jerusalem. We must therefore be careful about taking the narrative too literally. Depictions of the conflict involving horses and swords are no doubt time-conditioned symbols, prior to mechanized war—belonging to the Bronze Age rather than the twenty-first century. No doubt the end-time conflict will be a period of great persecution and tribulation for the saints around the world. They will suffer at the hands of an Antichrist figure, symbolically termed the beast, and his sidekick, the false prophet.

So why, then, should we consider Israel and Jerusalem as more than symbolic ciphers? Well, the fact is, many do. My own understanding of Jerusalem as the historic, geographic city is deduced from the fact that, while there are many symbols of a time-bound or apocalyptic nature in the related texts that need discerning and careful interpretation, war in and against Israel and Jerusalem is the one constant.

As we saw in the previous chapter, numerous texts may be marshaled to locate Israel not just theologically, but literally, and geographically, at the epicenter of end-time history. Zechariah 14:3f. tells us that the battle will end when Jesus comes with his holy ones (angels and church) to vindicate his people. He will place his feet firmly on the Mount of Olives. Joyce Baldwin correctly says, "The ascension of Jesus on the Mt. of Olives and in particular the promise of the angel concerning his return (Acts 1:11) draw attention to the significance of this prophecy and suggest a literal fulfillment."[18]

But what of Armageddon, where the conflict is being played out? John speaks of a place called Armageddon in Greek, which he claims stems from a Hebrew word—presumably *har meggido*, meaning Mount

Meggido. The problem is that, while there is indeed a Valley of Meg-iddo, no such place as the Mount (*har*) of Megiddo exists. The Valley of Megiddo is two days' walk north of Jerusalem, but there is no nearby mountain—although there is a Bronze Age tell at the spur of the Carmel ridge. The tell rises some seventy feet: hardly a mount![19] This site became the strategic pass between the coastal plains and the Valley of Esdron, guarding the plain of Esdraelen (the Vulgate translates this as the "plain of Megiddo"), and it is the intersection between the major trade routes linking Egypt with the Fertile Crescent and Palestine with the Phoeni-cian coast.[20] Eric Cline has shown that the site identified as Armageddon has for four thousand years been the place of decisive battles, fought by Egyptians, Israelites, Greeks, Muslims, Crusaders, Mongols, British, Germans, Arabs, and Israelis. All these have fought and died here.[21]

In seeking to identify a specific place, and recognizing the interpre-tative problems caused by the claim that it is a mountain, Hippolytus thought that the place John mentions might represent Mount Tabor (Judg. 4:6, 12). Some patristic scholars have posited that the root of Megiddo, *gdd*, meaning "cut/gash," suggests it is not a particular named place, but symbolically the place where the pagan kings would be gath-ered for "cut/slaughter."[22] Others think it is a mistranslation and in unpointed Hebrew would mean "fruitful," or "choicest," referring to Mount Zion.[23] John Paulien admits, "The abundance of solutions and the great creativity with which they have been developed suggests that it is unwise to be dogmatic about the etymology of Armageddon. Current scholarship generally settles on a link with Megiddo."[24]

G. B. Caird says that "no simple explanation of this word can be given" and concludes that it is "a composite image compounded of many elements."[25] Those elements represent Israel's history. Meggido was a place of triumph and celebration, where Deborah and Barak saw God's intervention and the destruction of the warring Canaanite kings (Judg. 5:19–20). It was also the ignominious place where the beloved and godly King Josiah was killed fighting against the kings of Egypt and Assyria (2 Kings 23:29), and was thus also a symbol of defeat and mourning (Zech. 12:10–11). In the Jewish mind Megiddo represented first victory and then disaster. Perhaps, prophetically, John reverses this: In Revelation, Megiddo would appear to be initially a place of impending disaster as armies gather, but ultimately it represents Israel's greatest victory as these kings are slain by the sword of Christ.

G. K. Beale, like certain Puritans mentioned above, understands Armageddon as a typological symbol of the last battle against the saints and Christ throughout the earth.[26] Robert Mounce believes similarly that it is a theological motif that speaks of the whole world at war:

> *Wherever it takes place, Har-Magedon is symbolic of the final overthrow of the forces of evil by the might and power of God. The great conflict between God and Satan, Christ and Antichrist, good and evil, which lies behind the perplexing course of history, will in the end issue in a final struggle in which God will emerge victorious and take with him all who have placed their faith in him. This is Har-Magedon.*[27]

Consequently, on the basis that no specific place exists as the Mount of Armageddon, and because Armageddon is named only once as the place of the last battle and even then in a highly symbolic text, and because Jerusalem is frequently referred to as the place of Christ's victorious visitation, I prefer to understand Armageddon as figurative and symbolic rather than literal and geographical. With John Hosier, I suggest that it is "event rather than place."[28]

All Old Testament prophecies of the final battle present it as occurring in Jerusalem, Mount Zion, or its surrounding mountains. John himself locates the final conflict directly outside Jerusalem (Rev. 14:20; 20:8f.), and if Revelation 20:1–8 represents the same final conflict as I have asserted, that also is in Jerusalem.[29] Unless Jerusalem, too, is a non-geographical typological symbol, then it would seem to be the exact geographical location for what Armageddon symbolizes. Nevertheless, because Armageddon is presented as the place where the demonic deceived kings gather, it is possible to understand it as the staging place before the march on Jerusalem, two days' walk to the north.

We should note that some people reject any interpretation of the end-time scenario that involves a war that wraps up history. One school of thought (known as Preterism) takes all the events depicted in Revelation as being historically fulfilled in the time of John, and Armageddon is believed to refer to the collapse of Jerusalem in AD 70. There are, however, too many problems associated with such a view. The army that attacked Jerusalem in AD 70 was Roman, not a coalition of ten kings. The Roman army in AD 70 was victorious and decimated Israel, whereas the coalition Armageddon army will be defeated in Israel. Moreover, in AD 70 the land turned into a wasteland for nomads, whereas after Armageddon, Christ will set up his glorious reign in the New Jerusalem, in the re-created heavens and earth (Rev. 21).

DAWN FOLLOWS DARKEST NIGHT

In considering an end-time final conflict between good and evil, God and Satan, the saints and the followers of the Antichrist, let us not miss the very vital New Testament truth that the decisive victory of Christ over sin, death, evil, and the demonic was at *Calvary*, not Armageddon. It was there, as Colossians 2:15 celebrates, that "having disarmed the powers and authorities, [Jesus] made a public spectacle of them, triumphing over them by the cross." This was where the cry went out, in Gustav Aulen's words, "Christus Victor!" The cross is the ultimate, decisive, disarming moment. At Calvary, as Christ bore the sentence for our sin, sentence was also mysteriously being passed on our satanic Enemy. Ever since Golgotha's victory, ratified by Jesus' resurrection, the clock on Satan's doomsday has been ticking. The only cause for delay has been the compassionate heart of God, who desires the gospel to be preached in all the nations: "The Lord is not slow in keeping his promise, as some understand slowness. He is patient with you, not wanting anyone to perish, but everyone to come to repentance" (2 Peter 3:9). Let us not undermine the Calvary of two thousand years ago, when our salvation was purchased, by overemphazising Armageddon as all-determinative.

Whatever or wherever Armageddon is—though I have tentatively opted for a final military showdown in Jerusalem—it expresses Satan's last-ditch attempts to thwart the plans for God's kingdom. Ultimately, however, it is the place where God has chosen publicly to display his final wrath against evil. Oscar Cullmann, in *Christ and Time*, used the Allies' conflict with the Nazis in World War II as an analogy for the work of Christ. He said that the cross represented a D-Day—the decisive landings of the Allies in Normandy that sounded the death knell for the Nazis. But many months of vicious fighting followed before the Allies marched on Berlin, the Germans surrendered, and VE (Victory in Europe) Day was declared. Similarly, history runs its course in time from Calvary, with continuing conflict against the Evil One, but the outcome is not in doubt. The demonic, death, and all that opposes God's reign will be defeated finally and unequivocally: They will meet their Armageddon. On Mount Golgotha, Satan went up against Jesus and was publicly disarmed. On Mount Armageddon he will make one last, renewed attempt and will be finally defeated.

While we need to be careful students of Scripture, awake and ready for Christ coming like a thief, prayerful and prophetic as Scripture's prophecies unfold, we must also be careful not to be too hasty in attempting to identify particular scriptural signs with current historical events. Many have rightly challenged the full-blown, highly detailed analysis and collation of biblical prophecy presented by the likes of Hal Lindsey. Such an approach misunderstands the nature of Old Testament prophecy, which was always being reappropriated in the progress of Israel's history. Failure to handle this properly resulted in the Pharisees' blindness to Christ when he came the first time: Their reading of the prophecies did not cohere with Christ's fulfillment of them. Hans Schwarz says that "even with the best imagination and the most diligent use of the Bible, we cannot predict the immediate future."[30]

Stephen Sizer has rightly cautioned that a carefully worked-out theology of Armageddon along the lines of a literalist, dispensationalist, or premillennialist model can have unhelpful consequences.[31] He suggests that it actually leads to a form of anti-Semitism, because implicit in the model is a Christian concern to get Jews back to Jerusalem, where they must face an end-time bloodbath when two-thirds will die and a third will finally become Christians (Zech. 13:8). Armageddon may end gloriously with evil crushed, but it is prefaced by considerable Jewish suffering. Christians who are keen to see the end come are regarded by many as trampling carelessly through the blood of the Jews. Indeed, because one theme within most premillennialist and dispensational theologies is the manifestation of an Antichrist who will establish a counterfeit peace in Israel for a limited time, so certain more extreme Zionists have rejected any attempts at negotiating peace settlements in the Middle East, because such settlements might involve unwitting complicity with the Evil One and history will end with war in Israel.[32] Sizer raises a significant point. Christian Zionists must understand that their model leads to another Holocaust.

How are we to respond? Here are some points to consider.

1. At the risk of clinical theological callousness, if indeed God has decreed the end as such, then it is written.

2. While the Lord is ultimately sovereign over this scenario, it is precipitated by the unholy trinity who summon the kings and seek to make war on the apple of God's eye, the Jews.

3. Life under the Antichrist will be no life at all: Death, destruction, oppression, and restriction of freedom will mark the latter part of his reign.

4. The numbers in the relevant Bible passages may be prophetic symbols and therefore not exact math.

5. History shows that Israel's security and peace have been constantly threatened and challenged, despite numerous attempts to meet the demands of others. Her very right to exist has been unrecognized by her enemies for sixty years. Peace agreements she has been willing to accept have been thrown back in her face.

6. Prayer and repentance (as in the story of Jonah and Nineveh) can change the prophetic decreed destiny of a people (Jer. 18:7–10). Who knows whether certain biblical prophecies may be averted through repentance or modified through the prayers and proclamation of the righteous?

7. Despite unimaginably terrible birth pangs, ultimately eternal life is initiated, evil is vanquished, and eternal glory is

established. The kingdom of God has been fully revealed in its power, splendor, and righteousness.

CONCLUSION: ANY TIME, ANY PLACE, ANYWHERE, THE LAMB WINS

As we saw in our study on the millennium, one passage in one New Testament book, shrouded in prophetic and apocalyptic motifs, does not a doctrine make. For the reasons outlined above, I prefer not to interpret Armageddon as an exact location for a final specific showdown between God and his adversaries. However, Old and New Testament texts may be marshaled to establish that there will indeed be a final military conflict of the sort, which Armageddon presents in Revelation 16:16f. Armageddon is to be understood as a theological motif, a symbolic *occasion* rather than a specific *location*—this latter being more readily identified from Scripture as taking place in Jerusalem, though Armageddon could be the place of gathering before the final push by the enemy's armies on Jerusalem.

Mention of the word *Armageddon* should cause the Evil One to quake with fear, but it should fill the faithful with hope. As a symbol it means that, despite the worst efforts of evil, Christ will triumph, the Lamb will win. Yes, Armageddon conveys the sense of terror and battle, but for us who believe in Christ, it also speaks of victory, the climax of history, and the gateway into glory and eternity.

TEN

THE RETURN OF THE KING

In a little while you will see me no more,
and then after a little while you will see me.
(John 16:16)

WHERE WILL IT ALL END?

As I sat in a coffee shop reading for this chapter on a warm spring day in Oxford, I was unaware that, three thousand miles away in Virginia, a college campus was under siege as a maniac went on the rampage, murdering thirty-two students and staff and injuring dozens more before eventually turning the gun on himself. It was a mind-numbingly horrific event that darkly frames human existence in the twenty-first century. For many people living in places like Iraq or Afghanistan or the Middle East, events such as this are their daily diet. The whole earth groans, awaiting the day of redemption. How long, O Lord?

Jesus told us that before he returns we will see an "increase of wickedness" and then the end will come (Matt. 24:12). Jesus is coming back—wickedness is increasing. Sometimes we feel he cannot come soon enough. There is a day that is fixed in the mind and map of God (Acts 1:7). Its delay is because God desires that none should perish and that the gospel should reach all nations and generations (2 Peter 3:9). But return he will, and when he comes, the injustices, immorality, and insanity of this world will be put right. When he comes, he will reward the faithful. When he comes, the chaos will be brought to order. This upside-down world will be turned right side up. Evil will be judged and consumed. All wrong will be reversed. Every tear will be wiped away. There will be no more Virginia Tech massacres, no more murders and murderers, no more mornings full of mourning. Those who live in Christ will wake to a new, pain-free, perfect world.

THE LONG-AWAITED HOPE

The return of Christ is a fundamental tenet of Christianity and the basis of Christian hope—promised by Christ, prophesied by angels, preached by the apostles, and written into the sacred Scriptures. It has been calculated that, in the 216 chapters of the New Testament, there are 318 references to the second coming of Christ: an amazing one out of every thirty verses. Twenty-three of the twenty-seven New Testament books refer to this great event. For every prophecy in the Bible concerning Christ's first advent, there are eight that look forward to his second! Its importance is second only to the saving work of Christ.

David Pawson rightly notes that there is so much material, it is a struggle to fit all the pieces of the jigsaw together.[1] Indeed, while all orthodox Christians agree on the fact of Christ's return, the voluminous material selected and arranged by the various traditions has led to rather different opinions on how the end pans out. The return of Christ is not an add-on extra for eccentric Christians: It is included in every major creedal statement developed by the early church fathers, as stated in the three main ecumenical creeds, the Apostles', Nicene, and Athanasian. The confession "He will come again in glory to judge the living and the dead and his kingdom shall have no end"[2] has rung out in church services for nearly twenty centuries. All major denominations include in their doctrinal statements the belief in the Lord's return. To reject it is to dissociate oneself from historic orthodox Christianity. Every time the church celebrates communion, she prophetically anticipates the return of Jesus Christ, who said, "I will not drink of this fruit of the vine from now on until that day when I drink it anew with you in my Father's kingdom" (Matt. 26:29). Paul states that we celebrate Communion "until he comes" (1 Cor. 11:26). Catholics and Anglicans both conclude their eucharistic liturgy with the historic cry, "Christ has died, Christ is risen, Christ will come again."

Despite the weight that Scripture gives to the return of Christ, an American survey surprisingly concluded that only 79 percent of those who call themselves "Christian" actually believe in the second coming of Jesus Christ, and far fewer consider Christ's return to be imminent. Just 20 percent of all Christians believe that Christ will return to earth in their lifetime.[3] While one does not expect non-Christians to believe in the return of Christ, it is alarming that many professing Christians do not accept the overwhelming testimony of Scripture and church tradition on this foundational doctrine. Perhaps it has something to do with bad theology, or the lack of basic theology.

NOT JUST A CHRISTIAN HOPE

Ironically, belief in the return of Jesus Christ has been incorporated into religions that on other accounts must be regarded as sub-Christian and unorthodox. Thus, while it should be accepted as a belief necessary to orthodoxy, it is not the sole criterion for orthodoxy. Let us take a brief look at some of the claims made by other religions.

- Within *Islam*[4] there is a strain of teaching drawn from the Koran that believes Jesus Christ was caught up to heaven and not crucified, another man having taken his place, and he is expected to return in the last days to wage war against the false messiah, or Dajjal, the Antichrist, and call humanity to Islam before the last judgment.

- The *Rastafarian*[5] movement claims that the Ethiopian emperor Haile Selassie was in fact the second coming of Jesus Christ, though he himself did not claim this. The Rastafarians expect him to return a third time to initiate the end-time judgment on the world.

- Devotees of the *Baha'i* faith believe that the second coming and other eschatological prophecies from other religions, including Buddhism, came to pass in 1844, its founder Baha'u'llah having himself fulfilled the prophecy of the return of Christ.[6] The Baha'i believe that the Lord's Prayer—"thy kingdom will come on earth as in heaven"—is fulfilled through their faith.

- *Swedenborgianism*[7] claims that the second coming occurred through the "ideas" revealed in Emanuel Swedenborg's theological works, and that the last judgment commenced and was completed in 1757. For them the second coming is in fact still taking place. The second coming is not an actual physical appearance of the Lord, but rather his return in spirit and truth, which is being articulated as a spiritual reality.

- In similar vein *Rudolf Steiner* believed that the coming of Christ would be a spiritual one in terms of enlightened individuals growing into communities. Steiner believed that this began in the 1930s.

- An interesting twist appears with *Sun Myung Moon*,[8] who is considered by many within the Moonies to have been given the vocation as "Lord of the Second Advent" by Jesus Christ on Easter on a mountainside when he was fifteen—with a calling to complete Jesus' task of ushering in the kingdom of God on earth and bringing peace to all humankind.

None of the claimed spiritualized, incognito visitations of Christ in these faiths measure up to the glorious global manifestation, the consummation of creation and the conclusion to history as presented in the Christian Scriptures.

THERE IS A DAY

The New Testament leaves its reader in no doubt that the return of Jesus is core to apostolic doctrine and Christian belief. Perhaps the most common term used to describe this event in modern usage is "the second coming." However, that is not strictly speaking a biblical term, and indeed there are a number of other terms used to convey the one event of Christ's return. These carry greater biblical and theological weight, not least because "second coming" could imply a third or fourth coming—whereas the return of Christ as King is the grand finale of both human history and the divine economy. Hebrews 9:28 has one of the clearest explanations of this: "So Christ was sacrificed once to take away the sins of many people; and he will appear a second time, not to bear sin, but to bring salvation to those who are waiting for him."[9] So what other terms are used to describe Jesus' return?

Arrival/Presence/Coming

The Greek word *parousia*, literally meaning "presence," "coming," or "advent,"[10] is generally translated "coming." It is often used synonymously with *erchomai*, which is also translated as "coming," and is widely used in the context of the return of Jesus. Although the two are interchangeable, *parousia* is a more technical and powerful word, classically used of a royal visitation or a manifestation of a deity, whereas *erchomai* is a more general expression.[11]

There are in fact several "comings" spoken of in Scripture:

- the coming of Jesus to the apostles following his resurrection (John 14:18f.; 16:16);
- the coming of the Holy Spirit (John 14:23; John 16:7);
- the coming of Jesus to visit his churches in judgment, comfort, or blessing (Rev. 2:5, 16; 3:3, 11, 20);
- the coming of Jesus to the world in judgment (Matt. 21:33–45; Mark 12:1–9).

Jesus himself used this idea of "coming" repeatedly in his major discourse on his return, reported in Matthew 24. The disciples had asked what would be the signs of his coming (*parousias*, v. 3). Jesus said his coming would be the end of the world as we know it (v. 14), and it would be global and visible, as when the lightning comes from the east and shines in the west (v. 27). Following the abomination, tribulation, and cosmic signs, the Son of Man would come (*erchomenon*) in glory in the clouds (v. 30). His coming (*parousia*) would be at a time unknown, just as in the days of Noah when the flood came suddenly and unexpectedly for most, though not for Noah (v. 37). We will need to be alert, for he will come (*erchetai*) like a thief in the night (vv. 42–44). This coming (*parousia*) will be to raise the dead (1 Cor. 15:22–23), to gather his elect to himself (2 Thess. 2:1), to destroy all evil (2 Thess. 2:8; 1 Thess. 3:13), and finally to hand over the renewed universe to the Father (1 Cor. 15:24f.).

The day of the Lord

This is a term that occurs repeatedly in the Old Testament prophetic literature and is taken up by the New Testament authors to describe the glorious return of Christ. Scholars debate how many actual references to this particular "day" may be found—the interpretative question being whether the "day" referred to by the prophet is in fact the "eschatological day of the Lord," or some other day.[12] All agree, however, that it is a major theme in the prophets and is found from the earliest prophet, Obadiah, right through to John's Apocalypse. It is a central theme in Joel and Zephaniah.

Some see this "day" not as a strict twenty-four-hour day, but as the period in which God and history enter their closing act. It certainly covers the period from the gathering of the world's armies in the final conflict and the outpouring of divine wrath, to the judgment that falls on unbelieving Israel (Isa. 2:6ff.; Jer. 30:4–17; Joel 1:15—2:11; Zeph. 1:14–16; Mal. 4:1), and it includes the cleansing and restoration of Israel (Isa. 4:2–6; Jer. 30:18—31:40; Micah 4:1–8; Zech. 12:10—13:2). The most sustained presentation of this eschatological day of the Lord is found in Zechariah 12—14:20. Here the author repeats the refrain "on that day" sixteen times. This "day" covers a possible period from Calvary through to Christ's glorious reign. Peter's use of Joel's words on the day of Pentecost suggests that this event has ushered in "the last days" (Acts 2:17).

The New Testament Epistles pick up this Old Testament theme and appropriate it for Christ. It is his day, generally referring to the very day he returns rather than the whole period leading up to it—the day when Christ will gloriously and victoriously return to bring history to an end and inaugurate the age to come, over which he will reign as King. That "day is almost here" (Rom. 13:12); it is the day of the soul's salvation

(1 Cor. 5:5); "the day of the Lord Jesus" (2 Cor. 1:14; Phil. 1:6; 1 Thess. 5:2); "the day of redemption" (Eph. 4:30); the day in which Jesus will be glorified by his saints (2 Thess. 1:10). Interestingly, Peter speaks of it as the glorious day of *God's* visitation, rather than Christ's (1 Peter 2:12). The day of the Lord, he says, will bring about the destruction and re-creation of the heavens and the earth (2 Peter 3:12).

Thus "the day of the Lord" is spoken of by the prophets, by Jesus, and by the New Testament writers. It can look like a single event, compact and definable, but it contains within it a time line that is considerably longer than might first have appeared, with a number of significant markings along the way—from the incarnation, death, and resurrection of Jesus, through Pentecost, to the final events of the rise of the Antichrist, Armageddon, and the decisive return of Christ, when the Lord will wrap up all history and all time in the final consummation of the day of the Lord.[13]

Manifesting/Appearing

The Greek term *epiphania*, meaning "appearing, or visible manifestation of divinity,"[14] is used to describe both the incarnation (1 John 1:2) and the crucifixion of Christ (Heb. 9:8; 1 John 3:5). It is used to convey the public, powerful spectacle of the Lord's return. This appearing will in itself bring the lawless one to nothing (2 Thess. 2:8). It will be the moment when Christ is revealed to reward the saints and hand out crowns of glory (1 John 2:28; 1 Peter 1:7; 5:4)—the moment of transformation for those who abide in him (1 John 3:2).

The end

The Greek word *telos*, meaning "termination," "cessation," "conclusion," "end," "goal,"[15] is a less frequently used term favored by Paul that conveys finality, completion, the reaching of the goal. History will run its course, time will run out, people's every action and intention will be instantly arrested: The coming of God stops everything. In 1 Corinthians 1:8, we read that Jesus will sustain the Corinthians to the end, and they will be guiltless "on the day of our Lord Jesus Christ." Mysteriously, Paul also says that this end can be understood as having already come upon the saints (1 Cor. 10:11), while they await the coming of the "perfect"[16] one who brings perfection (1 Cor. 13:10)—that is, Christ, who will hand over the kingdom to God after destroying every rule, authority, and power (1 Cor. 15:24). In that end, however, there will be a new beginning, a reclothing of the saints in immortality, a re-creation of heaven and earth.

Unveiling/Revealing

Similar in sense to *epiphania*, the Greek term *apocalypsis*, meaning "revelation," "disclosure,"[17] indicates that the coming of the day of the Lord at the end of history will be a revealing, disclosing, unveiling of Christ in all his dread-glory and majesty. There will be no cover-up, no veiling, but instead a public manifestation of his divinity when every knee will bow and every tongue will confess that he is Lord (Phil. 2:10f.). Peter favors this term in speaking of the praise, honor, and glory given to Christ on judgment day when he is revealed (1 Peter 1:7). Christ's unveiling will be an event of grace received (1 Peter 1:13), a day when there will be rejoicing in the revelation of Jesus' glory (1 Peter 4:13). It is primarily an unveiling of Christ, but it will also unveil the secrets of people's hearts in judgment, the future of the world, and the glorious saints (Rom. 8:19).

A scriptural certainty

All these terms and the numerous Scriptures behind them leave the reader in no doubt that the return of Christ is a scriptural certainty.

The day of the Lord, Jesus' arrival, his presence, his coming, his manifesting, and his full disclosure at the end of history will be welcomed with wonder by those who have long awaited him and with terror by those who have long rejected him. For the Christians this is their wedding day; for the unbelievers this is their doomsday.

Samuel Rutherford's name shines out in church history as a Puritan who suffered imprisonment for his faith but held faithfully onto Christ, and whose ministry of letter-writing brought great comfort and delight to the church. In his final letter, dated March 1661, he wrote:

> *The Lord calleth you, dear brother, to be still "steadfast unmoveable and abounding in the work of the Lord." Our royal kingly master is upon his journey, and will come, and will not tarry. And blessed is the servant who shall be found watching when he cometh.... It is possible that I shall not be an eyewitness to it in the flesh, but I believe he cometh quickly who will remove our darkness, and shine gloriously in the Isle of Britain, as a crowned king ... and this is the hope and confidence of a dying man who is longing and fainting for the salvation of God.*[18]

WHEN WILL JESUS RETURN?

We considered above several claims that Jesus has already returned, incarnated in various religious figures. Throughout Scripture and church history, (false) prophets within the church have set the date for the return of Jesus. Spurious claims that he had already returned may be the background to Paul's detailed discussion of Christ's return in the letters to the Thessalonians. In these letters Paul demonstrates a very real expectancy that some of them will be alive when Christ returns (1 Thess. 4:13–18). Clearly, the apostles believed they were living in the last days, ushered in by the events of Christ's life, death, and resurrection and the coming of the Holy Spirit (2 Tim. 3:1; Heb. 1:2; Jude 18). Revelation 22:20 ends with Jesus saying, "Yes, I am coming soon"—an exhortation to live in readiness. The early fathers, taking Peter's reckoning of a day as being a thousand years with the Lord (2 Peter 3:8), suggested that the six days of creation represented six thousand years, the length of time the earth would exist, after which, on the seventh day, the heavenly millennium, the eternal Sabbath rest, would come—in other words, AD 2000.[19] The medievalists had a heightened sense of the return of Christ at the end of the first millennium.

Catholic theologian John Knox[20] has shown in his exhaustive study on enthusiastic/charismatic movements that a marked feature of such groups is to prophesy the date of an imminent return of the Lord. Either because of political turbulence, or because of heightened spiritual experiences, such movements seem to write themselves into the last-day scriptural narratives and call time on history. Medieval mystic Joachim of Fiore dated Christ's return as 1260; the Anabaptists from Münster claimed a date of 1534; 1652 was the date chosen by Quaker James Milner; 1690 by the Huguenot Jurieu; 1734 by French Convulsionarie Nicholas of Cusa; 1790 by English Methodist George Bell; 1779 by the American Shakers, and 1823 by the Lutheran revivalist Ebel. William Miller of the Millerites prophesied the second coming as being October 22, 1844. When this event failed to materialize, the Millerites set later dates. Jehovah's Witnesses actually hold that the second coming occurred "secretly" in 1914—while the apocalyptic end-time manifestations will be visible subsequently. The late fundamentalist preacher Jerry Falwell predicted in 1999 that Jesus would return within ten years. Televangelist

Jack Van Impe has offered several predictions, each changing as the years roll on, the most recent being 2012. People have always tried to set dates for the return of the Lord. Up to the present time, those dates would appear to have been wrong—although Sir Isaac Newton dated the end of the world at 2060—1,260 years after the founding of the Holy Roman Empire in AD 800—and time will tell if he was right.[21]

It is notable that neither Jesus nor his apostles ever set a date for his return (Matt. 24:42f.). Why is this? Well, when he walked the earth in his humanity, Jesus made it abundantly clear that no one but the Father knew the date, not even himself (although conceivably now, sitting in resurrected glory at his Father's right hand, he is fully aware). Indeed, a question remains among Christians as to whether that date is set in the calendar, or whether it is flexible, depending on global spiritual circumstances. Those of a so-called Calvinist persuasion will lean toward saying the date is firmly fixed (Acts 1:7). Those of a more Arminian persuasion will believe that other factors may be brought to bear on the timing of Jesus' return, notably our faithfulness to build the kingdom, to pray for God's will to be done on earth, and effectively to evangelize the nations, which is the one major sign preceding Christ's return in which we have a part to play (Matt. 24:14). Peter says that, not only do we look forward to God's coming, but by living godly and holy lives we actually "speed its coming" (2 Peter 3:12).

While we may not date the return, we can locate it in terms of the signs that Scripture has told us will precede it. In the previous few chapters, we looked in detail at these. We noted that many of the signs have been regular features in the course of human life on earth, although we may expect their latter-day intensification. We are clearly living in a day when many of the signs described in Jesus' main end-time discourse have been or are being fulfilled (Matt. 24).

Most clearly, the great tribulation, the rise of the variously named Antichrist, and the establishment of his blasphemous global, spiritual, and fiscal world rule must precede the return of Christ (Rev. 13), as must the military conflagration of the battle of Armageddon (Rev. 16). Some see history hurtling toward such events on the political canvas, but we must be cautious. In view of the clear statement that the gospel must first be preached to the ends of the earth (Matt. 24:14; Acts 1:8), which is something yet to be accomplished, it would seem that Christ's return may be delayed yet a while.

Before we move on, let me touch on one further point about dating. While it would seem to be going beyond Scripture to try to deduce a date for the return of Jesus, some have suggested a "season" for it—for example, the Feast of Tabernacles occurring at the grape harvest, which is late autumn. The logic is this: Leviticus 23 commands the Hebrews to celebrate seven feasts, Passover, Unleavened Bread, Firstfruits, Pentecost, Trumpets, Day of Atonement, and Tabernacles. The last three occur during the autumn, and some biblical scholars believe that, while the first four have been fulfilled through Christ already, the last three speak prophetically of the end days—the Trumpets that herald the return of Christ, the Day of Atonement when judgment is passed, and the Feast of Tabernacles when the sojourn is ended and the messianic rest is entered into (Zech. 14:16–19). I find it an attractive proposition, but although it might indicate the "season," it gets us no nearer to the year![22]

HOW AND WHY WILL JESUS RETURN?[23]

Jesus will return personally

He promised the disciples, "I will come back and take you to be with me, that you also may be where I am" (John 14:3; see also John

14:23). Paul says that "the Lord himself" will return (1 Thess. 4:16). He will not send an envoy, an ambassador, or an archangel, but he himself will come.

Jesus will return physically

According to the angels at his ascension, the resurrected eternal Son of God who assumed human flesh at the incarnation will return, as "this same Jesus" (Acts 1:11). He who is the same yesterday, today, and forever, not just in character but also in form, now resurrected in his ascension to glory, will return as the Son of Man, Jesus Christ. He will not come, as some heretics have suggested, as a force, an energy, or an idea. The Gnostics in the second and third centuries despised the body as evil matter. Consequently, they rejected the incarnation and reinterpreted eschatology as a "spiritual" return of the Lord. By contrast early Christian apologists like Irenaeus argued from Scripture that there would be a bodily, physical return of Jesus, the eternal, enfleshed God.[24]

Jesus will return to a geographical location

Although debated by some, I believe that the prophecies in Acts 1:11, Zechariah 14:4, and Revelation presuppose a return to Jerusalem, specifically the Mount of Olives. From here Christ will execute judgment on the nations, re-creating heaven and earth (2 Peter 3:10–12).[25] Quite how every eye will see his return (Rev. 1:7) if he is going to come back personally and physically to a specific geographical location, we do not know—though some suggest the use of global communication networks such as the Internet! But I trust that Scripture is true and not contradictory. (The question of the geographical location of Christ's rule is explored further in chapter 4 on the millennium and chapter 12 on heaven.)

Jesus will return visibly

Scripture tells us that Jesus will return on the clouds with the angels and saints (Matt. 24:30), noisily with trumpets and the dead arising (1 Thess. 4:16), as blazing lightning shooting from east to west. Every eye will see him (Rev. 1:7). This is not the secret return that the Jehovah's Witnesses claim took place in 1914. It will be public, visible, and incontrovertible. All this, as David Pawson says, is in sharp contrast to Christ's first coming, when he came incognito, "invisible, hidden in the darkness of a womb."[26] This is the one event no one will miss—a truly world-shattering event of cosmic proportions.

Jesus will return unexpectedly

He will come like a thief in the night (Matt. 24:42f.; Rev. 16:15), like a flood as in the days of Noah (Matt. 24:32–51). However, Jesus also told us that numerous signs—political, military, economic, cosmic, and spiritual—will precede his return and prepare those with eyes to see.[27] Paul says that, although Christ's coming will be unexpected for many (1 Thess. 5:2), we Christian brothers and sisters "are not in darkness so that this day should surprise you like a thief" (v. 4): We are to be alert and ready.

Jesus will return once only[28]

Contrary to the dispensationalists and pretribulation millennialists who believe in two returns, one for the saints at the rapture and one with the saints at the end of time, we see just *one* return.[29] Only in the last 180 years has the notion of a twofold return been raised. Louis Berkhof rightly states, "It may be doubted whether anyone would have read the relevant passages in any other way if Revelation 20:1–6 (speaking of a millennium reign) had not been set up by some as the standard by which all the rest of the NT must be interpreted."[30] Not only is there a singular return of the Lord, but the events surrounding this are all taken up into a unified, singular whole. Thus the rapture in the sky, the resurrection of the dead, the resounding trumpets, the general judgment, the destruction of evil and the re-creation of the universe all coincide in that one event—the day of the Lord, his appearing, his manifesting, his perfecting end (1 Thess. 4:13—5:4; 2 Thess. 1:5–10; 2:1–10).

Jesus will return purposefully

The creeds state that he will return to judge the living and the dead and his kingdom will have no end. This indeed summarizes his work—to judge and to establish his perfect, permanent kingdom of righteousness. Jesus will manifest himself in glory (1 Peter 4:13), to reward everyone according to their due (Matt. 16:27; 2 John 8; Rev. 11:18; 22:12), to receive the worship that is rightfully his, and to exercise his sovereign rule (Phil. 2:10–11). His purpose is to conquer Satan and his evil angels (Rev. 20:10), to judge all sinners (2 Tim. 4:1; Jude 15; Rev. 20:11–15), to perfect his saints (1 John 3:2), to restore all things corrupted since the fall from his perfect intention (Acts 3:21), to re-create heaven and earth (Rev. 21; 2 Peter 3:10–12). and to reign with his saints (Rev. 21—22).

CONCLUSION

As a young Christian I remember hearing of a minister who began each day by pulling back the curtains and welcoming the Lord: "Is it today, Lord?" What a way to start the day! Whatever shadows came the day before, maybe today is the day of days, the glorious day when Jesus returns, when every knee will bow and every tongue confess that Jesus is Lord. While I have shown elsewhere that some signs predicted to precede his return have yet to be fulfilled, nevertheless we live in hope and readiness. His return is nearer now than ever before.

I began by saying that, during the hours I was reading for this chapter, the tragedy at Virginia Tech was occurring. As I sat typing this up, a friend came into the coffee shop where I was at work and said that a young student cyclist had just been run over and killed outside the shop. Another life made in the image of God and loved to death by Christ had been snatched away; another future robbed; another family distraught; yet more senseless, savage pain. Where will it all end? Will it ever end? How long, O Lord?

Yes, it will end, and it will end well. Scripture closes with a promise and a prayer. Jesus promises, "Yes, I am coming soon," and the saints pray, "Amen. Come, Lord Jesus" (Rev. 22:20).

ELEVEN

RESURRECTION AND LAST JUDGMENT

He will come again in glory to judge the living and the
dead. (Nicene Creed)

In the previous chapter we considered the day of the Lord, his so-called second and final coming, the *Parousia*. Its goal may be summarized as the fulfillment of the Lord's Prayer, the establishing of God's will on earth as in heaven. All self-will has to submit to his will; all darkness is driven out by his light; all hatred is dissolved in his love; all sin is purged by his blazing holiness; all wrongs are righted by his justice; all mystery is disclosed in his appearing. Louis Berkhof states:

> *In the usual presentation of scripture, the end of the world, the*
> *Day of the Lord, the physical resurrection of the dead, and the*
> *final judgment coincide. That great turning point will also bring*
> *the destruction of all evil forces that are hostile to God.*[1]

Indeed, the day of the Lord is multi-textured: It is the day of the resurrection of the dead; the day of the last judgment, when recompense for sin and reward for righteousness are dispensed; the day when eternities are entered; the day when evil is condemned and consumed; the day when Christ's bride is crowned and consummated; the day when the heavens and earth are created anew.

THE GENERAL RESURRECTION

Logically, the general resurrection must precede the final judgment, for all humanity must be present in order to give account. This definitive, universal, general resurrection is a concept unique to the so-called monotheistic religions that share sources, namely Judaism, Christianity, and Islam.

The Old Testament indicates a hoped-for resurrection, but this is generally an individual matter for the one who trusts in Yahweh (Job 19:25–27; Ps. 16:10; 71:20; 49:15; Isa. 25:8; 26:19; Ezek. 37:12–14). However, Daniel moves from an individual hope to a general resurrection when he states: "Multitudes who sleep in the dust of the earth will awake: some to everlasting life, others to shame and everlasting contempt" (Dan. 12:2). Inherent in his prophecy is the combining of judgment with resurrection.

The intertestamental era saw further reflection on the question of life after death and resurrection. Indeed, this was clearly a hotly contended issue among the religious groups, with the Sadducees rejecting any such notion and the Pharisees strongly believing it.

All three Synoptic Gospels (Matt. 22:23f.; Mark 12:18f.; Luke 20:27f.) include an encounter when Christ is tested by the Sadducees. They present a scenario of seven brothers who all end up marrying the same woman after each brother dies prematurely and the next in line takes responsibility for the woman. The Sadducees ask whose wife she will be at the resurrection, certain that their case shows up the absurdity of believing in any kind of resurrection. Jesus' answer powerfully dismisses them and sides with the Pharisees. He says that

they are in error for not knowing Scripture, which argues for a resurrection; that they do not know the power of God, which raises the
dead; and that they do not understand the nature of resurrected life,
which will be as angels experience it and will not include marriage.
Jesus then gives them the clincher in the oft-repeated statement from
Yahweh: "I am the God of Abraham, the God of Isaac, and the God
of Jacob." It is in the present tense, rather than the past tense, showing that Abraham, Isaac, and Jacob remain alive and in relationship
with their God. He is the God of the living, not the dead.

This issue was replayed when Paul was arrested and brought before
the Sanhedrin. He also took the side of the Pharisees against the Sadducees, saying, "I stand on trial because of my hope in the resurrection
of the dead" (Acts 23:6). Later, preaching before King Felix, Paul says
that this resurrection will be universal: "There will be a resurrection of
both the righteous and the wicked" (Acts 24:15).

John's gospel repeatedly refers to a general resurrection (John
5:25–29; 6:39, 44, 54):

> *Do not be amazed at this, for a time is coming when all who are*
> *in their graves will hear his voice and come out—those who have*
> *done good will rise to live, and those who have done evil will rise*
> *to be condemned. (John 5:28–29)*

Jesus (in Matt. 25) gives an unambiguous statement to the fact of
the general resurrection when he says that at his coming, he will sit on a
throne and all the nations (*ethne*, "peoples") will be brought before him
to be judged. The generic reference to *all* peoples implies more than
those currently alive. A judgment of all presupposes a general resurrection of all the dead. In a similar vein Jude 14–15 speaks of Christ coming

with a multitude of angels to judge all peoples for all the wrong they have done.

While a general resurrection may be implicit in Matthew 25 and Jude 15, it is explicitly stated in John's vision in Revelation 20:13f., which figuratively details the end-time fact of the dead being raised to judgment: "The sea gave up the dead that were in it, and death and Hades gave up the dead that were in them, and each person was judged according to what he had done."

This scriptural teaching is summed up in the three ecumenical creeds, which speak of Jesus returning "to judge the living and the dead." Thus his return involving judgment necessitates the resurrection of all to life. There are, of course, numerous other New Testament texts that speak of resurrection, but they generally refer to the resurrection hope of immortal life for the saints who have trusted in Jesus, rather than to the general resurrection of all. The hope of resurrection to eternal life and glory is at the heart of Christian doctrine. Without it we are no more than a merely ethical or moral society concerned with how we live with one another here on earth, with no reference to an eternal future (1 Cor. 15; 1 Thess. 4:16f.; John 8:51; 11:25f.).

DOES MY BOTTOM LOOK BIG IN THIS?

Belief in a general resurrection is belief in a *bodily* resurrection. The bodies will be raised, eternally enfleshed. "He who raised Christ from the dead will also give life to your mortal bodies through his Spirit" (Rom. 8:11). It is our spiritual bodies that will be redeemed and raised, joining with our eternal spirit, but our lowly bodies will be transformed into the likeness of Christ's glorious body (Phil. 3:20f.). Jesus rose from the dead in his flesh. He was recognized in his flesh. His flesh still bore the scars of the cross. His flesh was able to eat (Luke

24:42f.). However, that resurrected flesh was "reformatted"—it was transformed, glorified, able to enter rooms without coming through doors (Luke 24:36), able to disappear (Luke 24:31), and ascend into heaven on a cloud (Luke 24:50f.). Mysteriously, my body—dead, decayed, disintegrated—will be joined with my spirit at the resurrection. But clearly, that body will be transformed.

Paul offers a lengthy commentary on the nature of the resurrected body in 1 Corinthians 15:35–58. Even as a seed sown in the ground germinates and grows up as a blade of wheat, owing its origin to the seed but being completely transformed from the seed by God, so our body, dying as a seed, will rise transformed. It is still spoken of as a body, yet one that is now no longer perishable, but imperishable (v. 42); no longer dishonorable, but glorious (v. 43a); no longer subject to weakness, but powerful (v. 43b); no longer natural, but spiritual (v. 44); no longer bearing the likeness of Adam, but instead bearing the likeness of Christ (v. 49); no longer mortal, but immortal (v. 54). Paul tells us that flesh and blood cannot inherit the kingdom (v. 50)—thus this resurrection body, in all its corporality, will somehow be substantially different. This remains a mystery.

Joseph Ratzinger, wanting to emphasize the transformation of the body, speaks of a "pneumatic realism" to this body rather than a "physicalist realism."[2] However, while it is transformed and spiritual, it is also the same body raised and reconstituted. Job states his hope that, after his death, he will see the Redeemer "in my flesh" (19:26). The church fathers were clear: The dead body would be raised "in the flesh." The historic creeds initially spoke of the resurrection of the "flesh," not just the dead, to underscore the corporality of the event. The *Didache*, Barnabas, Clement, Irenaeus, Tertullian, and Hippolytus all emphasize the fleshly nature of resurrection. Against the Gnostics, particularly Valentius, who saw flesh as demonic and considered the resurrection to be a spiritual migration, the fathers rallied to rebuke such notions with widespread affirmations of a physical resurrection. Origen spoke of us being raised with "essential bodies" or "ideal bodies," while Justin Martyr stated very clearly, "The kingdom of God is life and this life also inherits the body, the flesh."[3]

Interestingly, Thomas Aquinas and other medieval scholars taught that we will rise again in the size and form that we would have had at the age at which Christ arose—that is, about the age of thirty-three. The reason Aquinas offers for this is that God will repair a perfect nature, but before or after that age, nature is more or less defective.[4] He also emphasized the primacy of the soul over the body, arguing that the body without a soul is a nonentity. The great dogmatic theologian of the later twentieth century, Jürgen Moltmann, argued against Aquinas's ideas: "In the dialectic of the resurrection, the soul does not have to withdraw itself from the body. On the contrary it will be embodied and become flesh."[5] For Moltmann, "hope for the resurrection of the body permits no disdain and debasement of bodily life and sensory experiences; it affirms them profoundly and gives greatest honour to them."[6]

This spiritual resurrection is more than a physical resuscitation. M. J. Erickson explains:

> *There is a utilisation of the old body, but a transformation of it in the process. Some sort of metamorphosis occurs so that a new body arrives. This new body has some connection with the old body, but is differently constituted.*[7]

Well said. But we are still not clear exactly *how* that body is constituted. Yet how could it be any other way, without the body of the resurrected Christ here and able to be tested in our laboratories? Even then, we would not have the categories in language or science to know what it was we were examining! Until the day of resurrection, when we are reclothed and know fully, it remains a mystery. Those who are alive at the return and general resurrection shall not die, but in an instant will also be transformed into their resurrection spiritual bodies that are able to meet Christ in the air (1 Cor. 15:51; 1 Thess. 4:17).

All this, of course, relates to the body of the believer, raised and transformed by the Spirit to be like Christ's resurrection body. We are uncertain what form the resurrected body will take for those raised to judgment and punishment—although the Reformed writer Francis Beattie speaks of this event as a "transmutation" of the body, which is made fit for its eternal abode, a change experienced by all, whether good or bad, righteous or wicked.[8]

The classic Reformed statement of doctrine, the Westminster Larger Catechism, closely coheres with Scripture and tradition. Four hundred years on, it still offers one of the best summaries.[9] Question 87 asks, "What are we to believe concerning the resurrection?" It answers thus:

> *We are to believe that at the last day there shall be a general resurrection of the dead, both of the just and unjust, when they that are then found alive shall in a moment be changed and the self-same bodies of the dead which were laid in the grave, being then again united to their souls forever, shall be raised up by the power of Christ. The bodies of the just, by the Spirit of Christ, and by virtue of his resurrection as their head, shall be raised in power, spiritual, incorruptible, and made like to his glorious body; and the bodies of the wicked shall be raised upon dishonour by him as an offended judge.*

The incarnation and resurrection of Christ *physically*, and the resurrection hope of the saints *physically*, is a divine "yes" to the body. We must affirm it too, not deny it for some misguided Gnostic spirituality. Sadly, many Christians emphasize the spirit or soul as the core of worship and religion, but in doing so they devalue, even negate, the body as worthless, rather than glorifying God in it (1 Cor. 6:20).

The following is an excerpt from an ancient Anglo-Saxon poem known as *Christ III*.

*Then mighty God will come, King of heaven's angels, into that
famed mountain; holy, glorious, he will shine out above the
hosts, the reigning God, and round about him that supreme and
noble multitude, the holy warrior-bands will shimmer clear, the
blessed company of the angels. In their inner thoughts they will
be trembling, fearful in the presence of the Father's wrath. It is no
wonder, then, that the impure species of worldly men, anxiously
grieving, should dread it acutely when this holy species, white and
heavenly-bright, the army of archangels, are afraid with fear for that
figure, and his bright creatures await in trembling the judgment
of the Lord. It will prove to be the most appalling day in the world
when the King of glory in his majesty punishes every people and
commands humanity to arise from out of their graves in the ground
and each single person, each member of mankind, to come to the
conclave. Then promptly all the kin of Adam will take on flesh; it
will have come to the end of its earthly rest and habitation. Each
one shall then rise up alive in the face of Christ's coming and take
on limbs and body and be young anew; upon him he will have
everything of virtue or of folly which in past days on earth he laid
upon his spirit with the passing of the years; he will have both body*

and soul conjoined. The display of his works and the remembrance
of his words and the intentions of his heart must come into the
light before the King of the heavens. At that time mankind will be
replenished and reconstituted by the ordaining Lord.[10]

JUDGMENT DAY

Most other religions envisage no final day of resurrection. Nor do they
believe in a last judgment—such an event being subsumed into the
experience at death, or in some cases the cyclic transmigration of the soul.
Only the three religions that share some doctrinal foundations—Judaism,
Christianity, and Islam—hold to such a belief. Interestingly, the universal
experience of the fear of death has been regarded by some as caused not
simply by fear of the unknown, or by regret for lack of continuity, but by a
deeper, innate sense of impending judgment. Indeed, the great philosopher
Immanuel Kant argued that the universal moral codes were based on this
innate sense of accountability to the deity on judgment day.[11] The idea has
found its way into popular culture and language, being used as the title
for movies and books, albeit with no religious bearing. And throughout
history, certainly in the West, the Christian conception of judgment day
has informed art and literature. Some of the greatest artists have been
inspired by this theme, including Michelangelo, Hieronymus Bosch,
Tintoretto, Giotto, Fiesole, Hans Memling, and Sir Edward Burne-
Jones. In Eastern Orthodox churches a depiction of the last judgment is
often located on the rear west wall, so that worshippers leaving church
are reminded by the images of divine reward and divine wrath to go out
and live holy lives unto the Lord.

The medieval period was marked by a sense of impending dread
at the horror of the day of judgment for sinners, rather than a sense
of excitement at its glorious welcoming, transforming, and rewarding

of the saints. The art of the time was full of vile images of torture, fire, disembodied limbs, demons, and such. Literature and drama carried a weighty awfulness. Anglo-Saxon poets wrote strikingly of the day of the Lord in such works as *Judgment Day I*, *Judgment Day II*, and *Christ III*. Sermons from such famous church figures as Aelfric and Wulfstan conveyed a powerful call for repentance before the dread day of the Lord. One medieval carol included the lyrics "gay, gay, gay, gay / think a drydful domisday."[12]

This sense of the return of Christ at the last judgment was certainly more doomsday than wedding day in popular conception. Chaucer's Parson in *The Canterbury Tales* calls pilgrims to repentance, reminding them of the certainty of doomsday. Christopher Marlowe's Doctor Faustus, nearing the end of his life, calls out, "Mountaines and lilies, come, come and fall on me and hide me from the heavy wrath of God" (see also Rev. 6:15–17). Similar images are found in Shakespeare's *Measure for Measure* and Cyril Tourneur's *The Atheist's Tragedy*. George Herbert wrote a famous poem entitled "Dooms-day," and the theme is picked up in Milton, Pope, Byron, Blake, Browning, and many other poets.

THINGS HAVE COME TO THIS

The term *judgment* (and its semantic family) occurs repeatedly in the New Testament.

In both noun and verb form (*krinein*, *krisis*, *krima*, *karakrima*, among others[13]), it is found well over a hundred times and speaks of the event and the act of handing over, judging, passing verdict, condemning, avenging. Numerous other texts that indicate the same event may not utilize this word group, speaking instead of coming wrath, condemnation, and separation. Judgment is unavoidable as a concept in Scripture and will be inescapable as a reality in human experience.

We have already noted that the general resurrection is for judgment, and the last judgment presupposes a general resurrection. The terms "last judgment" or "final judgment" are not biblical ones, although the concepts are. Speaking of "last" presupposes "previous" judgments. Scripture shows that various preliminary judgments have been passed by God, including the universal judgment of death on Adam and Eve and their heirs following the fall (Gen. 3), the judgment of destruction on the world by the flood (Gen. 7), the judgment on Korah and his family for their rebellion (Num. 16), and the judgment on Egypt for her refusal to release captive Israel (Ex. 7—12). Repeatedly the prophets spoke to the surrounding nations of the judgment that God was marshaling against them because of their sins (Jonah; Isaiah). The whole exile narratives are predicated on divine temporal judgment. Judgment fell on Nebuchadnezzar (Dan. 4) and Belshazzar (Dan. 5). Christ is the Judge who was judged in our place at Calvary (Isa. 53).

God is often spoken of as a Judge. He is one who will judge rightly (Gen. 18:25; Ps. 7:11). He will judge the earth (1 Chron. 16:33). His judgment is an overflow of his righteousness (John 16:8; Rom. 2:5; Rev. 19:11), which is his applied holy love. His judgment is universal, and all appear before it (Jude 14f.; Rom. 14:10). His judgments are perfectly just (Acts 17:31). He judges through his executive right hand, Jesus Christ (John 5:22). He will judge the living and the dead (1 Peter 4:5). He will judge the church (1 Peter 4:17), and with the church he will judge the angels (1 Cor. 6:3). His judgments are final and irreversible ("eternal," Matt. 25:46). Those who trust in Christ have somehow already passed over the judgment of Christ on the last judgment day (John 5:22–24).

We have already noted in chapter 3 that some within the Christian traditions believe in a "soul sleep" at death, a state of limbo, until the trumpet sounds and all the dead are awakened to be judged. This view would appear to be subscriptural, and the weight of the Bible leads us to believe that there is a preliminary judgment in spirit of the individual immediately at death (Heb. 9:27), based on whether that individual has lived righteously (Luke 16:19–31) or trusted in Jesus (Luke 23:43). This has generally been the view of the Eastern and Western churches. The parable of the rich man and Lazarus suggests that the individual will be sent either to a place of punishment or to paradise, and that this is fixed. There is no scriptural basis for the Catholic notion of purgatory, where advancement may be made on the benefit of prayers or good works. Our existence will run parallel with the course of human history until the day of the Lord, when those who are dead will be raised and, with all who are alive, will be taken before the final judgment seat.

JUDGING JUDGMENT

The early church fathers grappled with the concept of judgment and came up with some rather disparate views.[14] Many interpreted as figurative the scriptural teaching about specific days, specific seats, and specific books containing catalogs of sins. Cyril of Jerusalem understood the judgment to be spiritual remorse after self-accusation. Basil believed that the Judge's countenance would divinely illumine sin in our conscience—that our only accusers would be our own sins rising up in our memories. Ambrose said that the judgment seat was in the sinner's heart. Some, like Jerome, Basil, and Gregory of Nyssa, believed the judgment to be a purification process and therefore not perpetual punishment—a point of view from which the Catholic tradition flowed. Augustine, however, rejected these notions as unscriptural and based on a false notion of God's compassion.[15] He believed that history would be climaxed and that there would be an eternal, irreversible distinction made between the saved and the damned, between lovers of God and lovers of self.[16]

As we saw above, the medieval church's approach to the last judgment was overshadowed by fear. The hope of the resurrection was guaranteed only for some, and various means of securing a better standing were proffered, including the purchase of indulgences, participation in crusades, payment for Masses to be said for departed loved ones, pilgrimages, and the procurement of blessings. The increasingly dominant theology of purgatory gave some hope that the day of judgment was not the be-all and end-all: Efforts could be made by family and friends to help the departed on their way up.

The Reformation challenged all this with its focus on justification by faith in the finished work of Christ offering believers assurance of salvation. This in turn influenced members of the later pietistic movements, who shrugged off the fear and enjoyed fellowship with Christ and certainty of sins forgiven, while fueling the evangelistic mission by calling people to embrace Christ and find forgiveness before the day of judgment.

The underlying belief of the nineteenth-century liberals and their modern-day counterparts was summed up in the words of H. R. Niebuhr: "A God without wrath brought men without sin into a kingdom without judgment through the ministrations of Christ without a cross."[17] In a similar vein, dismissal of judgment was seen in the atheist German poet Heinrich Heine's deathbed comment in 1856 to a priest who proffered forgiveness: "Of course [God] will forgive me—that's his business."[18] This indeed remains the hope and belief of many. But it is a false belief and a false hope without any scriptural warrant. Tom Wright has said, "Not to speak of God's wrath is either to belittle the fact of evil, or to imply that God doesn't care about it and has no plans to deal with it."[19] David Pawson has rightly commented that the injustice of the world demands judgment: Most people do not pay for their crimes in this world, but they will in the age to come. The justice of God demands judgment: He is not mocked, and we will reap what we sow.[20]

The development in the mid-nineteenth century of premillennial and dispensational thought has led to a proliferation of judgments. The Scofield Bible offers seven distinct judgments, while others have found even more![21] Whereas the historic churches have understood there to be essentially three judgments—at the cross, at death, and at resurrection—some have suggested that the judgment of the sheep and goats (Matt. 25:31–46) differs from the judgment at the *Bema* ("judgment") seat of Christ (2 Cor. 5:10), which again differs from the judgment of the wicked at the "great white throne" (Rev. 20:11). This also is distinct from the judgment of the angels, which again must differ from the judgment of Israel. The semantic distinction between the "white throne" of Christ in Revelation 20:11 and the *Bema* seat of Christ in 2 Corinthians 5:10 is understood by some to indicate two separate judgments, divided temporally by the millennium.[22]

I rather feel that those who think this way have found texts with subtle terminological differences and forced unnecessary distinctions on them in order to fit with preconceived premillennial or dispensational schemes. Some see judgments at the cross, at death, when Christ comes for the church at the rapture, when Christ comes at the *Parousia*, and so on. Clearly there is a range of texts, but as James Garrett has said, there are no compelling reasons why the sheep and goats judgment (Matt. 25:31–46), the appearance before Christ's *Bema* seat (2 Cor. 5:10), and the "great white throne" judgment (Rev. 20:11) cannot all be identified with one eschatological judgment—Jesus, Paul, and John all recording their own description of the one location of judgment.[23] To try to make these into three distinct judgments rather stretches the imagination, but let us turn in greater detail to the texts and see what they tell us.

JUST TWO WAYS ABOUT IT: EITHER/OR
The sheep and the goats

The concept of the final judgment of all following the general resurrection is clearly inferred in Daniel 12:2: "Multitudes who sleep in the dust of the earth will awake: some to everlasting life, others to shame and everlasting contempt." This dual focus on judgment for some to everlasting life and others to everlasting shame may be reflected in Christ's parable of the sheep and the goats in Matthew 25:31–46. Here, at the coming of the King, Jesus the Son of Man will sit on a throne in glory and the angels will bring all peoples before him. Oscar Cullmann said that this coming judgment was "the primary eschatological function of the Son of Man."[24] Everyone will be judged on the basis of righteousness that is evidenced in graciousness to others. By their fruits they will be known.

The people are divided into only two groups, sheep to Christ's right and goats to his left. The judgment has only two outcomes and both appear to be final and irrevocable, on the basis that they are "eternal" (Matt. 25:46). One group, the sheep, those who have lived righteously, are invited to "come, you who are blessed by my Father; take your inheritance, the kingdom" (Matt 25:34). The other group, the goats, those who have acted unrighteously, are told, "Depart from me, you who are cursed, into the eternal fire prepared for the devil and his angels" (v. 41). The parable, told by Christ himself, then says, "They will go away to eternal punishment, but the righteous to eternal life" (v. 46). Here is both comfort for the sheep and terror for the goats, for, as Erickson says, "There is no hint that the verdict can be changed."[25]

Paul makes no reference to this stark parable, but he draws the same conclusions. In Romans 2:5f., Paul speaks of the day of God's wrath when his righteous judgment is revealed. On that day those who have sought glory, honor, and immortality will receive eternal life. Those who have been self-seeking and who have rejected the truth, following evil, will know wrath and anger. There will be trouble and distress for all who have done evil, but glory and honor for all who have done good. Again, as with the parable of the sheep and goats, there are only two camps, two groupings, two judgments. There is no halfway house, no middle ground: It is a clear either/or. God will give the judgment, based on what he knows of how we have lived and responded to him.

The judgment seat

Whereas Matthew 25 spoke of judgment taking place before Jesus sitting on a throne, Paul introduces the concept of a "judgment seat" (the Greek *bema*, *bematos*, means "step," "tribunal," "judicial bench," "throne-like platform"[26]). In Romans 14:10, Paul says that "we will all stand before God's judgment seat," and in 2 Corinthians 5:10 he says, "We must all appear before the judgment seat of Christ, that each one may receive what is due him." These are not to be understood as two different occasions at two different locations with two different judges. Jesus judges as God's executive—the throne from which he reigns is to us the judge's bench from which we are acquitted or condemned.

Our sins will be revealed

All of these texts presuppose a bringing to light of all of our actions, thoughts, and words. Jesus says, "Your Father, who sees what is done in secret, will reward you" (Matt. 6:18). Indeed, in Matthew 12:36, he warns, "I tell you that men will have to give account on the day of judgment for every careless word they have spoken." Paul says that God will judge the secrets of our hearts (Rom. 2:16). Nothing ever done, thought, or said by anyone at any time will be beyond his searching holy gaze. Everything will be laid bare before him.

The criteria of judgment will be the righteousness of our lives (Matt. 25:31–46) and our response to the truth of God in Christ (2 Thess. 2:12). The exposing of every sin is necessary to show the justice of God in punishing people's wickedness. G. C. Berkouwer says that this exposure will be "clearer, fairer, truer and more thorough" than any human judgments—a revelation of things as they truly are.[27]

Some Christians may argue that even to suggest that the sins of the saints are remembered is to contradict Scripture: After all, Jeremiah 31:34, Hebrews 10:17, and Micah 7:19 state that our sins are thrown to the bottom of the sea, buried out of sight—they are removed as far as the east is from the west (Ps. 103:12). Furthermore, some might claim that to suggest all sins are publicized undermines the precious doctrine of justification, whereby we are declared and established as righteous by faith in the blood of Jesus. They claim that the Christians' judgment is a judgment of reward, not a reminder of sin.

God forbid that I should ever do such a thing as undermine Scripture or the doctrine of justification. But I am personally inclined—in view of the New Testament texts cited above that indicate the universality of sins exposed—to conclude that all people's sins are revealed, those of both the sheep and the goats, the righteous and the unrighteous. The sins of the saints are revealed as *forgiven* sins, under the blood of Jesus, no longer incurring judgment and no longer bringing shame. It is like a bill stamped "Paid"—but the bill still shows what was paid. Indeed, our sins manifested as "forgiven sins" will simply serve to show the height and depth of Christ's love, dying for us to redeem us, and

this revelation will elicit from us more profound worship and gratitude. Many of us as Christians have no idea how sinful we have been
and are being, nor have we fully grasped what Christ endured at Calvary for us when he bore all our sins. The day of judgment will reveal
the magnitude of Christ's mercy that alone will elicit the magnificence
of praise that is his due.

Christians need not fear the day of judgment. Shame will have no
place for them on that day. The prodigal son's rich robe is made more
glorious by contrast with his former rags; the fatted calf is enjoyed all
the more by contrast with the pig fodder he served to his master's pigs
and with which he longed to fill his own aching stomach; the welcome
by his father as a son is enjoyed more intensely by contrast with the
demeaning servant role he knows he deserves (Luke 15:11–32). The
contrast between our sin and the tender mercy and forgiveness given by
the Father intensifies the experience and magnifies our worship. Then
we truly see and sing, "Holy is the Lord, worthy is the Lamb, for with
your blood you purchased men for God" (see Rev. 4:8; 5:9, 12–13).

Perhaps the insight of the character Marmeladov in Dostoyevsky's
Crime and Punishment provides a valid glimpse of how the revelation
and recognition of our sinful state will only serve to magnify Christ in
his gracious welcome of us at the last judgment:

> *And the wise ones and those of understanding will say, "Oh Lord,*
> *why dost Thou receive these men?" And He will say, "This is why*
> *I receive them, oh ye wise, this is why I receive them, oh ye of*
> *understanding, that not one of them believed himself to be worthy of*
> *this." And He will hold out His hands to us and we shall fall down*
> *before Him … and we shall weep … and we shall understand all*
> *things! Then we shall understand all … and all will understand.*[28]

When we see the magnitude of divine grace, made clear by the magnitude of our sins *forgiven*, then we will understand, fall down, and worship to an intensity never experienced before.

The great white throne

Revelation 20:11–15 has been described as one of the most sobering passages in the entire Bible.[29] It opens up to us a glorious image of "a great white throne" with Christ as King seated on it. As I mentioned above, I believe this to be the same as the throne described in the parable of the sheep and goats, and the *Bema* seat spoken of by Paul. John's vision continues:

> And I saw the dead, great and small, standing before the throne, and books were opened. Another book was opened, which is the book of life. The dead were judged according to what they had done as recorded in the books. The sea gave up the dead that were in it, and death and Hades gave up the dead that were in them, and each person was judged according to what he had done. Then death and Hades were thrown into the lake of fire. The lake of fire is the second death. If anyone's name was not found written in the book of life, he was thrown into the lake of fire. (Rev. 20:12–15)

While we may detect considerable apocalyptic symbolism here (white thrones, dead coming from the sea, books, fire), and while we may want to interpret many of the features in this passage as figurative, the facts surely speak for themselves. History concludes with a day of judgment before Christ, the righteous King and Judge, seated on a white throne. White speaks of his purity; the throne speaks of his authority. Everyone will be called before the King (all the dead are brought forth). Everyone will have his or her life scrutinized (in the book of works). Everyone who has trusted in Christ will live (their names are in the Book of Life). Those who have rejected Christ will join Satan and his demons (in the lake of fire).

CONCLUSION: JUDGE FOR YOURSELF

So what have we understood about the general resurrection and the last judgment? The points outlined below will help guide our conclusions.

1. *History will be wrapped up by Christ coming in judgment.* It will be swift, fair, and fierce. He will judge on the basis of his divine omniscience and his divine justice. He has given us fair warning. He who submitted to judgment on behalf of men and at the hands of men—the Sanhedrin, the high priest, Herod, Pilate—will himself as the vindicated Son of Man be the final Judge of all men.

2. *Each person (Rev. 20:13) must pass through this judgment,* whether living or dead, sheep or goats, good or bad, believer or unbeliever (2 Cor. 5:10). This is to show the utter impartiality of God and the absolute completeness of his judgment. Christ will judge Christians and expose their sins, but because they have fled to the cross, these sins will not be held against them. Their public record will only serve to demonstrate further the height, length, depth, and breadth of God's love and mercy. We who love him will not be humiliated on that day; we will only further glorify him who died to wash those sins away. Louis Berkhof has noted that, while Scripture leads us to believe that the sins of

believers will be revealed, they will be revealed as pardoned sins.[30]

3. *The standard by which our sins are judged is the perfection and glory of God* (Rom. 3:23). His judgment is an articulation of his just and loving nature, which must expose and blaze against sin while honoring righteousness. His judgment is a necessary vindication of himself. Emil Brunner says, "A conception of judgment flows necessarily from a recognition of the holiness of God. God is he who takes his will in absolute seriousness. He is not mocked."[31] God's judgment is his justice, which is his wrath, which is his love poured out to expunge evil and put everything in order. Judgment day is God's self-manifestation—it is a day of love, righteousness, and wrath. The latter "in this ethical sense is not only compatible with love, but in its purest form cannot exist apart from love. Righteous wrath cannot be based on self-concern, nor at its best is it consistent with any loss of self-control such as characterises the primitive emotion of anger."[32]

4. *Judgment is God's final word, but mercy was his first.* J. E. Fison notes that divine judgment in both testaments has a bias toward mercy.[33] While God's last just judgment is the expression of his righteousness, he desired and acted on our behalf that we might face it clothed by forgiveness. As Jesus said, "I did not come to judge the world, but to save it" (John 12:47).

5. *Judgment will manifest the majesty of Christ.* Francis Beattie has rightly stated that the highest end of judgment day will be the manifestation of the glory of God—on the one hand in mercy and grace to his people, on the other

in the damnation of the wicked.[34] Judgment is an act of
omniscience and omnipotence. God alone can do it, and in
doing it he displays the full panoply of his glory.

6. *Judgment for the unbeliever brings condemnation for sin;
   judgment for the believer reveals sins as forgiven in Christ.*
   Judgment day for the believer becomes a celebration of
   thanksgiving and an award ceremony (Matt. 5:12; 10:42;
   Heb. 11:26; 2 John 8).

7. *There is only one way by which we may pass through judgment
   unscathed and enter from it into heaven,* and that is through
   trusting in Christ as Lord and Savior, believing, accepting,
   and relying on his death for us at the cross. This offer is free
   and full for all, until that moment when an individual dies,
   or until the trumpet sounds, the Lord returns, and the day of
   judgment begins. Jesus promises:

> *For God so loved the world that he gave his one and only Son,
> that whoever believes in him shall not perish but have eternal
> life. For God did not send his Son into the world to condemn
> the world, but to save the world through him. Whoever believes
> in him is not condemned, but whoever does not believe stands
> condemned already because he has not believed in the name of
> God's one and only Son. (John 3:16–18)*

Let me conclude with words taken once again from the sublime
medieval English poem *Christ III*:

> *The great human multitude will rise up to judgement when the
> Lord of life looses the bonds of death. The sky will burn, the stars*

of heaven will fall, the ravening flames will ravage abroad and spirits will pass into an everlasting habitation. Not in the least will men be able to conceal that store, the thoughts of their heart, in the Ruler's presence. Not to him will their deeds be secret, for there in that momentous day it will be known to the Lord how each person has previously merited the life everlasting, and everything will be present that early or late they accomplished in the world. Not a whit of people's intentions will be hidden there but the notorious day will reveal all the store of their bosoms' vaults, the thoughts of their heart. Whoever is determined to bring to God a clear countenance when the blaze, scorching and gorily ravenous, assays before the triumphant Judge how souls have been cherished against sins, he must reflect beforehand upon his spirit's needs.[35]

TWELVE

HEAVEN OR HELL

Then they will go to away to eternal punishment,
but the righteous to eternal life.
(Matt. 25:46)

In the previous chapter we considered the day of judgment that
accompanies the return of the King. We saw that the inviolable law of
God's justice demands that judgment be the inevitable and inescapable
lot of all humankind—living and dead (1 Peter 4:5). God will exercise
his righteous judgment (Jer. 11:20) through his executive right hand,
the sovereign Lord Jesus Christ (John 5:27). The dead are brought
back to life and their bodies, along with those of the living, will be
transformed in an instant and made fit for their eternal destinations.
Judgment will be just (2 Tim. 4:8; John 5:30), based on the evidence
of our lives, words, thoughts, and deeds, and on our relationship with
Jesus Christ, all known according to the omniscience of God (Rom.
2:16). Judgment will be swift, with no equivocating or deliberating
by a mixed jury. Judgment will be final, with no court of appeal or
subsequent commuting of sentence. Judgment will fall into two prime
categories: sheep or goats (Matt. 25:32f.), wheat or tares (Matt. 13:24f.),
just or unjust (Acts 24:15), those with Christ or those against him (Luke
11:23). Judgment day is being delayed in order that many more may
be given the opportunity to accept the gospel and be found in Christ

(2 Peter 3:9). For those who side with Christ, judgment day is a day of reward. For those who have rejected him, it is a day of retribution (Isa. 62:11f.).

ETERNITY: SOMEWHERE OVER THE RAINBOW?

The afterlife is not some vague, spirited, disembodied, soulish existence. Jesus' physical resurrection, prefiguring our own physical resurrection, shows that the eternal state, though transformed, remains material, substantive, corporeal. Consequently, the eternal destination is not something insubstantial and vague, but a very real location—either with the presence of God in heaven, or shut out from that presence in hell. Eternity has a real destination. Jesus spoke of going to prepare "a place" for his disciples and said that he would return to take them there (John 14:2–4).

The ascension of Christ into the clouds and his promised return "in the same way" (Acts 1:9–11) has reinforced the conception of heaven as being somehow "above," in the heavens. Hell has been depicted as being somehow "below" the earth: The rich man "looked up" and saw Lazarus at Abraham's side in paradise (Luke 16:23; Num. 16:30; Job 26:5). Indeed, when the Russian cosmonauts went into space, they famously mocked that God was nowhere to be seen. This, however, is to parody Scripture, which presents to us a heaven and hell that are spatial but in a parallel dimension to our human existence. To speak of heaven above and hell below is to use figurative language, which correctly conveys the idea of such places as "real locations" but does not do justice to the reality of the dimensions. A geometrician or astrophysicist may have no problems with the concept of parallel universes or multidimensional space, but ancient biblical man thought more in terms of "above" and "below." There are repeated references in Scripture to heaven as a real existence that runs concurrently with human history, but which is seen only by revelation glimpsed by the saints. Note especially the visions of heaven experienced by Stephen and Paul (Acts 7:55f.; 2 Cor. 12:1f.), and John's apocalyptic revelation (Rev. 4).

SHEOL, GEHENNA, HELL, THE LAKE OF FIRE

The concept of hell is one with which most people are familiar. In nonreligious usage it has become a term to convey the horror of a situation someone faces—the soldier on a battlefield, the lover robbed of her beloved dying slowly of cancer, the depressive shrouded in darkness and despair. There is a notion of hell—as an underworld inhabited by demons, a place for the dead, where they are punished or purified—in most religions, from Greek, Egyptian, and Norse to the monotheistic religions of Judaism, Islam, and Christianity. Drawing on biblical imagery, the great literary works of Milton and Dante have conveyed powerfully to the Western mind the idea of hell as torment in an inferno.

Different terms for hell

The English word *hell* comes from the Anglo-Saxon word *hel* or *hol*, from which the term "hellhole" possibly derives. It originally meant "to conceal or hide," but was adopted in English usage to translate the biblical Hebrew term *Sheol* (sometimes translated as "grave") and the Greek term *Gehenna*, or *Hades*. Less frequent terms that are synonymous and are generally translated "hell" are the Hebrew *Abaddon* (Psalm 88:11) and the Greek *Tartarosas* (2 Peter 2:4).

Generally, the Old Testament concept of *Sheol* was of a shadowy, monotonous, meaningless existence beyond the grave where one was cut off from God (Job 7:9; Ps. 88). It was no respecter of persons, being the place of all dead, both high born and low (Job 3:17f.), an ethically neutral place inhabited by the righteous and the unrighteous.[1] Occasionally, the Old Testament treatment anticipates the familiar New Testament imagery of hell as a place of fire (Deut. 32:22). Not until Daniel do we see any unequivocal indication of a resurrection, reward, and recompense following death (Dan. 12:2). During the intertestamental period the theology of the afterlife and reflections on heaven and hell took a clearer form, then later on the teaching of Christ and the church gave further weight and content to our understanding. Judaism, however, continues to have no clearly defined doctrine of hell. Its mystic Kabbala stream articulates it in terms of a waiting room, a limbo, presumably influenced more by certain Christian traditions than by Old Testament Jewish roots.

The Greek word translated "hell" is *Gehenna*, which in the Septuagint, the Greek translation of the Old Testament, was used to convey the Hebrew concept of *Sheol*. The term *Gehenna* draws its name and imagery from the Greek word *Gehinnom*, which was the name of the valley outside Jerusalem where there was a perpetual fire consuming the detritus of the city populace. This fiery image comes into focus when Jesus says that anyone who calls his brother "you fool" will be in danger of the fire of hell (Matt. 5:22). Jesus warned that we should not fear those who can destroy the body, but we should fear God, "who can destroy both soul and body in hell" (Matt. 10:28). Similarly, James speaks of the tongue that leads to sin and directs the whole course of a person's life toward the fire of hell (James 3:6). This *Gehenna*, or hell, with its image of fire, is undoubtedly synonymous with the lake of fire in John's apocalyptic vision (Rev. 20:10, 15; 21:8).

The term *Hades* is sometimes translated as "hell" (Luke 16:23) and sometimes as "the depths" (Matt. 11:23; Acts 2:27). Interestingly, John speaks of this in the same breath as "death" and says that it will be destroyed in the lake of fire (Rev. 20:14 ; 21:8). Some believe that Hades is the intermediate location where those who die without faith in God are held before their resurrection, final judgment, and dispatch to hell, much as paradise is seen by some as the holding bay of the righteous at death.

The nature of hell

Theologians have always reflected on the nature of hell. Some great churchmen (such as Origen, Luther, and Calvin) have understood it in terms of experience rather than space. But in view of what was said above, I believe it is an experience that must take place in a space. This was certainly the view of church fathers like Basil of Caesarea and St. John Chrysostom, who believed in a literal fiery hell. It is my understanding that hell is a very real place, but the depiction of it as a lake of fiery sulfuric torment is figurative, intended to convey the terror of hell as well as the blazing, consuming wrath of our holy God against sin and evil. This theme of hell as fiery punishment is found in Jude, who writes of Sodom and Gomorrah "as an example of those who suffer the punishment of eternal fire" (Jude 7). But Jude can also change the imagery and speak of those "for whom blackest darkness has been reserved forever" (Jude 13). We are probably not meant to think that hell consists of both a chamber of fire and a chamber of darkness: Jude is simply employing powerful imagery to convey the awfulness of the destiny of those who die outside the faith.

We often find commentators diluting the horrors of hell by saying that the language used to convey it is metaphorical. However, as David White rightly points out, the metaphorical language of hell adopted by the New Testament authors surely points to a *greater reality* that is so horrible that plain language cannot bear its full weight. Biblical words and symbols cannot overstate the reality they convey, so hell must surely be beyond that imagined by biblical language.[2] Calvin helpfully says:

> *No description can deal adequately with the gravity of God's vengeance against the wicked—their torments and tortures are figuratively expressed to us by physical images—darkness, weeping and gnashing of teeth (Matthew 8:12; 22:13); unquenchable fire (Matthew 3:12; Mark 9:43f.; Isaiah 66:24); and an undying worm gnawing at the heart (Isaiah 66:24). By such expressions the Holy Spirit certainly intended to confound all our senses with dread.[3]*

There are, however, certain points we can establish:

1. *Hell is punishment from God.* Jesus spoke of the goats being separated and sent to eternal punishment (Matt. 25:46). Punishment is understood both directly and indirectly— directly as an experience of wrath, indirectly as a loss of blessing. This punishment is the inverse parallel to eternal life, depicted as a place of blessing by the Father, where those who are rewarded receive an inheritance in the kingdom prepared for them (Matt. 25:34).

2. *Hell is estrangement from God.* In several parables Jesus spoke of hell as a place "shut out." People are shut out from the wedding banquet in darkness, outside, weeping, and anguished (Matt. 22:13); they are separated from the Master, assigned "a place" with hypocrites, again "weeping and gnashing" their teeth in anguish (Matt. 24:51; 25:30).

3. *Hell is experienced sentiently.* Those shut out from the presence of the Father are aware of their condition and privation. They weep and gnash their teeth, presumably because they are overwhelmed by the realization of what they have lost.

4. *Hell is torment.* Revelation 20:10 speaks of the lake of hell, the lake of sulfur, as a place where the Devil and his cohorts "are tormented day and night for ever and ever." They are thrown there first and only then do the condemned souls join them (Rev. 20:15).

5. *Hell is permanent.* Surely for John to speak of "day and night for ever and ever" offers no hope of it ever ending. Note that Jude underscores both references to punishment as "eternal" (v. 7) and "forever" (v. 13).

6. *Hell is repayment.* It is not vindictive, but retributive for those who sin.[4] It is not some arbitrary action of an amoral or immoral God. Hell is the result of rejecting God and his gospel. Paul says that God is just, and he will inflict *(didontas)* vengeance *(ekdikesis)* in a just manner, punishing "those who do not know God and do not obey the gospel of our Lord Jesus. They will be punished with everlasting destruction and shut out from the presence of the Lord and from the majesty of his power" (2 Thess. 1:8–9).

We note that hell is for those who either reject the gospel of Christ or do not know God. While the gospel is the primary revelation of God, it is not inconceivable that God will judge those who have had no access to the gospel on their response and desire to know him— according to the modest revelation given through the light in creation and conscience. Thus the judgment of the sheep and goats indicates that many are declared sheep and enter eternal life, judged on their righteous service to Christ. Without, apparently, ever knowing they were doing it to Christ, they express surprise and ask, "When did we see you hungry?" (Matt. 25:37–40). I hope to see many in heaven who never entered a church, never partook of the sacraments, never read a Bible, yet, according to their light, stretched their lives longingly toward God, looking for him, seeking to live for him. I hope such people will receive mercy through the blood of Jesus applied to them and will become included among the saints.

ANNIHILATION, OR *APOKATASTASIS?*

Although most students of Scripture from the church fathers to Luther held to traditional concepts of hell as described above, many have protested against the notion of a perpetual tormented state in a place known as "hell." They do so for various reasons. Hell simply does not fit with their understanding of God, their understanding of the universe, and their reading of Scripture. It is suggested that an eternal punishment would be unjust for temporal sins, that an eternal punishment would not fit into a perfect universe where all evil was destroyed, and that God cannot permit anything that represents a negation of his will. It is further argued that a God of love could not possibly permit a hell, and that God's decree and his death in Christ make possible his will for all to enter heaven—and who are we to argue with that?

In view of such objections, two counteroptions appear:

1.   *apokatastasis* (from the Greek, meaning "restoration"[5])—no one will go to hell, for all will be redeemed in the love of Christ and enter heaven;

2. *annihilation*—the unbeliever destroyed permanently either at death or following the day of judgment.

Apokatastasis: universal salvation

As early as Origen some Christian fathers questioned the reality and eternity of hell. Many hoped for universal salvation, although the ecumenical Council of Alexandria in AD 400 declared the notion a heresy, as did the great Father Augustine.

Universalism is generally a doctrine held and hoped for by the liberal tradition, which emphasized a particular view of the love of God (not realizing that judgment and wrath are actions of love). Many even see the concept of an eternal soul as being unbiblical, more influenced by Platonic thought. Universalism is also hinted at within more evangelical traditions, notably by Karl Barth, for whom the decree and death of God must triumph over the will and negation of Satan and the flesh. God's yes is greater than his no, and in Christ he has said yes to the universe. He has reversed the death that came in Adam: Just as in Adam all die, so in Christ all will be made alive (Rom. 5:12–19; 1 Cor. 15:22–28). It is difficult to hold to a notion of all things brought together under one head (Eph. 1:10) if an eternal hell for evil exists as a constant reminder of separation. How then can we say that all things have been "brought together?"

The distinguished New Testament scholar I. H. Marshall has studied every New Testament text summoned to support universalism and has concluded that there are no grounds for such a view.[6] He emphasizes the eternal consequences of temporal sin, showing that the apostles were clear that those who practice works of the flesh will never inherit the kingdom (Gal. 5:21). Instead they will reap corruption (1 Cor. 6:9f.), condemned by God (1 Cor. 11:32), experiencing the final wrath of God (Rom. 2:5,

8–9; 5:9; 9:22; Phil. 1:28). Only those who do not persist in unbelief will be saved (Rom. 11:23). Surely the parables of Christ cited above that speak of the distinctions made between those inside the wedding banquet and those outside, between the sheep who go to eternal life and the goats who are sent to eternal judgment, close any hope some may have of universalism. Ulrich Luz says on Matthew 25:31–46, "Eternal life and eternal punishment are the consequences of the saying of the World Judge. Once again it is clear that Matthew believed that there will be a double conclusion to history—there is no suggestion of universal salvation."[7]

Annihilation

Annihilation[8] is a widespread view among groups such as the Jehovah's Witnesses and Seventh Day Adventists. It was historically found in some church fathers, including Origen, Gregory of Nyssa, and Justin Martyr. Interestingly, it has become increasingly popular among evangelicals and is supported as a possibility by such distinguished churchmen as John Stott and John Wenham,[9] Philip Edgecombe Hughes and Michael Green. Clark Pinnock has protested that the concept of eternal punishment in hell is barbarous and unworthy of the God revealed in Christ. He wrote a seminal work entitled *The Wideness of God's Mercy*, in which he objected to the classic doctrines of hell on the basis that God's redemptive purposes did not include just a very few evangelicals.[10] Elsewhere he has written:

> *I consider the concept of hell as endless torment in body and mind an outrageous doctrine, a theological and moral enormity. How can Christians possibly project a deity of such cruelty and vindictiveness? A God who would do such a thing is more like Satan than God.*[11]

Similarly, the Church of England Doctrine Commission's report, *The Mystery of Salvation*, rejects the notion that hell is eternal torment:

> *Christians have professed appalling theologies which made God into a sadistic monster ... hell is not eternal torment, but it is the final and irrevocable choosing of that which is opposed to God so completely and so absolutely that the only end is total non being.*[12]

The annihilationists do not rely merely on conjecture or emotive argument, marshaling scriptures and exegesis to support their view. They claim that the word *aionos*—rendered "eternal" in Matthew 25:46 ("eternal punishment") and "everlasting" in 2 Thessalonians 1:9—is wrongly translated and does not necessarily convey the sense of everlasting, but refers rather to the *aion*, the age of the life to come. Thus the sheep experience the age to come as an eternal blessed state, whereas the goats experience the age to come as destruction. However, while *aion* can carry the meaning of "the age to come," generally (and more normatively) it refers to the length of time as *eternal*.[13]

Annihilationists also note that the frequent use of terms such as "perish" (John 3:16) and "destroy" (Matt. 10:28) in relation to judgment suggest annihilation rather than preservation and permanent punishment. The imagery of fire lends itself more to understanding this as an event that brings an unrepeatable, total consuming: Once consumed by fire, how can one be continuously re-presented to it? They point out that death is often spoken of as a *returning to dust* (Gen. 3:19; Ps. 146:4; Eccl. 9:5, 10), and they suggest that the so-called "second death" (Rev. 20:6, 14; 21:8) may indicate annihilation. Old Testament texts may also hint at annihilation, portraying the reprobate shriveling up (Zech. 14:12), and in the eternal reign of God the saints look on the "bodies" of the reprobate, not their eternal tormented souls (Isa. 66:24), their existence apparently having ended.

However, such a position and such verses do not deal adequately with unequivocal statements to the contrary. The eternal punishment of the goats in Matthew 25 parallels the eternal reward of the sheep. While *aionos* may be translated "of the age to come" as well as "everlasting," that age to come is eternal and sentient for the sheep, and therefore presumably eternal and sentient for the goats also. Putting it simply: No eternal punishment—No eternal life; eternal punishment—eternal life!

Eternal punishment

The concept of eternal torment after death, not annihilation, became widespread in intertestamental Judaism (1 QS 2:15; 5:13; Psalms of Solomon 2:35; 15:11; 4 Macc. 10:15). How can death or the day of judgment bring total annihilation? Jesus comments that "it is better for you to enter life maimed or crippled than to have two hands or two feet and be thrown into eternal fire" (Matt. 18:8). Annihilation would render Christ's saying meaningless. Jesus is surely warning that if sin is not radically dealt with in this life, it will be severely dealt with in the next. And if all are annihilated, then where is the justice in that? The nonbeliever gets the same end as a Hitler? Is that fair? Of course, some might want to construct a doctrine of annihilation after partial and proportionate suffering following the day of judgment—Hitler suffering longer in hell than a mere unbeliever. But there is no evidence in Scripture for this, however appealing it might be.

Many object that the doctrine of eternal punishment is presented in parables, which are figurative and not meant to be the basis for constructing doctrine. Perhaps, however, there are also some nonfigurative statements to the same effect. Of particular significance is 2 Thessalonians 1:8–9, where Paul states that the ungodly who have rejected God and his gospel "will be punished with everlasting destruction and shut out from the presence of the Lord and from the majesty of his power." Now, while eternal destruction might conceivably imply annihilation, Paul qualifies this by speaking of being *shut out* from the Lord's presence. "Shut out" could be understood as the perspective on the destroyed held by those who "get in" to the Lord's presence, but Jesus clearly suggests that those who are shut out are *aware* of their plight (Matt. 25:11). This self-awareness, after being "punished with everlasting destruction" (2 Thess. 1:9), must challenge the interpretation of destruction as annihilation. If eternal destruction means annihilation, then the previous statement about being shut out from God's presence becomes redundant, superfluous: How can you be shut out from something if you no longer exist? This destruction is an ongoing experience of separation from God. For this text to mean anything, as Ernest Best notes, they would have to continue to exist.[14] We who exist in time cannot begin to comprehend what eternity outside time looks like. While many understandably want the New Testament texts that speak of destruction to indicate annihilation, the Jews, Jesus, and Paul all believed that "eternal" meant "eternal"!

One thought remains: Why would God decree an eternal punishment? I do not know. It is beyond my understanding. But we must trust that he who is absolute love and absolute justice, revealed in the nightmare of Golgotha, is doing what is most loving and most right. Ultimately, I must not put God before my human bar of judgment, questioning his actions—I must make sure I am right before *his* bar of judgment.

THE REALITY OF HELL CONVEYS
THE REVELATION OF GOD'S HOLY LOVE

I have no problem believing that Satan and his demonic workers deserve all the punishment and torment they will get for all the evil they have done (Rev. 20:10). I believe justice demands that such evildoers as Nero, Hitler, or Stalin get their just desserts—although we might ask whether, even for them, eternal punishment fits temporal crime. But I balk at the notion that people who have rejected Christ or not sought God will meet the same fate as a Satan or a Nero. Yet John states that all go the same way (Rev. 20:15). However, because God is righteous, his judgment must be equitable and proportionate. It would surely be unjust to sentence all humans and all demons to the same fate. Scripture's principle of "an eye for an eye, a tooth for a tooth" reveals the character of God and shows that sentence is proportionate and commensurate to the sin committed (Ex. 21:24; Matt. 5:38). Thus we can reasonably deduce that, while eternal hell awaits all who have rejected Christ and not sought God, within it there must be gradations or degrees of suffering and torment. Jesus says that some will be beaten with many blows, some with few (Luke 12:47f.). Abraham rightly says that God will make the just differentiation in judgment: "Will not the Judge of all the earth do right?" (Gen. 18:25). Judgment is God's, he knows everything, he will judge fairly.

That said, I would like to be a universalist, or at least an annihilationist. I echo C. S. Lewis, who said, "There is no doctrine I would more willingly remove from Christianity than [hell], if it lay in my power ... I would pay any price to be able to say truthfully: 'All will be saved.'"[15] At times in my Christian life, I have leaned strongly toward such notions, but I have always felt I was rather accommodating Scripture to my preferences. How can anyone not want everyone to enter heaven? God certainly does (1 Tim. 2:3–4), and in Christ he paved the way. How can anyone not want hell to be empty, bar the Devil and his cohorts? But the weight of Scripture and tradition leads me painfully to believe in a literal state of existence in an actual place where those who have rejected God and his gospel spend eternity suffering. To write or say such a thing lightly is to utter that which is ultimate horror. To be glib about hell, dropping it loosely into our preaching, is to know nothing of Calvary love. It has been well said that no one should mention hell without tears in their eyes. How true. God does not desire that any should perish (2 Peter 3:9), and God acted in Christ so that none need perish who trust in him (John 3:16). But how can they escape if they ignore so great a salvation (Heb. 2:3)?

What, then, must be our response if we reach such a conclusion?

1. It must lead to overflowing gratitude and praise, in *appreciation* of all that Christ went through at the cross when he assumed the consequences of our sin to redeem us from hell.

2. It must lead to passionate *intercession* for and *witness* to all, so that they might escape the horrors of hell and walk into heaven hand in hand with Christ.

3. It must lead to greater *revelation* of God's absolute hatred of sin and the absolute holiness that leads him to separate himself from it.

4. It should inspire our *proclamation* of hell as the dark backdrop, the shadow side to the glorious gift of eternal life. The great Puritan pastor Richard Baxter said of preaching on hell, "Many other things are desirable to be known but this must be known, or else our people are undone for

ever."[16] That said, I have heard preachers shamefully delight in describing hell! Notably, nowhere in the New Testament *kerygma*,[17] spelled out in the sermons in Acts, nor in Paul's massive New Testament corpus, is there a direct, detailed, specific mention of hell. Paul prefers to speak of "wrath" (Rom. 2:5) or "eternal condemnation" (Gal. 1:8–9), and the *kerygma* refers to "judgment."

HEAVEN: THINGS CAN ONLY GET BETTER

Google throws up one hundred and twenty million sites for heaven, beginning with a gay nightclub and ranging from corsets to chocolate. "Heaven" in modern parlance speaks of a state of bliss. It is a term loosely applied to anything giving pleasure, be it a warm bath, a beautiful sunset, or a moment's peace. Scripturally, "heaven" relates to three places:

1. the heavens above the firmament of the sky (Gen. 1:8; Ps. 19:1);
2. the spiritual realm where Satan and his demons contest God's rule and contend with the angels (Rev. 12:7; Dan. 10:13f.);
3. the "third heaven" (2 Cor. 12:2), referring to the dwelling place of God (Isa. 66:1).

Jesus taught his disciples to pray to "Our Father in heaven" (Matt. 6:9). It is the place from which Christ came at the incarnation and to which he returned at the ascension. It is the place from which he will return with the angels and saints at the end of time. It is the place where believers hold real estate (John 14:2–3; Eph. 1:3; 2:6; Phil. 3:20). It is the place from which God exercises his power and authority, mediated through the saints (Matt. 16:19)—that is, the church here on earth.

If hell is the retribution for refusing to honor God and accept the gospel, heaven is the reward for serving God and embracing the gospel. The parables that indicate hell as a condition of being shut out from God's presence also show that heaven is enjoyment of God's presence. Heaven is sharing in the "master's happiness" (Matt. 25:23). Heaven is shown figuratively as participation in the wedding feast (Matt. 25:10). Heaven is being blessed by the Father and inheriting the kingdom prepared (Matt. 25:34). Heaven is eternal life, not condemnation (Matt. 25:46). Heaven is receiving a reward (Matt. 5:12). Heaven is where our treasure is found (Luke 18:22). Currently, heaven has a provisionality about it: Its present form will pass away (Matt. 24:35) and it will find its reconfiguration and completion in the creation of a new heaven and new earth (2 Peter 3:13; Rev. 21:1).

BEYOND OUR WILDEST DREAMS

Surprisingly, one struggles to find a clear and systematic presentation of what heaven is like. Jesus spoke more about hell than about heaven. We may, however, deduce its content from the negative, it being the opposite of what evil on earth is like. Heaven being the opposite of hell tells us what heaven is not! The writer to the Hebrews says that the man-made tabernacle or temple is a type, a pale imitation or copy of that true sanctuary that is heaven (Heb. 9:11, 23f.). The garden of Eden, the theocratic land of Israel,[18] the city of Zion, the kingdom of God, all manifest traces of what God's design is like and therefore how his perfect rule in heaven will be. The prophets also give insights (Zech. 14; Ezek. 47; Isa. 65:17–25). Isaiah paints perhaps the most beautiful portrait of the new heavens and new earth, a term later picked up by Peter and John:

> *Behold, I will create*
> *new heavens and a new earth.*

The former things will not be remembered,
  nor will they come to mind.
But be glad and rejoice forever
  in what I will create....
I will rejoice over Jerusalem
  and take delight in my people;
  the sound of weeping and of crying
  will be heard in it no more....
He who dies at a hundred
  will be thought a mere youth....
My chosen ones will long enjoy
the works of their hands.
They will not toil in vain
  or bear children doomed to misfortune;
  for they will be a people blessed by the LORD....
The wolf and the lamb will feed together,
  and the lion will eat straw like the ox,
  but dust will be the serpent's food.
  They will neither harm nor destroy
  on all my holy mountain.
(Isa. 65:17–25)

Clearly, Isaiah's depiction is more figurative than descriptive. References to living more than a hundred years, and to children being born, suggest death and sex, both of which we know are not part of the new order (although some, taking it literally, for that reason relate it to a historical millennium rule—see chapter 4). Isaiah's intention is to convey the enjoyment, the peace, the security, the prosperity, and the proximity to God in heaven.

BEYOND OUR FINITE MIND

I am not surprised or bothered by the paucity of details about the heavenly existence. I believe it is because we can only understand according to the limits of our experience and language. We simply do not have the language to convey the intensity and extraordinary nature of heaven. It is so much more than the best of what we have so far experienced. Language, analogy, and metaphor will hint at it, but will inevitably fall short. Paul informs us that he was taken up to visit heaven (2 Cor. 12:1–4). He tells us nothing about the experience—not a thing![19] Why not? Paul appears not to know in what state he saw heaven, whether physically or spiritually (v. 3). He says "he heard inexpressible things, things that man is not permitted to tell" (v. 4). "Inexpressible" literally means "without words." Paul is saying that we simply do not have the language, and therefore do not have the ability, to comprehend heaven.

In 1 Corinthians 2:9f., Paul cites Isaiah and says, "No eye has seen, no ear has heard, no mind has conceived what God has prepared for those who love him." This relates to heaven. Paul continues by saying that "God has revealed it to us by his Spirit." The hope of heaven, the glimpse of its glory, the assurance of eternity, the rays that break through the gloomy shadows of our life, are all given by the Spirit, but no unresurrected human may yet fully understand and articulate it. Now we see "but a poor reflection as in a mirror." We know the tiniest part. But one day we will know fully, even as we are fully known (1 Cor. 13:12f.).

THE WEIGHT OF GLORY

The Gnostics argue for a dehumanized, dematerialized, overspiritualized existence in heaven, but I believe the opposite: Heaven will be a more material, more substantial, fully human experience, restoring what sin has dissipated. Jesus, God's eternal Son, is the perfect man in heaven, and we will be like him. Imagine a painting that over the years has seen the varnish darken, stained by the accumulation of dirt, dust, and smoke, only to have a master restorer strip off the layers of filth, letting the intensity of the artist's original vibrant colors burst forth once again. On earth, human existence is marked by the five senses: touch, taste, smell, sound, and sight. But in heaven I wonder whether we will have a proliferation of senses so that we may experience everything far more intensely.

C. S. Lewis, in his narrative of heaven and hell, *The Great Divorce*, makes a similar claim—that heaven is a coming out from the Shadowlands into the perfect, the authentic, the true, where everything is more "real."[20] Lewis imaginatively presents heaven as a place where the "bright solid people" exist. Phantoms, those on the hell-bound bus journey, find the grass too painful to walk on here; raindrops pass through them like bullets. They cannot pick the flowers because the stems are too strong. This sense of the heavenly being more real, more solid, finds scriptural support in the resurrected Jesus, who is visible, physical, able to touch, talk, and eat, and yet he can walk through walls into the disciples' upper room. The eternal reality is more real than the temporal, thus what appears solid, like a wall, is wispy in comparison with resurrected reality.

Lewis is on to something profound here, and it is further underscored by his essay "The Weight of Glory." In heaven the shining glorious people are somehow more weighty. The Hebrew word translated "glory" is *kabod*, and it conveys both gloriousness and weightiness. In heaven we regain that glory that we lost at the fall (Rom. 3:23), and we are fully transformed from one degree of glory into the likeness of Christ (2 Cor. 3:18). We become more substantial, more real, more weighty.

Robert Culver says, "Though presently unseen, heaven is the most real of all great realities."[21] We are limited by our three dimensions, by our five senses, and by our finite minds. It seems that in heaven, in our resurrection bodies, we will dwell in a multiplicity of dimensions, with a proliferation of senses and perfect knowledge making our experience what Jesus promised: life in all its fullness (John 10:10).

VACATION OR OCCUPATION?

Even as Scripture is sparse in its descriptions of heaven, it is also sparse in its depictions of what we will do in heaven. The absence of clear scriptural teaching must make us cautious in imagining what will happen. But we do have hints. Millard Erickson sums it up as three things: rest, worship, and service.[22]

God built *rest* into his creation. He rested from his labors on the seventh day and called humankind to follow suit (Gen. 2:2–3). He built rest into the farming cycle, ordaining that the land should rest from being cultivated every seven years (Lev. 25:1–7). He promised the Israelites that he would lead them into a land of rest (Deut. 12:9; Ps. 95:11)—when slavery in Egypt would be replaced by joy, peace, and prosperity in Canaan. God ordained that rest be applied to the annulment of debts and the freedom of slaves every fiftieth year (Lev. 25:8f.). Jesus came and offered rest for weary souls (Matt. 11:28), the rest that God had promised and for which humankind longed (Jer. 6:16). Christ offers entry into rest for those who believe in him (Heb. 4:3, 9). Heaven is the eternal city of rest. This rest is not a cessation of all labor, for here we will serve God. It is, rather, the end of strife, slavery, weariness, pain, suffering, trial, sin, debts. This rest is completion, wholeness, belonging, being home. From the fourth century in the Western church, baptisteries were shaped octagonally. The eight sides symbolized the eternal rest promised us by allegiance to Christ—an end to the seven-day cycle of human existence and, on the eighth day, permanent entry to the promised land of rest. Christians are eighth-day people, people of the rest, having partially entered that rest now by faith and the Spirit, and awaiting the eternal promised land of the new heaven and new earth.

Worship is central to our role in heaven (Rev. 5:8–10; 14:2f.; 15:2f.). Worship is laying down our crowns before the Lamb. But this is a repeated act, and presumably each time we fall on our face in worship, laying down our crowns at Jesus' feet, Jesus lifts us up and crowns us again. To worship is to fulfill our being. It is to be fully alive and whole. Jonathan Edwards was eloquent on the subject in his sermon entitled "Praise—one of the Chief Employments of Heaven":

> *When they behold the glorious power of God, they cannot*
> *but praise that power. When they see God's wisdom that is so*
> *wonderful, and infinitely beyond all created wisdom, they cannot*
> *but continually praise that wisdom. When they view the infinitely*
> *pure and lovely holiness of God, whereby the heavens themselves*
> *are not pure in comparison with him, how can they avoid with*
> *an exalted heart to praise that beauty of the divine nature! When*
> *they see the infinite grace of God, and see what a boundless ocean*
> *of mercy and love he is, how can they but celebrate that grace*
> *with the highest praise!*[23]

Service is also central to our role in heaven: "His servants will serve him" (Rev. 22:3). As with worship, heaven's service is not drudgery, but fulfillment. We are called to the privilege of being equerries to the King of Kings. That service may be understood perhaps in terms of government. In several parables (Matt. 19:28; 25:21f.), Jesus said that faithfulness on earth in stewardship will bring privilege in heaven to exercise executive rule—over angels and the redeemed. He has a kingdom to rule in love, and those who have proved faithful on earth will be given high privilege and honor in heaven.

NEW HEAVENS AND NEW EARTH

We sometimes speak of the saints going to heaven when they die, and rightly so. But heaven in its current state is provisional, as is the state of the souls departed, before the last day of resurrection, judgment, and the creation of new heavens and a new earth. As N. T. Wright notes, "That state is a temporary stage ahead of the time when God will restore all things and will renew his people to bodily life in the midst of the new creation."[24]

Isaiah spoke about "new heavens and a new earth" (Isa. 65:17). This is picked up by Peter (2 Peter 3:13), who speaks of the day of the Lord as a mighty conflagration when Christ will destroy the heavens by fire, melt the earth, and create "a new heaven and a new earth." Similarly, John in his great revelation spoke of God creating "a new heaven and a new earth" as "the first heaven and the first earth had passed away" (Rev. 21:1). Jesus himself spelled this out in Matthew 24:35. The new heavens and new earth will replace the old existing order. Currently, heaven may be thought of as an entirely separate universe with its own space and time that is nonetheless able to touch our universe, space, and time. However, at the end of our time, heaven will join earth and a whole new united, perfected universe will be established. The way that Scripture holds these two together—the new heaven and the new earth and the picture in Revelation 21 of a celestial city descending onto an earthly plane—leads me to believe not so much in a distinct heaven and distinct earth, but in a new order, in which the old order of separation is removed and heaven and earth fuse into one—a heaven on earth, a heaven that is earth.

Romans 8:19ff. speaks of the whole earth groaning as it awaits its day of redemption. That will be far more than a recapitulation to a pre-fall state. It will be its consummation when, like its inhabitants who have trusted in God, it is transformed and re-created, eternal, glorious, and perfect—fit for the King. N. T. Wright powerfully endorses this notion:

> *The great claim of Revelation 21 and 22 is that heaven and earth will finally be united. This is the polar opposite of all kinds of Gnosticism with their ultimate separation of heaven and earth … eventually heaven and earth will be impregnated with each other … God's heaven, God's life, God's dimension, impregnating, permeating, charging the present world, eventually producing new or renewed heavens and new or renewed earth integrated with each other.*[25]

A PICTURE PAINTS A THOUSAND WORDS: REVELATION 21:1—22:5

This is the finest and fullest depiction of the eternal heaven that Scripture offers. Commentators debate whether its sumptuous language is figurative or descriptive—but why not a bit of both? This new heaven and new earth is a *new heaven on earth*. Contrary to the dispensationalists and premillennialists, who believe in a literal reign of Jesus on earth from the old Jerusalem, we see the new true Jerusalem coming to the new earth from heaven. While Jerusalem in Israel has a significant role to play in God's revelation in history and geography, it will pass away in the new order.

The place of God's reign will then be with men on earth (Rev. 21:3). The goal of the Lord's Prayer is now complete: His kingdom is come, his will is done on earth as in heaven. Saints go to heaven when they die, but on the day of the Lord, when Christ returns, the saints and heaven come to earth. No longer is heaven the dwelling place of God and earth the dwelling place of humankind: The two come together in eternity. G. B. Caird says that the whole point of the descent (of the New Jerusalem) is that now God's dwelling is with humankind.[26] Revelation 21:3 reads: "Now the dwelling of God is with men, and he will live with them. They will be his people, and God himself will be with them and be their God." Robert Mounce believes that it is the presence of God and fellowship with him that forms the essential feature of the age to come.[27] The longing of humankind for intimacy with God their Creator, so long separated by sin and shame and space, is fulfilled. Heaven is God and humankind in a lovers' embrace. Heaven's God will be to us as bride to groom (21:2), as father to son (21:7).

"The coming of a city shows that 'heaven is supremely social'—no flight to the Alone, but life in the redeemed community of heaven."[28] In this New Jerusalem, this heaven on earth, certain things will be absent that were all too present in the old order. John tells us that the whole gamut of evil is evicted from life. Removed are the suffering elements that tear at our lives: no sea, no death, no grief, no weeping, no pain, no curse, no night. The sea is the place from which the Dragon manifested itself (Rev. 13:1). It has been seen as the great fear of the ancients, uncontainable, uncontrollable, terrifying, chaotic, the haunt of the Devil. Mariners kept to the shores in dread of him. But after being the symbol of evil and malevolent destruction, the sea is no more.

Hell is marked by weeping and gnashing of teeth, but no one weeps in heaven. God "will wipe every tear from their eyes. There will be no more death or mourning or crying or pain, for the old order of things has passed away" (21:4). Human history is haunted by tears and pain. Suffering scars all deeply. But as Thomas More famously said, "Earth has no sorrow that heaven cannot heal." Heaven is a healing place "for the healing of the nations" (Rev. 22:2). Not only does God make all things well, but in heaven God makes all things new (21:5)—not necessarily totally different, but totally new, pristine, perfect, straight out of the wrapper, without imperfection, and without life's scars or accumulated stresses. In Kazakhstan there was a city under Soviet control called Karaganda, whose nickname was "The City Where No One Smiles." In heaven a smile is the norm.

It is noteworthy who will not be present: "The cowardly, the unbelieving, the vile, the murderers, the sexually immoral, those who practice magic arts, the idolaters and all liars" will not be in heaven (21:8). The naming of these sinners and their exclusion does not imply that they will continue to exist in their sin. Rather these descriptive sins define those sinners who have rejected the offer of becoming saints, who will be thrown in the lake of fire. Heaven is a sin-free and therefore sinner-free zone. Only those whose names are written in the Lamb's Book of Life—those who have fled to hide in the rock of Christ—will be there (21:27).

John's descriptions of the Holy City stretch the imagination to the breaking point. I do not believe they are to be taken literally. Perhaps they are intended more as symbols of the glorious grandeur befitting God (21:11–27)—walls of jasper bejeweled with precious gems, gates of pearls, streets of pure gold. All reflect the glory of God and the Lamb. There is no temple (21:22), for Christ is the temple. There is no need for a priesthood, sacrifice, or religious cult, for all have now served their purpose. There is no light from sun or moon, for God's glory lights the new heaven on earth. The Lamb is the light of the world (21:23; 22:5). To this city the nations gather to give glory. The gates are always open, they are always welcome. No evil need be guarded against and shut out (21:24f.). And here the saints will serve Christ personally (22:3), see Christ face-to-face (22:4), and sit reigning with him forever (22:5). They will see, serve, and sit with him.

CONCLUSION

Such a hope, such a heaven, must have a powerful impact on our lives. The contemplation of it must lead to action. Let us *worship* the great Savior and Redeemer Jesus Christ, who opened up heaven for us. Let us *proclaim this great hope,* which is available to all while they yet have breath to say yes to Jesus. Let us *refuse to live as the world lives,* building bigger and better barns that will all be burned up—investing rather for a far greater reward in heaven. Finally, let us *rejoice and draw strength, courage and peace,* knowing that whatever the world may throw at us, "the best is yet to be, the last of life, for which the first was made."[29]

In C. S. Lewis's *The Last Battle*, Aslan, the Christ figure, has triumphed over evil. But Lucy looks sad. Aslan says to her, "You do not yet look so happy as I mean you to be."

Lucy replies, "We're so afraid of being sent away."

Aslan answers, "No fear of that.... The term is over: the holidays have begun. The dream is ended: this is the morning."

C. S. Lewis finishes, "And we can most truly say that they all lived happily ever after. But for them it was only the beginning of the real story ... which goes on forever: in which every chapter is better than the one before."[30]

Conclusion:
A Bride Prepared

We have come to the end of a long and stretching study of eschatology. The major themes we have considered include the following:

- the reach for the future, which is present within all life;
- Christian hope;
- the kingdom of God;
- death and eternal life;
- the nature and timing of the so-called millennium;
- the signs that indicate the end of the world;
- the mark of the Antichrist;
- the place of Israel in the end-time purposes of God;
- the tribulation and the rapture;
- Armageddon, the war to end all wars;
- the manner of the return of the King;
- the day of judgment;
- the new heavens and the new earth;
- our eternal destiny: heaven or hell.

We have approached these various themes from a commitment to Scripture as the inspired Word of God and thus the ultimate authority on the matter. However, we have repeatedly seen that, throughout the church's reflection on the relevant Scriptures, various—and at times wildly contradictory—interpretations and positions have been reached. I have tried to be fair in representing alternative positions, though invariably my own conclusions may have whittled away at evenhandedness. Each chapter has suggested how the Christian church should respond to that particular theme. As we conclude, Francis Schaeffer's famous question frames our final study: *How should we then live?*[1]

READY WHEN YOU ARE

Ideally, we are to live our lives as best we can in such obedience and conformity to Christ's will that, were he to come today, we would not be surprised, afraid, or ashamed. Some have walked so close to the Lord and felt themselves so at the center of his will that they have claimed they would change nothing in what they were doing if they knew Jesus was about to return. C. H. Spurgeon said, "If I knew that our Lord would come this evening, I should preach just as I mean to preach; and if I knew he would come during this sermon, I would go on preaching until he did." G. Campbell Morgan claimed, "I never begin my work in the morning without thinking that perhaps he may interrupt my work and begin his own."

One remarkable statement was made by John Wesley, when he was asked by a lady how he would spend his last hour if he knew he were to die at midnight the following day. He replied, "Why, just as I intend to spend it now. I shall preach this evening at Gloucester and again at 5 tomorrow morning. After that I shall ride to Tewkesbury, preach in the afternoon and meet the societies in the evening. I shall then repair to friend Martin's house, converse and pray with the family as usual, retire to my room at 10 o'clock, then in quiet faith and glad trust, commend myself to my heavenly father—lie down to rest and wake up in his home."[2] How inspiring that Wesley believed his life to be so in accord with the will of Christ that he would not change a thing if he knew he were about to meet him!

IN THE LINE OF DUTY

On May 19, 1780, a mysterious thick darkness, possibly caused by forest fires, descended on New England. Many were overcome by fear, believing that it was a signal of the end of time and the return of Christ. The Connecticut legislature was meeting that day, but the darkness was so thick by midmorning that many urged for an adjournment. Colonel Abraham Davenport resisted this: "Either the day of judgment is at hand or it is not. If it is not, there is no cause for adjournment; if it is, I wish to be found in the line of duty. Bring me candles."[3] Scripture has much to say about the details of the end times, and much about how we get "in the line of duty." We are offered some clear instructions on what the Lord will be looking for when he returns.

1. Readiness

> *So you also must be ready, because the Son of Man will come at an hour when you do not expect him. (Matt. 24:44)*

> *And his bride has made herself ready. (Rev. 19:7)*

Jesus informed us of the signs of the times that will precede his return. With one eye on Scripture and another on society, we will be able to discern the imminence of his return—a return that rapidly approaches and, in my view, may quite conceivably be fulfilled in this generation. History is on its last legs. The demonic is marshaling for its final manifestation. Paul says that we are to understand the present time.

"The hour has come for you to wake up from your slumber, because our salvation is nearer now than when we first believed. The night is nearly over; the day is almost here" (Rom. 13:11–12). Jesus will come like a thief in the night, but the church is to be alert to the signs, awake for the Master's return, and not taken by surprise (1 Thess. 5:4f.). We should have nothing to be ashamed of. Whenever he comes, we are to be faithful servants, awake and at work.

As a young man I was very briefly in the army. Within days of joining up, we were taken out on field exercise. We were put in pairs and told to do sentry duty through the night. We were warned sternly by the sergeant that, in war, lives depend on soldiers staying awake. To fall asleep on duty meant a fine and a brief period in the military jail. I think I was more afraid of my own color sergeant finding me asleep than of any potential enemy attacking. The church is to be alert and awake, on sentry duty, ready either for the enemy attack or for the coming of the general.

2. Steadiness

> You too, be patient and stand firm, because the Lord's coming is near. (James 5:8)

> Continue in him, so that when he appears we may be confident and unashamed before him at his coming. (1 John 2:28)

We saw in chapter 8 that before the end there will be an increase in the assault of the Enemy against the church. We will not, as some wishful thinkers assume, be rescued from the great tribulation. In J. R. R. Tolkien's *The Lord of the Rings*, Gandalf says to Frodo, "All we have to decide is what to do with the time that is given to us. And already, Frodo, our time is beginning to look black. The Enemy is fast becoming very strong ... we shall be hard put to it. We should be very hard put to it."[4]

The church has always been hard put to it—and this will increase. The Enemy will make a last-ditch effort to destroy the bride of Christ for whom the groom Christ Jesus returns. Some will fall away: The great apostasy accompanies the great tribulation. But to be forewarned is to be forearmed. Let us gird ourselves in prayer and the Word, building ourselves up in the most holy faith, contemplating Christ and his great sacrifice for us, meditating on the rewards that await us in heaven, so that we might be able to stand in that evil day. "When the Son of Man comes, will he find faith on the earth?" (Luke 18:8).

3. Holiness

The wedding of the Lamb has come,
*   and his bride has made herself ready.*
Fine linen, bright and clean,
*   was given her to wear. (Rev. 19:7–8)*

Live self-controlled, upright and godly lives in this present age,
while we wait for the blessed hope—the glorious appearing of our
great God and Savior.
(Titus 2:12–13)

But we know that when he appears, we shall be like him.…
Everyone who has this hope in him purifies himself. (1 John
3:2–3)

No groom ever watched his bride process down the aisle nonchalantly, in her gardening overalls, hair unkempt, nails broken, makeup smudged, and with her mind on other things. Jesus is returning for his beautiful bride—a bride who has made herself ready. Traditionally, brides have worn white to show they are virgin, pure, given exclusively for their groom. John says she will be clothed in fine white linen, which speaks figuratively of "the righteous acts of the saints" (Rev. 19:8b). Christ does not want to come for a grubby church. Christ is returning for a faithful bride, clothed in virgin's white, not a faithless harlot who has lifted her skirts to others.

A staggering comment is offered by Peter, who suggests that by living holy and godly lives we actually speed his coming (2 Peter 3:10–12). The term Peter uses is *speudein*, which generally means "to hasten or hurry."[5] There was a saying in the Talmud, reflected in Jewish thought, that if only the Israelites could really repent for a single day, the Messiah would appear (2 Esd. iv.38f.). That such a view informed the apostles' thinking is further seen when Paul speaks of repentance leading to times of refreshing and the Father sending Christ (Acts 3:19f.). How this works, I do not know—but the groom is eager to come when he sees the bride ready. Perhaps holiness works hand in hand with witness: A holy church attracts a longing world to Christ and when "the full number of the elect are gathered in," he returns. Holiness and gospel witness create the tipping point for the groom to return for his bride. That day, when those circumstances are met, is known and planned for by Christ, but we have a major part to play.

4. Joyfulness

> *When these things begin to take place, stand up and lift up your heads, because your redemption is drawing near. (Luke 21:28)*

We are not to be a "grubby bride," neither are we to be a "glum bride." No bride should be miserable on her wedding day. The signs of the times preceding the return of Christ are terrible, full of terror. While many shake with fear, it is not the time for the church to go into hiding. Such signs indicate the return of the King. Those who are his are to stand up and lift up their heads.

In the remarkable stage play and film *Jacob the Liar*,[6] we meet a man who bolsters the whole community of Jews in the ghetto by pretending he has a radio and is listening in on the BBC World Service. He fabricates stories of the victories of the Russians and their military advance, which will lead to the Nazi overthrow and the liberation of those being oppressed. The whole community is transformed by these stories of hope. Similar narratives may be seen in other treatments of Holocaust prisoners, who, on hearing the Allied bombers above or catching fragments of news that indicate that the Nazis are being defeated, are filled with hope and ecstasy, knowing that their redemption is drawing near. In *Jacob the Liar* the ghetto doctor informs Jacob that since he shared his message of hope, no one has committed suicide.

Christ is coming to collect us. Signs will show that his arrival is just around the corner. However fearful the signs, ultimately they speak hope for the saints. The saints are this world's heralds of hope.

5. Faithfulness

> *Who then is the faithful and wise servant, whom the master has put in charge of the servants in his household to give them their food at the proper time? It will be good for that servant whose master finds him doing so when he returns. (Matt. 24:45–46)*

Well done, good and faithful servant! You have been faithful with
a few things; I will put you in charge of many things. (Matt.
25:21)

God is looking for those with responsibilities to fulfill them. God
is looking for a return on his investment. He wants to see that we have
gone to work with what he has given us. The talents need to be invested,
the light needs to shine, the salt needs to improve taste and prevent corruption. Paul said to the Corinthians, "You do not lack any spiritual gift
as you eagerly wait for our Lord Jesus Christ" (1 Cor. 1:7). Those gifts
are not toys, but tools. They are to be put to work. Until he comes, the
church is expected to utilize in the service of the kingdom all that God
has invested in us. What has God put in our hand? What gifts, calling,
talents, responsibilities, and privileges has he afforded us? Are we fulfilling them? Are we becoming who we are called to be, being where we
are called to be, doing what we are called to do? The Lord is looking to
reward faithful servants. While salvation is secure for those who trust
in Christ, our position and privileges in eternity will be determined by
how faithfully we have discharged our responsibilities on earth.

6. Witness

And this gospel of the kingdom will be preached in the whole
world as a testimony to all nations, and then the end will come.
(Matt. 24:14)

The final sign before the return of the King is the gospel reaching
the nations. It is uncertain whether the exact date of Christ's return is
set, or whether the circumstances are yet right. Have all the nations

been reached with the gospel? The fact is that numerous tribes and peoples have still to receive an authentic gospel witness in their native tongue. The disciples asked Jesus before his ascension whether now was the time when he intended to restore the end-time kingdom to Israel (Acts 1:6). Jesus did not reply by saying their question was invalid, their theology flawed, their expectation misconceived. In fact his answer suggested the opposite: The kingdom reign of God on earth will be established, the Father has set the times and dates "by his own authority" (Acts 1:7), but the time is not yet right. The task ahead, which must take place before the kingdom is established in its fullness and glory, is to be "witnesses in Jerusalem, and in all Judea and Samaria, and to the ends of the earth" (Acts 1:8). Worship in heaven is to be facilitated by a choir with representatives from every tribe and language, people and nation (Rev. 7:9). For that to happen, the gospel must have reached every tribe and every tongue.

Jesus is not returning to a thin bride, but to a plump one, a large church. Hell must be depopulated and the world evangelized and won for Jesus.

7. Express it now

> *Your kingdom come,*
> *your will be done*
> *on earth as it is in heaven. (Matt. 6:10)*

We pray here to Christ for the coming of Christ the King and also for the advent of the new heaven and the new earth that he will establish. We are to express, to talk about, the future kingdom now. Looking forward to it, we work for it (2 Peter 3:13–14). G. E. Ladd said, "The church should always live with a sense of urgency, feeling the presence of the end."[7] That urgency must lead to activity, an activity that reflects in the present what we see by faith in the future. Stanley Grenz comments, "Eschatology is a call to action in the present based on God's future."[8]

As the church we are to model the eternal kingdom to come partially, proleptically (meaning "in anticipation/advance"), and prophetically. Partially, because heaven will come in its fullness only when Christ returns; proleptically, because it anticipates the future now; prophetically, because what we build is intended to focus others on what Christ is building. We do this through communicating the nature and character of that eternal rule of God, through our preaching, praying, praising, and practical works. We are an eschatological people, an outpost of heaven—the reign of God on earth. The church is a foretaste of tomorrow's eternal kingdom today.

We are to live, move, and have our being in the hope of the future. The Holy Spirit's coming was the inauguration of the new age and an anticipation of the eternal one (Heb. 6:4f.). We are called to partner with the Spirit in every aspect of his work in the world, to prefigure his eschatological reign. G. K. Berkouwer says, "Eschatology is not a projection into the distant future, it bursts into our present existence and structures life today in the light of the last days."[9] The Spirit drives the church forward, toward the coming of Christ in the future. Like gardeners, we have been tending the kingdom as she grows from a mustard seed toward her glorious eternal destiny to be worn as a garland in the crown of King Jesus at his second coming.

The eternal rule, the vision and powers of the age to come that we have glimpsed in the future, must season our life now. We do not simply batten down the hatches and wait for the Lord's return, working on our personal sanctification while we await our beatification. We are to seek the sanctification and beatification of all that frames human existence in the light of that glorious vision. In the renewed heaven on earth, there will be no room for ecological disasters caused by human greed and neglected husbandry. Let us learn to love, respect, and enjoy now what—once re-created—will be our eternal home.

A false, overspiritualized vision of heaven may lead us to abandon the present, the natural, the physical, and the material. But a vision of the earth re-created and renewed, physically, materially, should lead us to treasure and nurture it.

> *Let's get architecture redeemed, painting redeemed, technology redeemed, and dancing redeemed. Let's bring them back into the pure creature stream of God's love and let's rejoice in the fact that what is redeemed will have a place in our eternal home.*[10]

In heaven there will be no racism, no sexism, no elitism, and no intellectualism. All life will be recognized fully as reflecting God, precious to him and of infinite worth. Let us model heaven on earth by refusing to erect barriers and hold prejudices, and let us seek by the Spirit's help to model the true *liberté, égalité, fraternité*, for which secular idealistic states have longed but have been powerless to produce. David Lawrence powerfully provokes us, saying that "if beggars are at the banquet in heaven, this must surely influence who we invite to our banquets in this age."[11]

"COME, COME, COME"

Each day I take my two sons to school. I accompany Nathanael, the youngest (age seven) to his classroom and we go through a routine. He takes off his cycle helmet and hangs it on his peg, then he hangs up his rucksack, then his coat, then his hoodie, and finally we hug and kiss good-bye. On one occasion I was in a hurry to get to work so I said I didn't have time to wait for him to hang his kit up and could he just say good-bye quickly. He replied, hurt, "*NO—I save the best till last.*" Jesus may seem like he's taking his time—we may feel we would like him to get on with it—but he is not in a hurry, and he has saved the best till last, the embrace of his beloved church. In Revelation 22:17–20, Scripture draws to a close with two longing calls. The Spirit and the bride call out to a thirsty world to come and take the free gift of the water of life. The church exists to invite the world to "Come" to Christ while there is still time. Then the church cries out to our beloved, "Come, Lord Jesus"—longing for our glorious wedding.

ENDNOTES

INTRODUCTION

1. T. LaHaye and J. Jenkins, Left Behind series, 16 vols. (Wheaton, IL: Tyndale House, 1995 onward).

2. See, R. Cooper and R. Layard, eds., *What the Future Holds* (Massachusetts: First MIT Press, 2003).

3. See www.raptureready.com/rap2.html.

4. I am an Englishman, after all.

5. B. E. Daley, *The Hope of the Early Church* (Massachusetts: Hendrickson, 2003), 97.

6. R. A. Knox, *Enthusiasm* (Oxford: Oxford University Press, 1950), 110.

7. This constant unrealized expectancy of the end of the age is detailed in the classic treatment by I. Murray, *The Puritan Hope* (London: Banner of Truth Trust, 1971), xix.

8. W. Craig, *What Does God Know?* (Georgia: RZIM, 2002).

9. This summary is drawn from R. Culver, *Systematic Theology* (Tain, Scotland: Mentor Press, 2005), 1008; and J. Garrett, *Systematic Theology,* vol. 2 (Grand Rapids, MI: Eerdmans, 1995), 647.

10. Culver, *Systematic Theology*, 1008.

11. Quoted by Daley, *The Hope of the Early Church*, ix.

12. The great appearing of the Messiah at the close of the age.

13. F. F. Bruce, in W. A. Elwell, *Evangelical Dictionary of Theology* (Grand Rapids, MI: Baker Book House 2001). See mb-soft.com/believe/text/eschatol.htm.

14. Quoted by G. M. Burge in his article "Realize," in ibid. See mb-soft.com/believe/text/eschatol.htm.

15. K. Barth, *The Epistle to the Romans* (London: Oxford University Press, 1963), 314.

16. J. Moltmann, *Theology of Hope* (London: SCM Press, 1967).

17. Ibid., 16.

CHAPTER 1

1. *Educating Rita*, 1983, screenplay by Willy Russell, Acorn Pictures Ltd. Quoted in "Despair," in D. Lyle Jeffrey ed., *Dictionary of Biblical Tradition in Literature* (Grand Rapids, MI: Eerdmans, 1992), 198.

2. Oxford University Center for Suicide Research; see www.psychiatry.ox.ac.uk/csr/statistics.html.

3. Quoted in "Despair," in Jeffrey ed., *Dictionary of Biblical Tradition in Literature*, 198.

4. Quoted in Introduction, ibid.

5. J.-P. Sartre, *The Age of Reason* (London: Penguin, 1973), 49f.

6. A. Kelly, *Eschatology and Hope* (New York: Orbis Press, 2006), 209.

7. The following discussion is drawn from E. Hoffmann, "Hope," in C. Brown ed., *New International Dictionary of New Testament Theology,* vol. 2 (Grand Rapids, MI: Zondervan, 1986), 238–246.

8. B. E. Daley, *The Hope of the Early Church,* (Massachusetts: Hendrickson, 2003), 217.

9. See ibid., 217–220.

10. See T. Aquinas, *Summa Theologica*, 21-2ae.20.3.

11. See www.pathguy.com/julian.htm.

12. Quoted in I. Murray, *The Puritan Hope* (London: Banner of Truth Trust, 1971), xii.

13. Quoted in *Our Daily Bread*, 17 April 1995.

14. S. T. Coleridge, "Work without Hope," found at www.bartelby.net/101/554.html.

15. St. Augustine, *De Doctrina Christiana*, 1.15.14.

16. Hoffmann, "Hope," 239.

17. G. C. Berkouwer, *Studies in Dogmatics: The Return of Christ* (Grand Rapids, MI: Eerdmans, 1972), 11.

18. Hoffmann, "Hope," 244.

19. Ibid., 240.

20. Kelly, *Eschatology and Hope*, 211.

21. F. Kerstiens, "Hope," in K. Rahner, ed., *Sacramentum Mundi*, vol. 3 (London: Burns and Oates, 1969), 61.

22. Cited by Kerstiens, ibid., 62.

23. S. Grenz, *Theology for the Community of God* (Carlisle: Paternoster, 1994), 855.

24. Moltmann, *The Theology of Hope*, 225.

25. B. Haynes, in J. Colwell ed., *Called to One Hope* (Carlisle: Paternoster, 2000), 181.

26. Kelly, *Eschatology and Hope*, 212.

27. C. S. Lewis, *Mere Christianity* (London: HarperCollins, 2002), 116.

28. Words by Edmond Budry (1854–1932).

CHAPTER 2

1. W. Bauer, *A Greek-English Lexicon of the New Testament and Other Early Christian Literature*, tr. and augmented by W. F. Arndt and F. W. Gingrich, 2nd ed. (Chicago: University of Chicago Press, 1979); see entry for "Basileia", 134f.

2. See the article "Kingdom," at http://www.jewishencyclopedia.com/view.jsp?artid=225&letter=K. Here the author writes that Malkut Shaddai is synonymous with Malkut Shamayim; see also BAGD, "Basileia", 134f.

3. Quoted in J. Garrett, *Systematic Theology*, vol. 2 (Grand Rapids, MI: Eerdmans, 1995), 728.

4. J. Rodman Williams, *Renewal Theology*, vol. 3 (Grand Rapids, MI: Zondervan, 1996), 290.

5. W. D. Davies and D. Allison, *International Critical Commentary, Matthew*, vol. II (Edinburgh: T. & T. Clark, 1991), 340.

6. Garrett, *Systematic Theology*, 731.

7. In private correspondence.

8. J. Burgh, *Political Disquisitions: Or, an Enquiry into Public Errors, Defects, and Abuses* (London: E. & C. Dilly, 1774), 390.

9. S. Kim, "Kingdom of God," in R. P. Martin and P. Davids, eds., *Dictionary of the Later New Testament and its Developments* (Leicester: IVP, 1997), 629–638.

10. See www.bu.edu/wwildman/WeirdWildWeb/courses/mwt/dictionary/mwt_themes_200_augustine.htm.

11. Garrett, *Systematic Theology*, 733.

12. J. Calvin, *Institutes of the Christian Religion,* ed. J. T. McNeil (Philadelphia: Westminster Press, 1960), III.3.19.

13. See www.myriobiblos.gr/texts/english/christou_byzemperor.html.

14. See R. McBrien, *Catholicism*, 3rd ed. (London: Geoffrey Chapman, 1966), 1154.

15. Ibid., 1155.

16. See www2.gol.com/users/quakers/Hicks_Peaceable_Kingdom.htm.

17. For the full text, see www.kingdomnow.org/withinyou.html.

18. F. Nietzsche, *The Anti Christ* (Amherst, NY: Prometheus Books, 2000), 34.

19. See www.mises.org/books/socialism/part3_ch17.aspx; and www.anglocatholicsocialism.org/socialistchristiancatechiism.html.

20. See www.mbrem.com/eschatology/post1.htm.

21. (Rochester, NY, 1886), 887.

22. C. Caragounis, "Kingdom of God," in I. H. Marshall and J. Green, eds., *Dictionary of Jesus and the Gospels* (Leicester: IVP, 1991), 417–430, esp. 421.

23. G. E. Ladd, *Jesus and the Kingdom* (London: SPCK, 1966), 331.

24. Ibid., 334.

25. Caragounis, "Kingdom of God," 423.

26. L. Kreitzer, "Kingdom," in G. F. Hawthorne, R. P. Martin and D. G. Reid, eds., *Dictionary of Paul and his Epistles* (Leicester: IVP, 1993), 525.

27. H. G. Wells, *A Short History of the World* (London: Cassell, 1922), chapter 37.

CHAPTER 3

1. L. Boettner, "Death, Immortality and the Intermediate State," at www.gospelpedlar.com/articles/last%20Things/immortality.html.

2. V. White, *Life Beyond Death: Threads of Hope in Faith, Life and Theology* (London: Darton, Longman and Todd, 2006), 1. In this section I am indebted to White's excellent work. www.scienceblog.com/community/older/archives/G/ucb1004.html – 17k -

3. D. Thomas, *Collected Poems* 1934–1953 (London: Phoenix Press, 2000).

4. W. Schmittals, "Death," in C. Brown, ed., *New International Dictionary of New Testament Theology*, vol. 1 (Grand Rapids, MI: Zondervan, 1986.)

5. See shepherdpress.com/product.php?productid=16173&cat=0&page=1.

6. Boettner, "Death, Immortality and the Intermediate State."

7. M. J. Erickson, *Christian Theology* (Grand Rapids, MI: Baker Book House, 1983), 1171f.

8. M. Dahood, *The Psalms*, Anchor Bible Series, 3 vols (London/New York: Doubleday, 1995); R. McBrien, *Catholicism* (London: Geoffrey Chapman, 1966), 1159. The Catholic scholar Professor Dahood claimed that he saw numerous references to resurrection in the Psalms, while the Catholic scholar Professor McBrien found only glimmers of this in the later post-exilic materials.

9. See the detailed treatment of death in the New Testament in Schmittals, "Death."

10. The OT generally refers to "soul" as a person's inner, individual, eternal, unique being, whereas the NT Greek generally uses the term "spirit." Where both "spirit" and "soul" are found together in the NT, "soul" refers to the mind/intellect or will of the individual (1 Thess. 5:23).

11. See the interesting thoughts on this by Augustine in *The City of God*, Book XIII, Ch. 20.

12. J. Calvin, *Institutes of the Christian Religion*, ed. J. T. McNeil (Philadelphia: Westminster Press, 1960), III.25.997.

13. See H. Schwartz, in C. Braaten and R. Jensen, eds., *Christian Dogmatics* (Philadelphia: Fortress Press, 1984), 568.

14. Erickson, *Christian Theology*, 1179; see also Thomas Aquinas on purgatory through penal sufferings, in *Summa Contra Gentiles*, 4.91, and *Summa Theologica*, Q1, article 2.

15. McBrien, *Catholicism*, 1170.

16. See www.eliteskills.com/c/11892, full text and analysis of the poem "Death Be Not Proud."

17. See detailed essay about Martin Luther and William Tyndale on the state of the dead at www.aloha.net/~mikesch/luther-tyndale.htm.

18. Boettner, "Death, Immortality and the Intermediate State."

19. Calvin, *Institutes of the Christian Religion*, III.28.998.

20. R. Culver, *Systematic Theology* (Tain, Scotland: Mentor Press, 2005), 1034–42.

21. R. Latourelle, "Death," in *Dictionary of Fundamental Theology* (Slough: St. Paul's Press, 1994), 214.

22. See article on Bonhoeffer's faith, at www.religion-online.org/showarticle. asp?title=1928.

Chapter 4

1. J. Garrett, *Systematic Theology*, vol. 2 (Grand Rapids, MI: Eerdmans, 1995), 768.

2. P. Toon, *Puritans, the Millennium and the Future of Israel*, Library of Ecclesiastical History (Edinburgh: James Clarke & Co., reprinted 2002), 8f.

3. Eusebius, *History of the Church*, rev. ed. (London: Penguin Classics, 1989), 111.39, 11–12.

4. St. Augustine, *City of God* (London: Penguin, 2003 edition), 906–23.

5. The Donatists were a breakaway church movement who refused fellowship with any Christians who had handed over sacred writings in the persecutions under Diocletian. Ministers and bishops who had become "traitors" were reinstated by Constantine, but the Donatists refused to recognize their authority.

6. See Augustine, *City of God*, Book 20, Chs. 7–23, pp. 906–944.

7. Treated by B. E. Daley, *The Hope of the Early Church* (Massachusetts: Hendrickson, 2003), 131f.

8. See Toon, *Puritans, the Milliennium and the Future of Israel*, 17.

9. Quoted in Braaten and Jensen, *Christian Dogmatics*, 509.

10. J. Calvin, *Institutes of the Christian Religion*, ed. J. T. McNeil (Philadelphia: Westminster Press, 1960), XXV.5.995.

11. See Toon, *Puritans, the Millennium and the Future of Israel*, ch. 5.

12. David Pawson has suggested several subdivisions, including spiritual postmillennialism, political postmillennialism, skeptical amillennialism, and mythical amillennialism.

13. M. Wilks ed., *Prophecy and Eschatology, Studies in Church History 10* (Oxford: Blackwells, 1994), 236f.

14. See www.biblicist.org/bible/dominion.shtml.

15. The following has been suggested by David White in private correspondence.

16. See en.wikipedia.org/wiki/Dispensationalism.

17. Schwarz, *Eschatology*, 333.

18. See Garrett, *Systematic Theology*, 746f.

19. G. B. Caird, *The Revelation of St. John the Divine*, 2nd ed. (London: A. & C. Black, 1984), 249.

20. For lengthy balanced treatments, see S. Grenz, *The Millennial Maze* (Downers Grove, IL: IVP, 1992); D. Pawson, *When Jesus Returns* (London: Hodder & Stoughton, 1995); M. J. Erickson, *A Basic Guide to Eschatology: Making Sense of the Millennium* (Grand Rapids, MI: Baker Book House, 1999).

21. Helpfully summarized by Garrett, *Systematic Theology*, 750.

22. S. Grenz, *Theology for the Community of God* (Carlisle: Paternoster, 1994), 799–810.

23. Pawson, *When Jesus Returns*, 259.

24. I am grateful to Neville Jones who in private correspondence has offered this view, which I find compelling.

25. J. Moltmann, *The Coming of God* (London: SCM, 1996), 201.

26. G. K. Beale, *The Book of Revelation, New International Greek New Testament Commentary* (Carlisle: Paternoster, 1999), 1018.

27. L. J. Kreitzer, "Apocalyptic," in R. P. Martin and P. H. Davids, eds., *Dictionary of the Later New Testament and its Developments* (Leicester: IVP, 1997), esp. 62.

28. Note that the key eschatological texts about the Day of the Lord have no sense whatsoever of the restraining of the Enemy for a thousand-year period while Christ reigns, before the last conflict and final judgment. See Matthew 24; 1 Thessalonians 4:16—5:11; 2 Peter 3:10–13.

29. R. Mounce, *The Book of Revelation, New International Commentary on the New Testament* (Grand Rapids, MI: Eerdmans, 1977), 351.

30. Beale offers the most careful presentation of an amillennial reading of the first resurrection and second death.

31. See J. Rodman Williams, *Renewal Theology*, vol. 3 (Grand Rapids, MI: Zondervan, 1996), 421.

32. Beale, *The Book of Revelation*, 991.

33. Ibid., 983f.

34. Quoted by G. C. Berkouwer, *Studies in Dogmatics: The Return of Christ* (Grand Rapids, MI: Eerdmans, 1972), 294.

35. Ibid.

36. Schwarz, *Eschatology*, 337.

CHAPTER 5

1. See www.abcog/nh/signs.htm.

2. See www.raptureready.com.

3. A remarkable, if rather dense, treatment of this is E. Weber's *Apocalypse: Prophesies, Cults and Millennial Beliefs throughout the Ages* (London: Hutchinson, 1999).

4. J. Hosier, *The Lamb, the Beast and the Devil* (London: Monarch Press, 2002), 65f.

5. BAGD: W. Bauer, *A Greek-English Lexicon of the New Testament and Other Early Christian Literature*, tr. and augmented by W. F. Arndt and F. W. Gingrich, 2nd ed. (Chicago: University of Chicago Press, 1979), see Tote, 823f.; Telos, 811f.

6. For the complete account by Josephus, see www.preteristarchive.com/JewishWars/.

7. F. D. Bruner, *Matthew*, vol. 2 (Dallas: Word Publishing, 1990), 876.

8. U. Luz, *Matthew 21—28, Hermeneia Commentaries* (Minneapolis: Fortress Press, 2005), 84.

9. Ibid., 184–189. This summary, like the rest of the commentary, makes it stand out from the crowd.

10. H. Schwarz, *Eschatology* (Grand Rapids, MI: Eerdmans, 2000), 383.

11. G. C. Berkouwer, *Studies in Dogmatics: The Return of Christ* (Grand Rapids, MI: Eerdmans, 1972), 243.

12. Ibid., 245.

13. Hosier, *The Lamb, the Beast and the Devil*, 66.

14. Berkouwer, *Studies in Dogmatics*, 245.

15. D. Pawson, *When Jesus Returns* (London: Hodder & Stoughton, 1995), 18–30.

16. J. Ratzinger, *Dogmatic Theology of Eschatology—Death and Life* (Washington DC: Catholic University Press of America, 1988), 196–200. Ratzinger takes the abomination that causes desolation to be a person who desecrates God's sanctuary, and believes Romans 11:26 and the conversion to

Israel within historical time is a necessary preliminary before the ending of time (196–197).

17. See www.thepost.coza/index.php?/articleID.

18. See en.wikipedia.org/wiki/Famine.

19. See www.earthquake.usgs.gov/regional/neic; www.indiadaily.com/editorial/13772. asp; www.planet-x.150m.com/quakes.html.

20. See www.human-rights-and-christian-persecution.org.

21. See http://www.avert.org/uksummary.htm.

22. See www.crimestatistics.org.uk.

23. See http://www.lausanneworldpulse.com/peoplesoftheworld/25/09-2005.

24. That said, it is conceivable that the population migration and ethnic integration will speed gospel presentation: There will be less need for witnessing to indigenous peoples in the jungle or outback, and consequently less need to learn their own tribal tongue, as they are moving toward the cities and learning generic languages such as Spanish, English, Chinese, Urdu, Hindi, and Arabic.

25. Weber, *Apocalypse*, 50.

26. Ibid.

27. Ibid., 101.

CHAPTER 6

1. The most comprehensive historical presentation of this is E. Weber's *Apocalypse: Prophesies, Cults and Millennial Beliefs throughout the Ages* (London: Hutchinson, 1999), to which I am indebted throughout this section.

2. Quoted in ibid., 75f.

3. Ibid., 76.

4. J. Calvin, *Institutes of the Christian Religion*, ed. J. T. McNeil (Philadelphia: Westminster Press, 1960), IV.7.

5. See www.wels.net/cgi-bin/site.pl?2617&collectionID=795&contentID=4441&sho rtcutID=5297.

6. Weber, *Apocalypse*, 205.

7. See www.unaoc.org.

8. B. D. Forbes and J. Halgen Kilde, eds., *Rapture, Revelation and the End Times—Explaining the Left Behind Series* (New York: Palgrave, Macmillan, 2004), 168f.

9. A substantial text that explores many of the latest designated antichrists and exposes many of the moves toward a global religious system is the Catholic Lee Penn's *False Dawn* (Hillsdale, NY: Sophia Perennis, 2004).

10. See the syncretistic religious agenda at www.uri.org.

11. Such a view misinterprets this phrase; "the desire of women" could refer to any number of things, including marriage, security, Israel, peace, the Messiah ...

12. For further discussion and challenge to the supposition of a Jewish Antichrist, see F. Wright ed., *Israel, His People, His Land, His Story* (London: Monarch, 2002), 310.

13. D. F. Watson, "Antichrist," in R. P. Martin and P. Davids, eds., *Dictionary of the Later New Testament and its Developments* (Leicester: IVP, 1997), 51.

14. As Stephen Smalley suggests, and not without merit. See S. Smalley, *1, 2, 3 John, Word Biblical Commentary* (Milton Keynes: Word, 1991), 99.

15. See J. Hosier, *The Lamb, the Beast and the Devil* (London: Monarch Press, 2002), 107; Smalley, 1, 2, 3 John, 99.

16. H. Schwarz *Eschatology*, (Grand Rapids, MI: Eerdmans, 2000), 385.

17. Smalley, *1, 2, 3 John*, 100.

18. A point recognized by New Testament exegete J. Green, *The Letters to the Thessalonians*, (Leicester: Apollos, 2002), 317, who sees the parallel between 2 Thessalonians 2 and 1 John 2—between the plural antichrists preceding the coming of the one Antichrist and the secret power of lawlessness preceding the appearance of the Lawless One.

19. Among the most recent, judicious, and substantial evangelical interpretations, carefully weighing the alternative positions, is G. K. Beale, *The Book of Revelation, New International Greek New Testament Commentary* (Carlisle: Paternoster, 1999).

20. G. C. Berkouwer, *Studies in Dogmatics: The Return of Christ* (Grand Rapids, MI: Eerdmans, 1972), 261.

21. R. Mounce, *The Book of Revelation, New International Commentary on the New Testament*, (Grand Rapids, MI: Eerdmans, 1977), 249.

22. Ibid., 259.

23. A. J. Beagley, "Beasts, Dragons, Sea conflict motif," in Martin and Davids (eds), *Dictionary of the Later New Testament and its Developments*, 127f. See also Mounce, *The Book of Revelation*, 252.

24. Quoted in Mounce, ibid., 258.

25. For a detailed discussion of gematria, and the numerous possible titleholders of 666, see Beale, *The Book of Revelation*, 718–728.

26. See www.sacred-texts.com/cla/sib/sib03.htm.

27. See en.wikipedia.org/wiki/Antichrist.

28. Quoted in Mounce, *The Book of Revelation*, 265.

29. I am grateful to Stephen Rathbone, historian and student of eschatology, who has helped me considerably in thinking through this chapter.

CHAPTER 7

1. America is perhaps Israel's only sustained supporter, but the relationship is complex. America is widely disapproved of because of her relationship with Israel, and Israel because of her relationship with America.

2. "Zionism," in *The Shorter Oxford English Dictionary*, 6th ed. (Oxford: Oxford University Press, 2007).

3. See en.wikipedia.org/wiki/UN_General_Assembly_Resolution_4686; en.wikipedia.org/wiki/United_Nations_General_Assembly_Resolution_3379.

4. It is possible, however, that Carey acted as he did because he perceived that to call a ministry to the Jews by this name would naturally cause defenses to go up before any dialogue concerning the gospel could be started—that is, his intention was not to stop evangelizing Jews, but rather to respect their integrity in first listening to them, and only then expect them to listen to the gospel.

5. D. Moo, *The Epistle to the Romans, New International Commentary on the New Testament* (Grand Rapids, MI: Eerdmans, 1996), 710.

6. Throughout this section I am relying on the detailed work in the Wikipedia electronic encyclopedia article "Christianity and Anti-Semitism." This is one of the best articles I have found on the Web, full, footnoted, accurate, and scholarly.

7. See R. Gellately, *Backing Hitler* (Oxford: Oxford University Press, 2001)—a scholarly work proving that the Nazi machine operated with the consensual knowledge of German society at large.

8. B. Schlink, *Israel My Chosen People* (Basingstoke: Marshall Pickering, 1987), 13.

9. I. Murray, *The Puritan Hope* (London: Banner of Truth Trust, 1971), 41.

10. P. Toon, *Puritans, the Millennium and the Future of Israel, Library of Ecclesiastical History*, (Edinburgh: James Clarke & Co., reprinted 2002), 115f.

11. Quoted at www.mideastweb.org/britzion.htm.

12. Murray, *The Puritan Hope*, 100.

13. Quoted in *A Nation Called by God*, published by Love Never Fails, 2–4.

14. Ibid.

15. See F. Wright ed., *Israel, His People, His Land, His Story* (London: Monarch, 2002), 289–290.

16. See www.shoaheducation.com/balf.html.

17. On the Hussein/McMahon correspondence, see www.israelipalestinianprocon.org/bin/procon/procon.cgi?database=5-H-Subs.db&command=viewone&id=31&op=.

18. See en.wikipedia.org/wiki/Palestine_(mandate).

19. For a detailed account of this foundation of the state of Israel, see M. Gilbert, *Israel a History* (London: Black Swan Publishers, 1999), which presents the tumultuous days leading up to and following the declaration of independence and the complex web of political relations. Note especially chapter 8.

20. Some commentators like David Pawson and Derek Prince have suggested that the dismantling of Britain's empire, which began the year they relinquished the mandate, was a divine judgment on Britain for her failure to act righteously. Others reject this, noting that Britain actually saw her empire crumble only after Suez, when Britain supported Israel. In fact the end of the empire was a consequence of the shift in geopolitics following World War II, when all colonial empires—France, Belgium, Britain—saw the collapse of their power.

21. The scriptural boundaries of the land are set out in Deuteronomy 1:7f. and Joshua 1:4f., from the Euphrates to the Mediterranean—hence the design of the Jewish flag, with two blue stripes representing the water-marked boundaries, while the white in the middle represents the land over which is the morning star of David.

22. Neville Jones in private correspondence.

23. Wright ed., *Israel, His People, His Land, His Story*, 288.

24. D. Block, *Ezekiel 25—48, New International Commentary on the Old Testament* (Grand Rapids, MI: Eerdmans, 1998).

25. G. Burge, *Whose Land, Whose Promise?* (Carlisle: Paternoster, 2003).

26. This makes sober reading: see www.dci-pal.org/english/PrinterF. cfm?DocId=504&CategoryID=16.

27. Joan Peters, *From Time Immemorial* (Chicago: JKAP Publications, 2002).

28. See www.yale.edu/lawweb/avalon/mideast/israel.htm.

29. The history of the Zionist/Arab conflict is a very complex one and we find blood on the hands of both sides. A powerful and exhaustive work is B. Morris, *Righteous Victims* (New York: Vintage Books, Random Press, 2001).

30. Burge, *Whose Land, Whose Promise?*, 240.

31. Quoted in N. T. Wright, *Jesus and the Victory of God* (London: SPCK, 1996), 212.

32. N. T. Wright, "The Letter to the Romans," commentary in E. L. Keck et al. eds., *The New Interpreter's Bible* (Nashville: Abingdon Press, 1971), 698.

33. C. Chapman, *Whose Promised Land?* (Grand Rapids, MI: Baker Books, 2003), 282.

34. See the decent presentation of this view in S. Wohlberg, *End Time Delusions* (Shippenburg, PA: Treasure House, 2004), 153–157, a book that elsewhere is popular and perhaps quirky.

35. See the detailed essay on Jesus the True Israel at www.leithart.com/pdf/jesus-as-israel-the-typological-structure-of-matthew-s-gospel.pdf.

36. Quoted in J. Hosier, *The Lamb, the Beast and the Devil* (London: Monarch Press, 2002), 117.

37. Burge, *Whose Land, Whose Promise?*, 172f.

38. See Chapman, *Whose Promised Land?*, 160f., for the counterargument.

39. G. C. Berkouwer, *Studies in Dogmatics: The Return of Christ* (Grand Rapids, MI: Eerdmans, 1972), 348.

40. See Wright's New Interpreter's commentary, "The Letter to the Romans," on this verse. Wright did his DPhil on Romans 9—11, and he moved to this view from the classic evangelical one. He writes of this shift on his Web page, www.ntwrightpage.com/Wright_My_Pilgrimage.htm. He has taken this line just as most scholars have rejected it.

41. Discussed in J. Fitzmyer, *Romans*, Anchor Bible Commentary (London: Geoffrey Chapman, 1992), section 41.

42. Ibid., 623.

43. J. Dunn, *Romans 9—16, Word Biblical Commentary* (Dallas: Word Publishing, 1988), 681.

44. C. E. B. Cranfield, *Romans IX—XVI, International Critical Commentary* (Edinburgh: T. & T. Clark, 1979), 577.

45. Ibid., 575.

46. This appears to be the drift in J. Doukhan, *Israel and the Church, Two Voices for the Same God* (Peabody, MA: Hendrickson, 2002).

47. M. J. Erickson, *Christian Theology* (Grand Rapids, MI: Baker Book House, 1983), 1043.

48. L. Lambert, *The Uniqueness of Israel* (Eastbourne: Kingsway, 1980), 146.

49. J. Rodman Williams, *Renewal Theology*, vol. 3 (Grand Rapids, MI: Zondervan, 1996), 323.

50. Ibid., 15.

51. Hosier, *The Lamb, the Beast and the Devil*, 125.

52. D. Prince, "Our Debt to Israel," www.derekprince.com, 2.

53. Moo, *The Epistle to the Romans*, 726.

CHAPTER 8

1. J. Ratzinger, *Dogmatic Theology of Eschatology—Death and Life* (Washington, DC: Catholic University Press of America, 1988), 197.

2. S. N. Gundry, ed., *Three Views on the Rapture* (Grand Rapids, MI: Zondervan, 1996); M. J. Erickson, *A Basic Guide to Eschatology: Making Sense of the Millennium* (Grand Rapids, MI: Baker Book House, 1999).

3. S. E. Porter, "Tribulation and Messianic Woes," in R. P. Martin and P. Davids, eds., *Dictionary of the Later New Testament and its Developments* (Leicester: IVP, 1997), 1179–1182.

4. Erickson, *A Basic Guide to Eschatology*, 153.

5. Surely the book of Job is the classic scriptural witness to such a thesis. Did Jesus not learn obedience through the things he suffered (Heb. 12)?

6. Erickson, *A Basic Guide to Eschatology*, 152.

7. J. Rodman Williams, *Renewal Theology*, vol. 3 (Grand Rapids, MI: Zondervan, 1996), 378, 364.

8. Quoted in R. Mounce, *The Book of Revelation, New International Commentary on the New Testament* (Grand Rapids, MI: Eerdmans, 1977), 120.

9. J. Hosier, *The Lamb, the Beast and the Devil* (London: Monarch Press, 2002), 30.

10. An idea suggested to me by Neville Jones.

11. Possible interpretations are discussed by G. K. Beale, *The Book of Revelation, New International Greek New Testament Commentary* (Carlisle: Paternoster, 1999), 784f. He concludes that a futurist view is possible in understanding chapter 15 as the final events of history, though he opts to understand them not as last in the course of history, but as last in the visions representing the complete expression of God's wrath. Beale sees them as a retrospective historical experience of judgment, explaining in greater detail God's wrath on the world "before what is depicted in ch. 14" (p. 786).

12. Some premillennialists would alter this outline, placing the millennium rule in it and the rapture either before or after this.

13. R. G. Glouse, "Rapture," in *Elwell Dictionary of Theology*, online at mb-soft.com/believe/txw/rapture.htm.

14. For a whole host of dispensational and rapture-ready Web links, see www.bibleprophecy.org/links.htm.

15. J. F. Walvoord, *The Rapture Question* (Grand Rapids, MI: Zondervan, 1979).

16. See www.leftbehind.com/channelendtimes.asp?pageid=518&channelID=71.

17. Cited and discussed in B. D. Forbes and J. Halgen Kilde, eds., *Rapture, Revelation and the End Times—Explaining the Left Behind Series* (New York: Palgrave, Macmillan, 2004), 80.

18. D. Pawson, *When Jesus Returns* (London: Hodder & Stoughton, 1995), 179.

19. See BAGD: W. Bauer, *A Greek-English Lexicon of the New Testament and Other Early Christian Literature*, tr. and augmented by W. F. Arndt and F. W. Gingrich, 2nd ed. (Chicago: University of Chicago Press, 1979), 'harpaxo', 109.

20. R. Culver, *Systematic Theology* (Christian Focus Publications, Mentor Press, 2005), 1132.

21. J. Green, *The Letters to the Thessalonians* (Leicester: Apollos, 2002), 229.

22. Discussed by Forbes and Kilde eds, *Rapture, Revelation and the End Times*, 80ff.

23. Pawson, *When Jesus Returns*, 189.

24. See www.according2prophecy.org/rapsec.html; www.pre-trib.org/article-view.php?id=252; www.raptureready.com/featured/RaptureBeforeTribulation.html.

25. This powerful story is told in Pawson, *When Jesus Returns*, 199.

26. Williams, *Renewal Theology*, 379.

27. Erickson, *A Basic Guide to Eschatology*, 160.

28. H. Schwarz, *Eschatology* (Grand Rapids, MI: Eerdmans, 2000), 335.

CHAPTER 9

1. R. Schell, "Armageddon," in D. Lyle Jeffrey, ed., *Dictionary of Biblical Tradition in Literature*, (Grand Rapids, MI: Eerdmans, 1992), 55f. Note the title of the military history work by Max Hastings: *Armageddon: The Battle for Germany*, 1944–1945.

2. Justin Huntly McCarthy, "Armageddon," 1914.

3. See www.authorsden.com/visit/viewpoetry.asp?AuthorID=26717&id=145119.

4. See www.mexicanmuralschool.com/gallery2/gal33.htm; www.ebsqart.com/ ArtShows/cmd_71_Exhibition_Entries_4_5_G.htm.

5. See www.urbandictionary.com/define.php?term=armageddon&page=3.

6. For example, in the recent book by B. McGuire, *Surviving Armageddon—Solutions for a Threatened Planet* (Oxford: Oxford University Press, 2005).

7. H. Lindsey, *The Late Great Planet Earth* (Grand Rapids, MI: Zondervan, 1970), 58.

8. Ibid., 153–160.

9. H. Schwarz, *Eschatology* (Grand Rapids, MI: Eerdmans, 2000), 320.

10. See Schell, "Armageddon."

11. I am indebted to the scholarly article by R. W. Cogley, www.britannica.com/ magazine/print?query=cognizant&id=40&minGrade=&maxGrade=.

12. See www.apologeticsindex.org/b10.html.

13. Schwarz, *Eschatology*, 315.

14. G. K. Beale, *The Book of Revelation, New International Greek New Testament Commentary* (Carlisle: Paternoster, 1999), 833.

15. Ibid., 833. See also chapter 4 in this book, "The Millennium Maze."

16. Ibid., 830.

17. Ibid., 833.

18. J. Baldwin, *Haggai, Zechariah and Malachi*, Tyndale Old Testament Commentaries, (Leicester: IVP, 1972), 201.

19. R. Mounce, *The Book of Revelation, New International Commentary on the New Testament*, (Grand Rapids, MI: Eerdmans, 1977), 301.

20. Schell, "Armageddon," 55.

21. E. H. Cline, *The Battles of Armageddon* (Ann Arbor, MI: University of Michigan Press, 2001); www.press.umich.edu/titleDetailDesc.do?id=11583.

22. J. Paulien, "Armageddon," in N. Freedman, ed., *The Anchor Bible Dictionary*, vol. 1 (New York: Doubleday, 1992), 394f.

23. Ibid., 395.

24. Ibid.

25. G. B. Caird, *The Revelation of St. John the Divine*, 2nd ed. (London: A. & C. Black, 1984), 206.

26. Beale, *The Book of Revelation*, 836.

27. Mounce, *The Book of Revelation*, 302.

28. J. Hosier, *The Lamb, the Beast and the Devil* (London: Monarch Press, 2002), 135.

29. Beale, *The Book of Revelation*, 836.

30. Schwarz, *Eschatology*, 321.

31. This is the thesis of the whole book by Stephen Sizer, *Christian Zionism— Roadmap to Armageddon* (Downers Grove, IL: IVP, 2004).

32. Ibid., 196–199.

CHAPTER 10

1. D. Pawson, *When Jesus Returns* (London: Hodder & Stoughton, 1995), 7.

2. See www.creeds.net/ancient/nicene.htm.

3. See people-press.org/reports/display.php3?ReportID=287.

4. See www.islam.tc/prophecies/jesus.html.

5. See www.letusreason.org/Cults15.htm.

6. See bupc.montana.com/index.html.

7. See www.Swedenborg.org/tenets.cfm.

8. See www.unification.org/rev_mrs_moon.html.

9. See J. Garrett, *Systematic Theology*, vol. 2 (Grand Rapids. MI: Eerdmans, 1995), 705.

10. BAGD: W. Bauer, *A Greek-English Lexicon of the New Testament and Other Early Christian Literature*, tr. and augmented by W. F. Arndt and F. W. Gingrich, 2nd ed. (Chicago: University of Chicago Press, 1979), 629.

11. See "Second Coming," in D. Lyle Jeffrey, ed., *Dictionary of Biblical Tradition in Literature*, (Grand Rapids, MI: Eerdmans, 1992), 688f.; also L. Y. Kreitzer, "Parousia," in R. P. Martin and P. Davids eds, *Dictionary of the Later New Testament and its Developments* (Leicester: IVP, 1997), 837.

12. James Garrett cites research suggesting there are 28 references, while David Noakes accounts for 107 references to the phrase "in that day," of which 80 refer to the future day of the Lord; see "The Day of the Lord," in F. Wright, ed., *Israel, His People, His Land, His Story* (London: Monarch, 2002), 38–58.

13. Thanks to Debbie Flint for this apposite illustration.

14. BAGD, 304.

15. Ibid., 811.

16. The term telos here in 1 Corinthians 13 has been read by some to mean not the return of Christ the "perfect one," but all that is associated with the perfecting he brings—total knowledge, immortality, the church in all her spotless perfection at Christ's coming, etc. Some, however, take it to mean the canon of Scripture.

17. BAGD, 92.

18. *The Letters of Samuel Rutherford* (Edinburgh: Banner of Truth Trust, repr. 1973), 192.

19. J. N. D. Kelly, *The Epistles of Peter and Jude* (London: A. & C., Black, 1969), 463.

20. He shares only his name with the famous Scottish Puritan John Knox!

21. This calculation is complex, but based on the significant end-time scriptural dates offered as "time, times and half a time," or three and a half years, a lunar year averaging 360 days. Thus 3.5 x 360 days = 1,260 days. Some take the day here to refer to a year, and thus "time, times and half a time" is taken to mean 1,260 years. For "time, times and half a time" equalling 1,260 days/42 months, see Daniel 7:25; 12:7; Revelation 12:6, 14. For a day as a year, see Numbers 14:34; Ezekiel 4:6; Daniel 9:24. Further information on this calculation can be found at http://biblelight.net/times.htm.

22. See www.gotquestions.org/Jewish-feasts.html.

23. I am drawing heavily on David Pawson's clear presentation on this point.

24. J. N. D. Kelly, *Early Christian Doctrines* (London: A. &. C. Black, 1977), 463.

25. All the details that depict the day of the Lord may happen as a single event, as the bride meets the Lord in the air, the heavens and earth are rolled away and re-created, and men and women are resurrected.

26. Pawson, *When Jesus Returns*, 15.

27. See chapters 5—10 for the catalog of signs that will precede the return of Christ and prepare the watching saints for this event.

28. See the excellent argument in M. J. Erickson, *Christian Theology* (Grand Rapids, MI: Baker Book House, 1983), 1190f.

29. We studied this in some detail in chapter 8.

30. L. Berkhof, *Systematic Theology* (Edinburgh: Banner of Truth Trust, 1939), 707.

CHAPTER 11

1. L. Berkhof, *Systematic Theology* (Edinburgh: Banner of Truth Trust, 1939), 707.

2. J. Ratzinger, *Dogmatic Theology of Eschatology—Death and Life* (Washington, DC: Catholic University Press of America, 1988), 169.

3. Ibid., 174.

4. Revd Arthur Devine, "The Resurrection of the Body," www.angelfire.com/ms/seanie/newage/creedex11.html.

5. J. Moltmann, *The Coming of God* (London: SCM, 1996), 66 (although Jesus made it clear that we would not be given in marriage in heaven and presumably the sensory experience that goes along with sex is sadly not on offer!).

6. Ibid.

7. M. J. Erickson, *Christian Theology* (Grand Rapids, MI: Baker Book House, 1983), 1198.

8. F. Beattie, "The Presbyterian Standards—a commentary on the Westminster Catechism," http://www.shortercatechism.com/resources/beattie/wsc_be_038.html.

9. See www.reformed.org/documents/larger1.html.

10. From an Anglo-Saxon apocalyptic poem entitled *Christ III*, lines 1007–61; see www.apocalyptic-theories.com/literature/christiii/mechristiiib.html.

11. See www.faithnet.org.uk.

12. This section draws on the ever-useful article by R. K. Emmerson, "Last Judgment," in D. Lyle Jeffrey, ed., *Dictionary of Biblical Tradition in Literature* (Grand Rapids, MI: Eerdmans, 1992), 434f.

13. See detailed analysis in T. M. Comiskey, H. Beck and W. Schneider, "Judgment," in C. Brown, ed., *The New International Dictionary of New Testament Theology*, vol. 2 (Grand Rapids, MI: Zondervan, 1986), 362–371.

14. J. N. D. Kelly, *Early Christian Doctrines* (London: A. &. C. Black, 1977), 480f.

15. Ibid., 484.

16. Augustine, *City of God*, Ch. 15:1–6.

17. H. G. Niebuhr, *The Kingdom of God in America* (New York: Harper & Row, 1937), 193.

18. Quoted in E. and C. de Goucourt, *Memoires de la vie litteraire,* Journal, 23 February 1863.

19. "How Jesus bore our sins," in *Church Times*, see www.anglican-mainstream. net/?p=1607.

20. See D. Pawson, *When Jesus Returns* (London: Hodder & Stoughton, 1995), 54f.

21. See J. Garrett, *Systematic Theology*, vol. 2 (Grand Rapids, MI: Eerdmans, 1995), 782f.

22. Pawson, *When Jesus Returns*, 55.

23. Garrett, *Systematic Theology*, 784.

24. Quoted in J. Hosier, *The Lamb, the Beast and the Devil* (London: Monarch Press, 2002), 65.

25. Erickson, *Christian Theology*, 1203.

26. BAGD: W. Bauer, *A Greek-English Lexicon of the New Testament and Other Early Christian Literature*, tr. and augmented by W. F. Arndt and F. W. Gingrich, 2nd ed. (Chicago: University of Chicago Press, 1979), 140.

27. G. C. Berkouwer, *Studies in Dogmatics: The Return of Christ* (Grand Rapids, MI: Eerdmans, 1972), 160. In particular, Berkouwer emphasizes the judgment beginning with the church, see 1 Peter 4:17; Jeremiah 25:29; Ezekiel 9:5.

28. F. Dostoyevsky, *Crime and Punishment* (London: Everyman), ch. 2.

29. Hosier, *The Lamb, the Beast and the Devil*, 168.

30. Berkhof, *Systematic Theology*, 732.

31. E. Brunner, *Eternal Hope* (London: Lutterworth Press, 1954), 173.

32. *Church of England Doctrine Commission, Doctrine in the Church of England* (London: SPCK, 1938), 71.

33. Quoted in Garrett, *Systematic Theology*, 776.

34. Beattie, "The Presbyterian Standards."

35. *Christ III*, lines 1007–1061; see www.apocalyptic-theories.com/literature/christiii/mechristiiib.html.

CHAPTER 12

1. "Hell," in D. Lyle Jeffrey ed., *Dictionary of Biblical Tradition in Literature* (Grand Rapids, MI: Eerdmans, 1992).

2. Drawn to my attention in private correspondence.

3. J. Calvin, *Institutes of the Christian Religion*, ed. J. T. McNeil (Philadelphia: Westminster Press, 1960), vol. 2, IV.25.12.

4. E. Best, *The 1st and 2nd Epistles to the Thessalonians* (London: A. & C. Black, 1972), 259.

5. See www.newadvent.org/cathen/01599a.htm.

6. I. H. Marshall, "Does the New Testament Teach Universalism?," in J. Colwell, ed., *Called to One Hope* (Carlisle: Paternoster, 2000), 17ff.

7. U. Luz, *Matthew 21—28, Hermeneia Commentaries* (Minneapolis: Fortress Press, 2005).

8. See the useful article at www.theologicalstudies.org.uk/article_destroyed_gray.html.

9. See the moving book by J. Wenham, *Facing Hell, An Autobiography 1913–1996* (Carlisle: Paternoster, 1998).

10. C. Pinnock, *The Wideness of God's Mercy* (Grand Rapids, MI: Zondervan, 1992).

11. Frequently cited in discussions on this subject. See, e.g., E. Donnelly, *Biblical Teaching on the Doctrines of Heaven and Hell* (Edinburgh: Banner of Truth Trust, 2001), 7.

12. Church of England Doctrine Commission, *The Mystery of Salvation* (London: Church House Publishing, 1995).

13. BAGD: W. Bauer, *A Greek-English Lexicon of the New Testament and Other Early Christian Literature*, tr. and augmented by W. F. Arndt and F. W. Gingrich, 2nd ed. (Chicago: University of Chicago Press, 1979), 27: recognizing that *aion* can mean "the age to come," it defines its initial meaning as "very long time, eternity."

14. Best, *The 1st and 2nd Epistles to the Thessalonians*, 262.

15. C. S. Lewis, *The Problem of Pain* (London: Geoffrey Bles, 1940), 94.

16. R. Baxter, *The Reformed Pastor*, abridged ed. (Edinburgh: Banner of Truth Trust, 1974), 113.

17. *Kerygma* is a term derived from the Greek kerusso, "to preach." The kerygma refers technically to the "preached word," the gospel presentation, and hell is absent from the sermons recorded in Acts.

18. The biblically presented, historic Israel dwelling in the land when they were ruled by God through his covenant with them given by Moses.

19. Unlike many who have claimed a vision of or trip to heaven and then make a living and a ministry informing others about it, I find the depictions of their experiences and descriptions of heaven generally unimpressive!

20. C. S. Lewis, *The Great Divorce* (San Francisco: HarperSanFrancisco, 2001). It is a concept more Platonic than clearly scriptural, but I find it compelling. Heaven is surely not a Gnostic dehumanizing, but a divine intensifying of that good creation.

21. R. Culver, *Systematic Theology* (Tain, Scotland: Mentor Press, 2005), 1103.

22. M. J. Erickson, *Christian Theology* (Grand Rapids, MI: Baker Book House, 1983), 1229f.

23. See www.biblebb.com/files/edwards/praise.htm.

24. N. T. Wright, *New Heavens, New Earth: The Biblical Picture of Christian Hope* (Cambridge: Grove Books, 1999), 6, 20.

25. Ibid., 10–11.

26. G. B. Caird, *The Revelation of St. John the Divine*, 2nd ed. (London: A. & C. Black, 1984), 263.

27. R. Mounce, *The Book of Revelation, New International Commentary on the New Testament* (Grand Rapids, MI: Eerdmans, 1977), 372.

28. A. M. Hunter, quoted in ibid., 370.

29. R. Browning, "Rabbi ben Ezra" (1864), stanza 32.

30. C. S. Lewis, *The Last Battle* (London: Harper Collins, 1997), 171–2.

CONCLUSION

1. F. Schaeffer, *How Should We Then Live?* (London: Crossway Books, 1983)—an important study in which Schaeffer looks at the philosophical influences that have shaped modern culture and considers the church's response.

2. This is an oft-repeated story, and I am unable to locate the original source.

3. For a full account, see www.freerepublic.com/focus/f-news/1407171/posts.

4. J. R. R. Tolkien, *The Lord of the Rings—The Fellowship of the Ring* (London: HarperCollins, 1995), 50.

5. J. N. D. Kelly, *The Epistles of Peter and Jude* (London: A. & C. Black, 1969), 367.

6. See en.wikipedia.org/wiki/Jacob_the_Liar.

7. G. E. Ladd, *Jesus and the Kingdom* (London: SCM, 1966), 334.

8. S. Grenz, *Theology for the Community of God* (Carlisle: Paternoster, 1994), 851.

9. G. C. Berkouwer, *Studies in Dogmatics: The Return of Christ* (Grand Rapids, MI: Eerdmans, 1972), 19.

10. D. Lawrence, *Heaven—It's Not the End of the World* (Bletchley: Scripture Union, 1995), 141.

11. Ibid., 135.